My Beautiful Bahrain

A collection of short stories and poetry about life and living in the Kingdom of Bahrain.

COMPILED AND EDITED BY
ROBIN BARRATT

miracle PUBLISHING

Compiled & Edited: **Robin Barratt**

Consulting Editor: **Dina Fakhro**

Cover Art: **Ella Prakash**

Designed and Published by

miracle PUBLISHING

PO Box 10013, Manama, Kingdom of Bahrain
T. +973 77022222 F. +973 77022221
www.miracle.com.bh
miracle@batelco.com.bh

First edition published in The Kingdom of Bahrain, 2012.

ISBN: 978-99901-37-47-7
Bahrain National Library Listing: 2012/10008 د ع

For full list of books from miracle PUBLISHING please visit www.miracleshop.com.bh

MY BEAUTIFUL
BAHRAIN

CONTENTS

FOREWORD

With lots of fascinating personal 'life' stories, quite a few tourist-type information and fact based contributions, some wonderful poetry, an occasional piece of fiction (set on the island) and a mixture of other diverse and captivating prose, with fifty contributions from forty writers from fifteen countries, *My Beautiful Bahrain* is both varied and unique, and an undeniably indispensable guide for travellers and visitors to the island, as well as a 'must-read' book for people living here, doing business here, or just interested in what life is like living on this tiny, tiny island in the Arabian Gulf. And a Brit, editing and compiling a book called *My Beautiful Bahrain* written by both Arabs and foreigners about life on the island, is most definitely unique!

The call for contributions for this book was simple and straightforward; to write about life and living here with no other - or hidden – agenda. The only conditions for contributing were that there was to be no political or religious criticism of any kind and writers *should always* keep in mind the title: *My Beautiful Bahrain*. The aims and goals of this book are to show the world that; firstly, there are a great many terrific and talented writers on the island that most definitely should be read and heard, and secondly - and more importantly - for most people here, Bahrain is actually a wonderful place to live!

Although many contributors to this book are members of the Bahrain Writer's Circle, contribution was open to anyone; Arab or foreign, young, old, published or not and whether a veteran writer with many years experience or a beginner stumbling through their first few words. And because of this, aside from obvious errors in grammar and spelling, as much as possible all contributions have been kept as original as possible, highlighting just how many people can write such wonderful prose and poetry even when English is not their mother tongue! And to this end a very big thank you goes to all the wonderful contributors; Aaron Maree, Ana Corradini Boreland, Anita Menon, B.M.Engel, Bron Vanzino, Catherine Purchase, David Hollywood, DaVonda St.Clair, Dilraz Kunnummal, Eva

Burns, Fahad Ali, Faridah Serajul Haq, Fatima Dincsoy, Hameed Al Qaed, Hasina Patel, Heera Nawaz, Jim Scalise, Joanne Jones, Kathleen Dodd, Kevin Howarth, Lillian Mills, Lorraine Charlesworth, Madhavi Tiwary, Maeve Kelynack Skinner, Mary Coons, Nadia Muijrers, Namit Bhatia, Natasha Khan, Nawf Al Basam, Omar Ahmed, Osama Arshad, Phari Poitier, Pooja Rajpal Kasala, Rohini Sunderam, S Krishna Kumar, Shauna Nearing Loej, Steve Royston and Zahra Zuhair. Also, of course, a huge thank you goes to artist Ella Prakash for painting the beautiful cover picture and to Miracle Publishing for publishing *My Beautiful Bahrain* and helping to make it a huge success across the region.

And lastly, of course, a massive thank you goes to everyone buying a copy of this book, thus helping to showcase this wonderful, beautiful island of Bahrain and its writers to the world!

THE BAHRAIN WRITERS' CIRCLE

The Bahrain Writers' Circle (BWC) was formed early 2011 especially for writers and authors (or indeed budding writers and authors!) based in the Kingdom of Bahrain. It warmly welcomes writers of any age, any genre, whether published or not. Whether sixteen or sixty, a professional writer writing for a living or still waiting to see your first few words in print, The BWC welcomes anyone and everyone interested in the written word. Our members include authors, poets, bloggers, journalists, magazine editors, freelance writers, commissioned writers, coaches, reporters and publishers.

The main reasons for forming the BWC are:

- To get fellow writers and authors together once a month to talk informally about writing. We focus on different topics every month which could include novel and short-story writing, writing for children, magazine writing, freelancing, genre-specific writing, getting published, research, editing, proofing your work etc.

- To invite guest speakers e.g. publishers, well-known local writers, magazine editors, journalists etc., to talk about their speciality and / or to read extracts from their work.

- To network with other like-minded souls fascinated by the written word!

- To organise writing competitions and projects.

- To publish and promote works from the group.

- To act as a go-between local writers and publishers.

- To promote writing and the written word on the island!

- To publish The Word, a magazine about writing, for writers across the region.

Since forming in February 2011, the BWC has grown to almost one hundred members representing a huge range of nationalities; it is undeniably now the biggest group of international writers to have ever been formed on the island! The BWC aims to be a significant feature for both Arab and foreign Bahrain based writers.

Monthly meetings are on the first or second Sunday of every month, with a calender of events including creative writing and poetry workshops, literary festivals, book clubs and much more! All writers and budding writers based on this little island welcome! So whatever your field, and whether you are experienced or a novice, join us now.

www.BahrainWritersCircle.com

My

[mahy]

Pronoun - Possessive (a form of the possessive case of 'I' used as an attributive adjective)

Beau·ti·ful

[byoo-tuh-fuhl]

Adjective - having beauty; having qualities that give great pleasure or satisfaction to see, hear, think about, etc.; delighting the senses or mind.

Bahrain

[bah-reyn, -rahyn, buh-]

Noun - a sheikdom in the Arabian Gulf, consisting of a group of islands.

GLOSSARY OF FOREIGN TERMS

Abbaya/abaya	*a cloak or loose over-garment, essentially a robe-like dress.*
Agaile	*flavoured sponge type cake.*
Adamantine	*mythical material, and an adjective referring to non-metallic, brilliant light reflecting and transmitting properties e.g. diamond.*
Baqâra	*boat.*
Bisht	*men's formal woven cloak.*
Cardamom	*plant used as flavourings in food and drink, and as cooking spices.*
Carnelian	*a brownish-red mineral.*
Chaat	*Indian savoury snacks.*
Chai	*tea.*
Chana Masala	*vegetable dish whose main ingredient is chickpeas.*
Chapatti	*flat bread.*
Dalla	*Arabic coffee pot.*
Damask	*a reversible figured fabric of silk, wool, linen, cotton, or synthetic fibers.*
Dandiya	*traditional Indian folk dance.*
Dhow	*generic name of a number of traditional sailing vessels found across the region.*
Diwali	*a festival 'of lights' celebrated between mid-October and mid-December.*
Dorim	*a herb used by women as makeup.*
Dugong	*a large marine mammal.*
Dussera	*an Indian state-festival.*
Estecaan	*Persian tea cups.*
Ex-pat	*an abbreviation of expatriate.*

Gawha	*coffee.*
Gawha cursi	*long wooden benches, literally coffee seats.*
Gujarat	*a state in western India.*
Gutras	*clothing.*
Habibati	*'dear'.*
Halaal/Halal	*any object or an action permissible according to Islamic law.*
Halwa	*sticky sweet Arab toffee.*
Hamour/Hammour	*type of fish.*
Harim	*women's quarters.*
Hijab	*headscarf.*
Hilal	*new moon.*
Hummous/Hummus	*dip or spread made from cooked, mashed chickpeas, blended with tahini, olive oil, lemon juice, salt and garlic.*
Iftar	*during Ramadan, the meal that breaks the fast at sunset.*
Imam	*leader of a mosque.*
Insh'allah	*'God willing'.*
Jalabeeya / Jalabiyas	*traditional flowing robe or kaftan.*
Jinn	*supernatural creatures in Arab folklore.*
Kandura	*an ankle-length garment.*
Khaleej	*Arabic word which means 'Gulf'.*
Khanjar	*traditional dagger of Oman.*
Lehenga	*traditional clothing of women in Rajasthan and Gujarat.*
Mahrem	*relations.*
Majles	*traditional reception type rooms.*
Malayalam	*one of the four major languages of southern India.*

Mashrabiya	*decorative wooden balconies.*
Muharram	*the first month of the Islamic calendar.*
Naham	*elderly man.*
Nashal	*wedding robe.*
Niqab	*full-face covering.*
Obsidian	*naturally occurring volcanic glass.*
Onasadya	*Indian festival.*
Oud	*a pear-shaped stringed instrument.*
Patou	*blanket.*
Puttu	*rice cakes.*
Qu'ran/Quran/Koran	*the central religious text of Islam.*
Saffi	*a type of fish.*
Salwar	*traditional dress worn by both women and men where legs are wide at the top and narrow at the ankle.*
Samosa	*Indian fried turnover filled with minced meat or vegetables.*
Saree/Saris	*a garment worn by Hindu women, consisting of a long piece of cotton or silk wrapped around the body with one end draped over the head or over one shoulder.*
Shamal	*hot and dry, dusty wind from the north or north-west in Iraq, Iran, and the Arabian Peninsula.*
Shisha/Sheesha/ Hubbly-Bubbly pipes	*traditional eastern way of smoking using a water pipe in which the water cools the smoke.*
Shwarma/Shawarma	*Eastern Arabic-style sandwich usually composed of shaved lamb, goat, chicken, turkey, beef, or a mixture of meats.*
Souq/Suq	*market.*

Struldbrugs	*In Jonathan Swift's Gulliver's Travels, Struldbrugs were humans born seemingly normal but are in fact immortal.*
Sumboosa	*deep fried, savoury saffron sponge.*
Tabouleth/Tabbouleh	*is a Levantine Arab dish, often used as part of a mezze.*
Tagleedi	*traditional folkloric dance.*
Thobe/Thawb	*llong white robe normally made of white cotton, typically worn by men in the Arabian Peninsula.*
Thobe Al Nashal	*traditional male wedding robe.*
Tumuli	*heap of earth or stones placed over a grave.*
Wothoo	*ritual washing before prayer.*
Yanaan	*fish similar to sea bass.*

Currency

Bahrain Dinar (BD or BHD). One BD is divided up into 1000 fils.

INTRODUCTION

by

Robin Barratt

Beauty is, of course, subjective. Each and every one of us has our own personal idea of what beauty is, or of what we find beautiful (or indeed not). And beauty does, of course, manifest itself in many, many different ways for many different people. But I believe it is fair to say that there are certain things in the world that are, by it's very definition, visually beautiful to almost everyone; perhaps snow-capped mountains, or rolling green hills, or the oranges and reds and yellows of a forest in the Fall, or perhaps a painting, a sculpture, or even the way someone looks. There are things that almost all of us would most definitely immediately classify as 'beautiful', and few would disagree. Therefore, by this definition alone, it would be hard to place Bahrain into the visually 'beautiful' category. Sure, there are some places on the island that you could say are very attractive; a few pretty parks, a handful of nice promenades along the sea-shore, a number of majestic buildings, but it would be hard to say that Bahrain is 'beautiful' by definition, (even though, when you tell people that Bahrain is a tiny island in the Arabia sea - by that description alone it suggests it should be!). Bahrain's beauty is not aesthetic, it is not visual - its beauty is much deeper, hidden, and much more personal. In this way, and to many people, Bahrain is beautiful. And, as many of the stories in this book will demonstrate, Bahrain's beauty is fundamentally the subtle, gentle beauty of the island, its way of life and the friendliness and compassion and openness and warmth of its people.

At the time of writing this, I have been living on the island for almost three years. I am English, and therefore can only compare my life here in Bahrain to my life back in England (although for me 'home' now is Bahrain). And I have to honestly say my life here has - so far - been far better and infinitely more relaxed and meaningful, and I rue the day I would ever have to leave. I can have a lifestyle here in Bahrain that would be both extremely difficult, and extremely costly to replicate in the West.

But Bahrain isn't perfect, actually it's far from perfect, but having travelled extensively and spent time living and working in many places around the world, I have come to understand that actually no country or place is perfect. There is no Utopia. There is good and bad with everything, and for sure there are some bad things about Bahrain (which I'll briefly touch upon shortly) but, in my opinion, the good things here far outweigh the bad, the light overwhelms the dark, there are far more positives about living on the island than negatives. And this is why both Bahrainis and foreigners either chose to stay here, or to eventually return, and call Bahrain 'home.'

For many and for me, the beauty of Bahrain is both personal and individual. For me, one of the most fundamental aspects I really find beautiful about Bahrain is the respect most of the population shows to each other, and their kindness and compassion. For me this stands out above almost everything else, and can be perceptibly compared to the way people treat and respect each other in the West. Here, aside from the current unrest, there is actually little vandalism, very little crime, the streets are clean, strangers smile and greet you every single day, people are helpful and polite without any hidden agenda, and you can feel comfortable without ever feeling threatened or intimidated. In my three years here I have never once witnessed any street-type aggression or even heard any raised, angry voices. One summer, within two days of returning to the UK, I witnessed a street brawl, a group of intimidating thugs in a public park being threatening to passers-by, and a street arrest. You rarely see anything like this here. For me, coming back to Bahrain, a weight is literally lifted off my shoulders and I breathe a big sigh of relief. Here you can live every day of your life with a certainty that you are unlikely to ever be the victim of any crime and this relatively crime-free environment makes a huge difference to a person's quality of life. And I love this about Bahrain. Sure there is crime; with a population of just over a million in a country roughly the size Isle Of Man (UK) or Singapore, there is bound to be some crime, but there is so much less than a UK city with roughly the same population (for example Glasgow). So far here I have not heard or read about a single house burglary, not one! I am sure it does occasionally happen, but it is so rare (I wonder how many house burglaries happen in Glasgow every day, let alone over the past three years!?). I always walk to my local DVD shop, and every single time I pass two or three cars parked outside an adjacent supermarket; keys in the ignition, engines running (to keep the air-conditioning on), no one inside - owners probably shopping. Cars here are almost never stolen. How many high-streets in England could you leave your car running by the side of the road while you popped out do some shopping? I did read in a daily newspaper here once that a British women had her handbag snatched whilst leaving the British Embassy. It made front page headlines. Apparently the man was caught and was given a year in prison. I also read that someone was given a three-year prison sentence for stealing a credit card. Three years! I also once passed an electrical shop and outside the shuttered shop (it was Ramadan and most shops are closed during the day), were about ten boxed, new Sony flat-screen televisions that had been delivered while the shop was closed. They were just left sitting outside the shop. Again, how long would they last in England - someone seeing them would have made a few calls and in just a few minutes they would have disappeared. But not in Bahrain.

There is low crime here for a number of different and very important reasons; firstly punishments for even the smallest crimes are severe, which makes any form of criminal behaviour a real deterrent. In the UK it is impossible to punish people as severely simply because there is just so much crime! And because there is so much crime, prisons are full, and because the prisons are full, people can be more criminal because they know they just won't get severely punished. It is a terrible, downward spiral that blights society in the UK - and the West. But not here. In Bahrain, if you steal from someone, no matter how much you steal, you have acted disrespectfully and have gone against the fundamental laws of Islam so you are going to prison, end of story. Wonderful! This is how religion here is integrated into everyday life, unlike the West.

And another crucial reason crime rate is so low is because a large part of the working population here are expats and migrant workers who send money back home to their families, and in many cases whole families are dependent upon the income of just one family member working in Bahrain. If they break the law and lose their jobs, not only do they go to prison and eventually deported, their whole families suffer. There is a huge commitment and responsibility to others which again we don't see so much in the UK. And so, people here live their lives relatively free of the fear of crime and I love this about Bahrain.

Another thing I really think is beautiful about Bahrain is of course the weather. It is undoubtedly wonderful to live in a place where the sun shines every single day, without fail. Sun definitely makes people happier, friendlier and much more easy-going. After three years, I still can count the number of cloudy days on both hands (and perhaps a couple of toes), and the days it rained on one hand. There was a storm once too, for a couple of hours in the middle of the night one March, but by the morning the sun was out again. The sun makes everyday life here so very different compared to England, where for much of the year it is bleak and grey and cold and damp, and where weeks and weeks of brilliant sunny days in a row are rare. Although I must say that when I was back in the UK in June 2010 I did remember almost two weeks straight of sunshine, and then it rained for a few days to compensate! And the really good thing about living in such a hot and sunny country is that never, ever do you wake up in the morning and wonder what the weather is going to be like. Never! Unlike England, where weather is the main topic of conversation, no one here talks about the weather because it is the same, every single day. That may sound boring, but believe me it is not! And during the winter you can plan outside events weeks or months in advance knowing that the weather will never affect your plans, unlike England. Standing on a crowded grey, bleak railway platform in the pouring rain in the middle of winter waiting for the train or Tube for your daily commute into work, just does not happen here! And this is most definitely something to love about Bahrain. Be warned though, some days here during mid-winter you might need to wear a jumper or even a jacket once or twice, on really chilly days. The downside to this however, is that while the winters here are lovely, the summers are just too hot; the heat is relentless and the sun scorching. By February or March you have got so used to the lovely winter climate, when you can sit outside in the cafés or take a stroll along the promenade, or just walk to the shops, you have actually forgotten all about the heat of the summer. But as sure as it rains in the UK, from around early June the heat arrives in Bahrain. And in July and August temperatures frequently reach 45° Celsius or 113° Fahrenheit when even a five minute walk to the local shop is a real effort and will leave you drenched with sweat and sunburnt. Furthermore, with it being so hot during the peak summer months of July and August, you have to stay inside almost all of the time, and more or less confined to air-conditioned buildings and cars and shopping malls. But is this better than months and months of cloudy, drizzly, grim, grey, cold England? For sure.

Compared to England, there are many other things I just love about living in Bahrain and its health care system is certainly another of them. While I was back in the UK, unfortunately I had to see a gastroenterologist. The procedure to see him was thus; first I had to make an appointment with my General Practitioner (doctor) which took just under two weeks, he then had to write a letter to the hospital to request an appointment, another two weeks. Then I received a letter in the post telling me that, in order to make a hospital appointment, I had to telephone a central appointments line with my unique password, which I did. My appointment date; two months later. It took me almost three months to make an appointment with a specialist. In Bahrain I called the Bahrain Defence Force (BDF) hospital appointments line and saw a specialist just two days later (they even apologised for the delay!), although as a foreigner, my treatment at the BDF wasn't free and so I did have to pay 15BD (about 25GBP / 40USD), but even if I opted to go private in the UK, it would have cost at least 100GBP for the consultation and I would have still had to wait a few weeks at least. Bahrainis don't pay for their hospital care and they still get an appointment within just a few days.

I also like having a maid to clean the apartment once or twice a week, and to do the ironing. Here, having a maid or home-help is the norm and not a luxury. I also really like the fact that fuel is less so much cheaper than in the UK and can fill my car for about 6BD (10GBP /

16USD). In the UK it would cost seven or eight times this much. Running a car here is not a weekly living cost, and because petrol is so cheap and there is virtually no car crime, people here drive the cars they would never consider driving anywhere else. There are Mercedes, Porsches, Ferraris, BMWs, Hummers and American Muscle cars just about everywhere, and you can drive them without some jumped-up idiot decrying "gas guzzler," or scratching it in envy.

And of course, I love that there is no income tax or corporate tax, and no VAT. It is great to go to work every day and then rewarding yourself by buying what you want knowing that a big chunk of your salary, and then another chunk in VAT, won't be going to the government. There are taxes here, for example a five percent levy on hospitality (e.g. restaurants) but nothing compared to the excessive and often hidden taxes on just about everything in the UK.

Also, for such a tiny island there is just about every brand represented – from high-street to designer luxury. The shopping malls are excellent and extensive, the cinemas are brilliant (even if most films are censored and edited), there are lots of nightclubs and great bars, and there are probably more really good restaurants per square kilometre here than just about most other countries. It is a tiny island though and, according to Wikipedia, one of the most densely populated countries in the world, behind Hong Kong and Singapore, so you can get stir-crazy. But Bahrain connects to almost everywhere and nowhere is too far by plane.

Lastly, I like the choice of rented accommodation available and the fact that normally everything is included in the monthly price. When you rent a villa or apartment here you don't have to leave a damage deposit (as you would naturally replace anything you damage anyway), and unlike England where on top of your rent you also have to pay Council Tax, gas, electricity, water rates and television licence, here all bills are included in the one monthly payment which almost always includes the internet as well. Plus, most apartment blocks also have a pool and a gym! Also if you need anything fixed, or a bulb changing, the landlord does it. Not in England!!

So what's bad about Bahrain?

There is one thing I dislike the most; the contrast of the locals once they get behind the steering wheel of the car! It's like mass schizophrenia. Normally everyone is so laid back and relaxed, friendly and kind and considerate to others, and then they get into a car! God help anyone who takes more than a nanosecond setting off from the traffic lights; drivers in Bahrain beep their horn incessantly for any and every reason and often for no reason at all. They also jump red-lights, change lanes without signalling, stop in the middle of the road for no obvious reason, park wherever they want with no consideration for anyone else, use their mobile phone, eat and drink while driving (yes, I once saw a lady in a hijab driving, but in one hand she was chatting on her mobile phone, the other hand she held a McDonald's cup! Tell me...how?). Traffic police do very little and fines are so small anyway, unlike other crime, getting caught for traffic offences is not much of a deterrent. And because of this, I have read that Bahrain has comparatively one of the highest traffic accident rates in the world. But it's not really surprising as the level driver instruction here is said to be terrible and often reported in the local press as corrupt, and many foreigners driving here originate from countries where driving instruction and road etiquette is even worse. Road etiquette here not as bad as some countries, but it is worse than many and unbelievable compared to the UK. By placing speed cameras (that work!) on all the major highways, cameras at traffic lights, deterrently hefty fines, perhaps a 'penalty points system' (as in the UK) and put loads more traffic cops on the streets, overnight the government could make driving much safer and even mildly enjoyable. I think they should, but they don't, hence the incredibly high traffic accident rate and the stress most people endure while driving. This is the one main thing that I, along with many others, really dislike about Bahrain.

One thing that I find really annoying more than anything, is that for at least six months of the year the weather really is nice enough to walk, yet walking anywhere is very difficult, if not impossible. There is little provision for pedestrians; crossing the major highways to the lovely promenades along the sea-shore is, in many cases, extremely dangerous and in most cases virtually impossible. The government builds really nice sea-shore promenades

– which are meant to be for walking along - but no way to get to them other than by car. They also do lay some really nice pavements around the island, but many, if not most, then have big road signs or advertising hoardings slam-bang in the centre and cars almost always park across them, forcing you into the road to get round them! Or a nice new expensive pavement will suddenly stop or crumble into nothing. This is really annoying for many of us that actually like to walk!

While on the subject of sea-shores, Bahrain is an island yet there are very, very few good public beaches and what beaches there are, most don't have any public facilities and are often unkempt and dirty. Bahrain could have the most glorious beaches (for both Muslims and non-Muslims) in the Gulf and could become a magnificent beach destination, but it doesn't forcing people to use the small and over-priced private hotel and club beaches.

Another thing I and many others really don't like, not just about Bahrain but about the region in general, is that labour here is a cheap commodity and with many migrant workers earning just 100BD or around 300USD a month, coupled with a standard six-day, fifty-hour week, the standard of service and workmanship can often be appalling. And that's being kind! Employers here don't seem to realise that you won't get the best out of someone if you pay them just over a dollar an hour! Also, it never ceases to amaze me why entrepreneurs here frequently invest so much money setting up a business only to then find the cheapest labour they can to run it! And they then wonder why business is bad, blaming the economy and / or the recent unrest and / or anything and everything else but they fail to look at their own backyard and at the service they are providing which is, in many cases, the real reason why they are not doing well. Just a one of many examples; I recently went to a café in the Lagoon area on Amwaj island. The owner had previously told me he had been badly affected by the unrest. I used to go there a lot, it was a lovely place, with great service and good food. On that particular occasion however I waited over thirty minutes just to get served, even though I was their only customer! The main course was brought first and I had finished it before my drink arrived, the food was bad too. I decided not to order a dessert and left after (reluctantly) paying the bill. I wouldn't ever go back - it was the service and the quality of food that had, over time, driven people away, not the economy or the unrest as, all over the island, there are plenty of other consistently good cafés and restaurants that remain constantly full. When I told the owner about my experiences, he then blamed their ongoing staff problems.

In Bahrain I have found there are always excuses and reasons not to do something, or for doing something badly. Here few people take ownership for their mistakes and always, always blame someone or something else. And I mean always!

Good, bad, ugly, pretty, annoying, indifferent, whatever you like - or dislike - about Bahrain, all together it is nevertheless undeniably a brilliant, exciting, unique and most would say beautiful place to live. I love it here, and many others love it here too. Bahrain markets itself as 'Business Friendly' as it is one of the easiest countries in the region for both foreigners and locals to start a business and the entrepreneurial spirit here is huge, but I believe the country should also market itself internationally as 'Living Friendly Bahrain' because, despite the few bad and annoying things, for most people, young, old, rich poor, local, foreign, living here truly is much better, much easier and much more relaxed that in many, many other places around the world, and the people here are undeniably some of the friendliest.

Welcome to *My Beautiful Bahrain*...

THE BIRTH OF A PEARL

by

S. Krishna Kumar

Just as someone sprayed grey stars into a fading sky
An unseen hand with artistic flourish
Brushed in random shades of orange and pink
The blob of a remorseful sun licked
On cotton candy clouds blushing with borrowed hues
As the waters washed up tidy rocks
Feverishly rising in an act of romantic kiss

Just then.....
With quiet and subtle humour
A pearl broke open from an oyster
And bubbled up from the Arab waters
Settling calmly, bashfully
Hesitating but boldly reticent
Peeking slowly at the artwork of a benevolent creator
Winking smilingly as the supreme artist welcomed
A delightful introduction of

A little pearl
In the vast canvas of the painting
Shining, glimmering in the sheen of a white moon
Giggling with the tickle of a new born baby
That looked like a drop of water which stayed afloat
As the jaws of nature dropped
The sky scratched its head with the tail of a distant comet
The sands of dunes crossed paths hurriedly
Whispering in awe
As the pearl shaped up
And started growing
Coming alive, vibrating with heart beats
Smiling at an ever changing sky

And until now…
Some unseen hand caresses its majestic head
Blessing it, loving it
As the pearl gently dances
To a perfumed breeze which sings its name as it passes by:
Bahrain.

A BACKWARD GLANCE

by

Maeve Kelynack Skinner

A burst of clapping broke out as the Gulf Air flight from London landed at Muharraq airport on 1st November 1976. I joked to myself that they were welcoming me to Bahrain but apparently it wasn't unusual for Bahrainis to give a round of applause for the Captain who brought them safely back to their homeland.

I stepped out of the aircraft and was hit by a wave of humidity and the nostalgic smell of tangy sea air mingled with heat and dust and pungent kerosene fumes. The last rays of the setting sun glimpsed through distant palm fronds silhouetted against a turquoise sea, shimmered like liquid gold. I sighed happily. This is where I was meant to be.

I was born on the tropical island of Penang, Malaysia, and grew up crunching my toes on sandy beaches as I ran beneath rustling palms and splashed in sparkling blue seas. My teens were spent in an Irish boarding school followed by a few years working in the endless cold of Dublin. One morning walking down a dismal grey street with the rain trickling down the back of my raincoat, I yearned for the sunny lifestyle of my childhood and decided that I'd had enough. My criteria for a new job was to live in a land of 'Sun, Sea and Palm Trees' and within a couple of months, I was winging my way to Bahrain. I was to be the PA to the chairman of one of the Gulf's oldest merchant families. My posting was for two years – that was thirty-five years ago.

Bahrain was a heady mix of adventure, fun and fascinating people. Everyone had a story to tell of why they had set out to find their fortunes in the world's newest and biggest honey-pot. It was only forty-four years since oil had been discovered in Bahrain; the first place in the Arabian Gulf to untap the massive oil fields that lay beneath the desert and which transformed forever the lives of its people.

For the first few months my feet didn't touch the ground. Except for having to be in the office at 7.15am from Saturday until Thursday noon, life was one big party. I shared a flat in a small two storey block for junior overseas staff with a stunning English girl called Gudrun, the only other European female in the company. Our view was the municipal graveyard which was always busy and adjacent to us was Andalus Gardens where, on Friday evenings, local dancers and musicians played traditional Arabic music with the women ululating loudly and clapping their hands, filling the night with their joyful sounds.

We drove to work through sandy winding lanes and potholed tarmac streets, flanked by wind-tower houses, decorated with mashrabiya where ladies were able to view what was going on without being seen. Past the American Mission Hospital and down Government Road we reached the car-park; a patch of sandy gravel near the original National Bank of Bahrain tower, on what is now Manama's multi-storey car-park. Latecomers paid no regard to parking etiquette and blocked others in, which resulted in daily scraps and shouting matches usually refereed by Isa, the tall, dignified chief car washer. Now slightly stooped and frail, Isa continues to clean cars for a few fils a day in the government car park opposite Bahrain Financial Harbour (BFC). From his earnings, he educated five children, each of whom went to university and now have sound jobs in the private sector.

The once thriving dhow port of Mina Manama stood on the site of the traffic lights opposite the BFC. Here, dhows from neighbouring countries unloaded cars, tractors, refrigerators, sheep and other livestock, the latter held in warehouses on the site of the Regency InterContinental Hotel. When the wind blew in the wrong direction, Manama suffered from the sickly stench of lanolin and soggy wool.

"The Manama bazaar claims with justice to be the emporium of the Gulf" wrote, James Belgrave, a long-term English resident, in his book Welcome to Bahrain published in 1953. It gives a fascinating insight into Bahrain before and after the discovery of oil, particularly its commercial status as the hub of the Gulf before the ripple effect of black gold brought undreamed of prosperity to the Gulf and the tribal outposts of Dubai, Abu Dhabi, Oman and Qatar. Before the shopping malls invaded the land like giant tripods, the souq was the vibrant heart of Manama where you could buy anything and everything, even things you didn't know existed, or had only read about in old text books. Most products came from India, Iran, Egypt, Jordan and nearby countries, until the influx of cheap goods from Japan and China squeezed out genuine high quality items.

Our office overlooked Bab Al Bahrain and even before the hand-carved wooden shutters opened at 8am, the souq was alive with novel sounds, scents and colours; the drone of air-conditioners, the blare of horns, the searing brightness and humidity evaporating as the sun rose higher. At any opportunity I'd nip onto the fourth-floor veranda and watch the bewitching scene unfold below, like turning the pages of an Arabian fairytale.

As befitted this oil rich nation, spanking new Rolls Royce, Mercedes and Cadillacs cruised down the streets parading their individually commissioned liveries of emerald, purple or gold. Small white donkeys pulling carts of hand-painted drums containing drinking water, stood submissively, their ears twitching and bodies artfully decorated in henna, as their owners sold cups of water to passers by. Curious shoppers stopped to inspect the latest electric gadgets or feel the texture of a Persian carpet or Kashmir shawl, or query the price of outdated Western style dresses, suits and sharp shoes. Indian stall holders dangled fake Rolex and indicated to wind-up mosque alarm clocks which gave an ear-splitting call to prayer, 'hubble-bubble' pipes, halwa, the sticky sweet toffee so loved by the Arabs - anything and everything appeared to be on sale.

Streets were literally lined with gold where rows of shop windows gleamed with glitteringly ostentatious yet intricately crafted displays of gold, pearls and precious stones. Jewel studded necklaces, woven bridal caps with chains dangling like plaits from the sides, decorated with half-moons, coins, balls and other shapes. Rings for each finger, linked by golden strands to a bracelet, ornamental ear, nose and toe rings. The complexity of designs was mesmerising – but essential for a bride. Gold was a vital commodity for her dowry in case she became divorced, widowed or replaced by another wife. It was common to see black robed women inside shops, their sleeves pulled back to reveal armfuls of gold which they would barter for cash. Gold was so cheap that it didn't matter much if you lost a piece, you could replace it for a few dinars. If you couldn't decide which ring or necklace you liked best, the jeweller allowed you to take a few items home to decide which one you preferred –a custom I never heard being abused. Deeper inside the souq, were the pearl merchants who displayed their precious pearls, graded according to size on a piece of red cloth, resting in bowls on the counter. Some of these pearls were over one hundred years old and would sell for a fortune.

The material souq wound its way like a rainbow through lanes and alleys of multi - hued fabrics that billowed out from stalls crammed with Indian silks and satins, sequin trimmed saris, woven damask from Syria and Egyptian cottons that would cost a small fortune in Europe. Locals and expatriates sought bargains for the best quality material which would then be made up by a local tailor into the latest fashion. As in traditional Arabic bazaars, alleyways were laid out like supermarket aisles, each dedicated to particular goods. One was filled with suitcases of every size and shape, others of shoes and sandals, towels and bedding, thobes and gutras, abbayas and hejabs, colourfully stacked spices - their aromas mingling with intriguing potions, exotic perfumes and expensive oud bark. From dark alleys the clanging of metal drew you further to see shadowy figures crouched on wooden stools crafting coffee pots and incense burners out of flat sheets of copper or silver.

A mesmerising buzz of Arabic, Urdu, Farsi, Pashtun, Hindi, Malayam, floated in the air from residents from all sections of society including the labour force of fierce eyed Afghanis sporting bushy henna dyed beards, their heads covered in flamboyantly large turbans with one end hanging over their right ear, tall handsome Pathans from the high Karakormans, their ruddy complexions and green eyes strangely at odds with their billowing trousers and long tailed shirts, Gujarati ladies in neatly embroidered cotton bonnets and capes walked in pairs like nuns, whilst all around were cheerful black robed, plump shapes who chattered non-stop, taking up half the street as others squeezed by.

The only female sellers appeared at the weekly Wednesday Market near the Delmon Hotel; a great crowd puller. Here, village women dressed in colourful, long cotton dresses, their faces covered in shiny black 'beak' masks, set up stalls to sell their hand embroidered, gold trimmed thobe al nashal (wedding robe) and bisht (men's formal woven cloaks), embroidered sheets and pillow cases, woven baskets and mats and pottery, halwa and bottled chutneys.

The two main food stores frequented by Westerners were Jawad Cold Store standing where Yateem Centre is today and Al Jazira in Adliya. Otherwise it was the meat and fish markets at the far end of the souq, which were not for the faint-hearted. Covered by strips of cloth to provide shade, the wooden counters were piled high with haunches of mutton and goat. There were no fans, nor air-conditioners, and the meat sellers' aprons were very, very bloodstained and the stench of meat was overpowering. But it was packed with housewives carefully examining each joint, as was the adjacent fish market but at least the fish were kept in water containers, and the fantastic selection of prawns, crab, hamour, shark, mussels, oysters and more, made up for the odour. The vegetable and fruit market was picturesque. Traders would perch above their colourful displays, tempting shoppers to taste a peach or nectarine. Over the years these food markets were moved to the Central Market with initially fans installed, before air-conditioning.

One of my favourite places – and still is – are the coffee shops where the male shopkeepers and elders gather throughout the day. Seated on gawha cursi (long wooden benches, literally coffee seats) their legs tucked under their thobes, they sipped cardamom flavoured gawha or lemon chai, served from hole-in-the-wall kitchens and discussed the events of the day and latest gossip.

Life in Bahrain was – and is - so easy. No need to battle through a downpour to haul a petrol line to your car; here attendants filled up your car at a few fils a litre, boys stacked your shopping and carried it out to your car and drivers were courteous. Rather than being second-class citizens, women were respected, especially when it came to queues. Whether in the post office, a hospital, supermarket or shop, women were summoned to the front of any queue and served before the poor men, no matter how long they'd been waiting. Sadly this practice seems to have been discontinued!

The new Sea Road, or King Faisal Highway, named in honour of a State visit to Bahrain by the late King Faisal bin Saud in 1975, began at the junction of the Budaiya Road and Sanabis and continued past the dhow building yard - later reclaimed as the Pearl Roundabout junction - past Manama and Government House, until it veered right at the Hilton, Bahrain's first international hotel, now the Golden Tulip. The Sheraton, Diplomat Radisson and Crowne Plaza didn't exist. The Diplomatic area was being reclaimed, so the highway connected with Government Road near the British Embassy and continued up Old Palace Road, past the fishing village of Hoora until it reached the palm groves of Juffair village and the Gulf Hotel.

Night-life was limited to a few hotels or restaurants and the Gulf Hotel, built on an island of reclaimed land, was the place to go on a Thursday night. Outdoor dances were held in the gardens by the pool with entertainment provided by dark skinned Muharraqi males wearing thobes with gutras tied around their hips who danced to rhythmic, tribal music played by black-robed female musicians, some wearing old fashioned shiny black 'beak' masks as they beat drums made of stretched goat hide. Sometimes camels were brought along to ride, which added to the exotic flavour of the night. The best curry lunch in town was served at the Omar Khayyam Hotel, now hidden behind urbanisation in Hoora. It then overlooked the sea and the yacht club, which consisted of a wooden hut and a rickety pier.

An intriguing night spot was the Pearl Restaurant on top of the former Jashanmal building near the Yateem Centre. Owned by two Lebanese brothers, it was dark, seedy and smoke filled, with velvet seating around the dance floor and a buffet of Arabic cuisine garnished by the odd cockroach. Troupes of singers, dancers and circus stars from Cairo, Beirut, Istanbul and other foreign ports performed tantalising and daring routines; the females in eye-boggling skimpy attire, much to the delight of local and expat audiences. The persistent jamming of the elevator between the ground and 11th floor, also added to the thrill of a night out at the Pearl.

Julianna's, Bahrain's first disco, opened in the Delmon Hotel which had a large pool in a palm fringed garden that backed onto the sea. Julianna's attracted society's young bloods; many of the young men looking hilarious as they jived and twisted in their thobes and gutras. Bahraini ladies never dined in public, nor went to nightclubs - unlike today, where whole tables are often taken over by groups of sophisticated and confident Bahraini ladies.

Expatriates usually entertained at home and hosted dinner parties, barbeques, film shows or fancy dress parties which were highly popular – often with no-holds barred. One American couple held a party where each guest was given one metre square of black cotton and one safety pin and told to undress and cover themselves as best they could with the cloth, with some hilarious results.

We were often invited to the Company's guest house by the sea at Zellaq, where we met visiting dignitaries and senior family members from Saudi and the UAE. I was warned to have a snack before I went because, although we arrived at about 9pm, dinner wouldn't be served until after midnight, after which the guests would leave immediately. Bahraini weddings were lavish affairs, generally held in hotel ballrooms. This was an opportunity for the young women to dress in the latest Paris gowns where they could dance and mingle with young men and hopefully catch the eye of a handsome suitor. The more traditional families held separate wedding venues with only the bridegroom and the bride's immediate male family members invited into the ladies' 'do'. Great stamina was required for the bride and groom who sat on thrones on a stage arranged in bridal décor and received well-wishers for hours on end, not moving until dinner was served at about 2am.

The month of Ramadan was celebrated quietly. Muslims fasted all day then gathered at each other's houses at sunset for the Iftar meal. There were no khaimas or qaqbas held at hotels. We never knew when Eid would be declared as the sighting of the hilal - new moon - depended on when it was announced in Saudi. It must have been a tense time for Bahraini housewives to plan ahead when they didn't know which date would be Eid.

Sometimes we'd actually be at work when the word would spread that "hey – it's Eid – a three day holiday!"

Few expats had their own boats, so dhow trips were the best option on Fridays. About twenty of us would hire a dhow from Abdulla, a retired pearl diver and captain who was a great character. We climbed aboard his dhow moored at the Muharraq jetty with blocks of ice bought from the ice factory - as no one had cold boxes then - which we dropped into a large wooden box which served as a fridge. Armed with cocktails and curry, we skimmed across the turquoise Gulf to Al Bain (the spring), a sand-spit off the north-west coast, now absorbed into the Saudi Causeway. Al Bain's main attraction was a stone hut that sheltered a pipe from an underground aquifer that poured out cool, sweet water which was a glorious relief for our salt encrusted bodies in the blazing sun. The aquifer must have also appealed to pregnant shark as the shallows around Al Bain were filled with (harmless) baby shark, so plentiful that we could catch them in our hands. Fortunately we never met their mums or dads!

Once renowned as 'the land of a million palm trees' because of the abundance of fresh water springs – ains – that flowed beneath the islands, this marine phenomenon gave Bahrain its name – Land of Two Seas. In Arabic, 'bahr' means sea and 'thnain' means two. In centuries past, seafarers sailing to Bahrain were astounded by the thousands of aquifers that gushed from the seabed to mingle with the salty sea that created a unique confluence of velvety sweet water which also gave Bahraini pearls their exceptional lustre. Pearl divers could remain at sea for months by diving to the seabed and filling their leather water bags with sweet water to sustain them.

Sailing home beneath a pink twilight with a fresh breeze caressing our skins, a stunning sight was the setting sun as it dipped behind acres of date palms that stretched along the coast from the shoreline of Sanabis village – site of the Bahrain Exhibition Centre - to Janabiya and Zellaq. Knowing the sea like the back of his grizzled palm, Abdulla would drop anchor at certain spots where we would leap in to refresh ourselves in fresh springs that once flowed beneath where the Ritz Carlton and the reclaimed land as far as The BFC now stands.

A BACKWARD GLANCE

{ MAEVE KELYNACK SKINNER }

For it's tiny size, Bahrain has an exclusive, yet intertwined history and heritage, unique to anywhere in the world. It was the first place to discover oil along the Arabian peninsula, had fresh water aquifers beneath the seas which gave the island its name, it produced lustrous pearls sought after by emperors and royalty for centuries, and had the five thousand year old burial mounds which pre-dated the pyramids. Until the 1980s, more than one hundred thousand burial mounds stretched like buns on a baking tray across the island from A'Ali, flowing across the sands over what is now Hamad Town and Dumistan to Shakhura and near the Janabiya coast. They remained virtually undisturbed until the 1950s when the Danish Archaeological Expedition excavated some of the tumuli and other sites including the Barbar Temple where Bahrain's iconic copper bull's head was discovered.

Archaeologists have excavated a few hundred tumuli which yielded fascinating information of earlier occupants of Bahrain dating back to 3500BC when the Sumerians sailed from Mesopotamia to seek the secret of eternal life which they believed lay in the pearls found in the confluence of sweet and salt waters of Bahrain. They named it the Land of Dilmun and built a city at Saar, near the Saudi Causeway. Two thousand years later in 1500BC, Alexander of Greece detailed some of his navy to sail down the Gulf where they discovered the islands which they renamed Tylos and settled here for several hundred years. Both the Sumerians and Tylos civilisations buried their dead in circular tumuli, with pearls and jewellery, clay pots, pieces of iron and coins. A distinctive feature of the Tylos tombs were statues found at the head of each grave which named the interred bodies. These finds, including the exquisite Dilmun Seals are on display at the Bahrain Museum. Sadly for Bahrain's cultural heritage, the majority of tumuli have in the past thirty years, been bulldozed in favour of urbanisation. I once I asked a senior ministerial official why the tumuli were allowed to be destroyed and he replied "We don't need these old graves, we have some in the museum to show people. We need the land for housing." Perhaps he was right but Bahrain, and the world, has lost an irreplaceable part of history.

A single track road led from Manama through Riffa to Awali – the high place - an American style town built in the 1940s for expatriate employees of Caltex, the US oil giant which formed the Gulf's first joint venture with Bahrain Petroleum Company, now BAPCO. It was a world of its own with a private school, hospital, shops, cinema, offices and a club. A local joke was that Awali expats never left their compound until they flew out of Bahrain on leave. Members of Awali Golf Club, Bahrain's first, used to carry their own plastic green mats which they placed on the oil-brown earth to tee off from.

Driving south from from Awali was a journey into the Empty Quarter with the whole desert and the Jebel Dhukan to choose from for picnics by the sea or on the rimrock. Local families preferred to picnic beneath the shade of the acacia plantation near to Sakhir, a former Ruler's palace. Near the Tree of Life we regularly saw herds of dainty Reem gazelle, jackals or foxes, hares and giant lizards which spread themselves across the warm, potholed road. Walking in the desert after heavy winter rains, desert blooms spread a riot of colour across the dips and ridges of the terrain. Scattered across the surface where rain had dislodged the sand, you could pick up ancient pottery sherds, bottles, iron age arrow heads and other treasures.

A wonderful weekend getaway was to obtain a permit to camp for a couple of nights at Ras Al Bar, the very tip of the south of Bahrain. Usually only Western expats were mad enough to camp out in the heat, but we had great fun as the pristine beach was long and the sea was deep and cool. We often spotted pods of dolphin playing at sea, or the secretive dugong that lived off the sea grass in the shallows. Fishermen paddled their handmade reed boats into the shallows where the fish were so plentiful that they could spear hamour, saffi and other varieties on their long oars. They would offer us fat, gleaming hamour for a few fils which we would cook on the barbeque. A timeless sight when returning home at sunset was a ruined stone palace perched on the rim-rock at Riffa; silhouetted against the soft pink sky, it epitomised the ethereal beauty of Bahrain.

Another welcome seaside option was a private beach for Westerners to swim without being hassled. The gardens were a delight of manicured lawns running down to the beach shaded by fragrant citrus, almond, frangipani trees and date palms. Streams ran through the gardens where children could catch tadpoles and crabs. The sea was very shallow for about five hundred yards which was safe for toddlers and young children and when we got too hot, we cooled off in a fresh water pool in a covered bathhouse. Cold fizzy drinks were free and in the late afternoon, white clothed tables and chairs were set up on the beach where tea, sandwiches and cake were served.

Beyond Zellaq the road petered out to a sandy track where we nearly always got stuck, so everyone carried a rope, spade and old carpet in the car boot. A favourite spot was Thompson's Beach, now known as Al Jazira Beach. Here we would hold sunset barbeques and sing songs and swim in the sparkling phosphorescent sea until late at night when we would head home along dark unlit tracks, driving carefully to avoid camels which often lurched into the headlights.

The Budaiya Road was pure countryside with farms lining either side, interspersed with villages and a few country homes of some of Bahrain's older families. Stables were aplenty and you could ride from the Bahrain Fort along the beach to Jazra, then swing inland and gallop across the desert to the old racecourse – near Saraya Two – and watch the horse and camel races which sometimes ended in fisticuffs between rival owners. All fun and games on a Friday afternoon.

Nabi Saleh island off the Sitra Causeway, was a picture postcard island, a homage to palm trees which once stood tall and elegant, their fronds sheltering the village houses. Villagers here wore coloured dresses and veils and it was common to see them carrying jars on their heads having drawn water from the many aquifer wells on the island. Bahraini friends fondly recall family outings to Nabi Saleh to swim in its cool, sweet water pools and picnic beneath its shaded palms and to paddle in the shallows to catch small fish and prawns and especially to be there for turtle hatching, when baby turtles scuttled out of their sandy nests to race into the sea.

The Bahrain Rugby Football Club was originally established at the old RAF base at Muharraq airport and passengers were often treated to a quick glimpse of a rugby match as they landed. When the airport was expanded, it was decided to move the BRFC to its second location behind the large Saar Mosque in Budaiya. To raise funds for the new clubhouse, one of Bahrain's first Walkathons was held with strong virile club members walking from the airport site across the island to Budaiya. Several hours later, a raggle-taggle band of beer swilling, sunburnt and footsore members staggered into the new grounds where they plunged like sardines into the tiny swimming pool to revive their spirits. The Club was, and still is, one of the island's most popular venues and is fondly remembered by many for its infamous Rugby Reviews and for the high jinks that occurred during visiting team matches from around the Gulf.

One of my fondest memories is of a scavenger hunt. One task was to count the number of flags on the 'Irish Embassy' in Bahrain. This referred to a motley pile of green bricks decorated with forty shades of green flags. It was actually a shrine that stood at a crossroad between Sehla and Isa Town. The green painted mosque that replaced the shrine is still referred to by some as the 'Irish Mosque'.

A particularly memorable occasion was when President Hillary of Ireland arrived on a state visit in 1979. The rain that February would have done St Patrick proud, as the roads were flooded and a howling shamal was in progress. Undaunted, a group of valiant Bahraini workers clambered up every lamppost in Manama to hang the Irish tricolour. Just hours before the President arrived, an irate Irishman rang the Ministry of Foreign Affairs to complain why Bahrain was flying the Italian flag instead of the Irish one. A few hours later, up the lampposts went the stalwart crew to remove the offending green, white and red Italian flags to replace them with the green, white and gold of Ireland.

Bahrain's terrain changed dramatically in 1986 after the opening of the King Fahad Causeway linking us to Saudi Arabia and again in 1991 after the Gulf War. Large areas of wilderness have been replaced by main arterial roads linking Mina Salman to Janabiya, the Isa Town highway to Awali, Hamed Town was built and linked by the Shaikh Khalifa Highway to Seef and Manama. Yes, progress has spoiled much of our heritage and beauty spots but that has happened all over the world, yet the spirit of Bahrain remains unchanged and undaunted.

For five thousand years, Bahrain has welcomed adventurers to its shores. In recent times we expats have described it as 'the world's best kept secret'. Many people have left and returned on new postings by choice, as they know what a special place this is. Despite many changes to their traditional way of life, the Bahrainis are still the friendliest, most hospitable and amusing people you can meet. Overseas, if you catch someone's eye in the street or bump into someone, they usually look through you, whereas in Bahrain, people immediately break into a warm smile – and you automatically smile back - and feel the better for it.

Hospitals provide excellent medical care – you rarely have to wait more than a week for an appointment with a top surgeon. Educational standards in most schools deliver 'A' grade pupils who get into the world's top universities. Nowhere is more than an hour's drive from the airport where we can connect to anywhere in the world and the weather is only really hot for three or four months a year and, we have air-conditioning. For the rest of the year, temperatures are as pleasant as the Mediterranean.

Bahrain has been good to me and I realise how lucky I am to live here. I met my husband on my first day, his eldest son grew up with us in Bahrain and our two younger sons were born here and we've made wonderful friends from all over the world. The Bahraini family I came out to join so many years ago have been my family overseas. We lived as neighbours and our children were brought up together. Now we hope to retire here, because nowhere is as comfortable and easy to live in as Bahrain.

My Beautiful Bahrain is epitomised in a recent incident. I parked at a meter in Manama and after fumbling in my wallet realised that I'd no change. Sighing in frustration, I felt a tap on my shoulder and spun round to see an old beggar to whom I often gave a few fils. He'd uncoiled himself from his cardboard seat and handed me two hundred fils. That says it all.

BAHRAIN: MINARETS AND PALM TREES

by

David Hollywood

Minarets and palm trees,
Possess my pictured gaze,
Of heights within a vision,
In heat and sun and haze.

Exotic in appearance,
And elegant they stand,
In noble perseverance,
Amongst the warming sand.

As each reflects their setting,
Elusively and tall,
The harshness of the landscape,
Increase their statures call.

And as they summit skyward,
In search of heavens hall,
This Garden born of Eden,
Holds zeniths that enthrall.

THE JOURNEY HOME

by

Faridah Serajul Haq

Leila was trying her best to stay calm. She was returning to a familiar place; the country of her birth. Yet she could not help feeling apprehensive about her whole idea of returning to Bahrain, to heal the wounds of the last ten years. It had been a long time and Leila could not help but wonder if she'd made the right decision. She gave a long sigh, tears began to well in her eyes. She wiped them quickly before five-year old Sara could see her mother feeling sad. Sara had seen pictures of her mother's family and home and is excited to see grandma and grandpa, and all the presents she expects to receive.

"Mum, why are you crying?" Sara asked quizzically.

"Nothing dear, I was just remembering the movie we saw." Leila avoided a direct answer.

"But that was ages ago! Why are you remembering it now?" Sara questioned her mum just like any precocious five year old would do.

"OK, I promise not to cry again. Are you excited about seeing Bahrain?" Leila tried to change the subject and put on a happy voice.

"Yes, Yes. I feel tired now but I want to see so many things after I have slept for two whole days." Sara was serious about catching up on her sleep.

Poor child, the journey was too long and exhausting. Leila and Sara were practically at farewell functions for more than a week. If it was not a farewell lunch, it would be a farewell dinner and more invitations to attend. It was hard for both of them to say goodbye to so many wonderful people. Life is a journey that has many twists and turns, and Leila felt this journey to Bahrain was needed for a long time but she could not anticipate the outcomes for her and her young child. Her thoughts drifted to her own mother's words years ago…

It was a phone call that changed her life.

Umm Ahmed was so distraught, that her emotions shifted from anger to sadness. Then back to anger again in an attempt to let her daughter know that her decision is unacceptable to her family. "I want you to come home this instant, Leila." Umm Ahmed was practically yelling from thousands of miles away.

"What difference would it make, Umi? I have decided and I will do what I have made up my mind to do." Leila insisted on her opinion.

"You are not shameful of your behaviour? No woman in our family can be so disrespectful like you! What you are going to do is wrong! Wrong for our religion and wrong for our culture!" Umm Ahmed was about to lose her mind.

"Please Umi, I know what I am doing. I am not a child and I am not going against my religion or my culture. I am doing the right thing. Please try to understand Umi, please!" Leila begged for her mother's understanding.

" Leila, *habibati* I have only this to say to you. Leave that man and come home now! You have been away too long, you have forgotten your tradition. You cannot hurt me like this. I will never forgive you if you marry that American!" Umm Ahmed was wailing.

How can Leila forget this conversation. Her mother said she could never forgive her. What is so wrong about marrying John Anderson? He was a good man, a good husband and a good father. It was unfortunate that Umm Ahmed did not get a chance to meet and know John.

He was also a good Muslim.

Leila had been married to John for six years and it was a wonderful six years. Some people wait for a lifetime to find the love Leila and John had for that brief period. Leila was confident from the beginning that she made the right decision to stay in Wisconsin with John. However, her sadness persisted when she lost all contact with her family. Umm Ahmed practically disowned her, and forbid her family from communicating with Leila her 'lost' daughter.

The birth of Sara changed everything and Leila poured out her love on her child. She carried this life in her womb, just like Umm Ahmed had once carried her. Leila was beyond ecstasy when Sara was born. A million questions raced through Leila's mind as her apprehension grew the closer she was getting to her 'homeland;' how could she ever stop loving her? And so how could Umm Ahmed never want to see her daughter Leila again? Will she want to see and forgive her now? Has time healed the wounds and broken hearts?

She gazed at the clouds in the sky. Each like a cotton ball floating in the air. The sky was unbelievingly blue. It was on a similarly gorgeous day like this that John left his home in Madison, Wisconsin. Leila stood at the door to wish him a wonderful day. John just looked straight at her, a strange smile dancing on his face. Leila stood on the porch everyday to wish him goodbye but today was somewhat different.

"John, is something wrong? Are you OK?" Leila looked into John's eyes.

"I just want to take a good long look at my beautiful Leila before I go." John continued with the same strange, forlorn smile.

"Before you go? You never said things like that before. Is there something you want to tell me?" Leila hated asking such a question but she needed to know what was going on.

"Yes, there is something I want to tell you, I want you to remember it all the time; I love you very much. I thank you for our wonderful life together." John was unusually serious that morning. The next thing she knew, John hugged her tightly, went to his car and turned back to smile and wave at her.

The announcement from the cabin crew jolted Leila from her thoughts. The 'fasten your seat-belts' sign was flashing on the screen. The cabin crew was busy collecting earphones, pieces of plastic cups, and telling the passenger to straighten their seats and prepare for landing.

Leila thought to herself how appropriate was this reminder. She needs to also fasten her psychological seat-belt and prepare for the rough landing with Umm Ahmed. Her heart begins to pound in her chest. But seeing the happy smile on Sara's face made her calm down for a while.

"Mum, we are finally here. Yeah, Bahrain." Sara could not contain her excitement.

"Yes sweetie we are at last here. We are home." Leila felt the word 'home' seemed like a distant and unfamiliar term. Was not Wisconsin home as well? Or was it a resting place on the journey home?

All the passengers began to disembark, some rushing for connecting flights while others waited in their seats for the crowd to clear. Leila held Sara's hand and led her to the door. Sara clutching her Winnie the Pooh backpack was glaring at everything, a happy smile perpetually on her face. Leila feels that she too needs to have a similar happy smile.

The weather is steaming despite a soft whirl of evening breeze. Dragging her bags while making sure Sara is by her side, Leila looks around for an available airport taxi. Her eyes look directly at a tall, slender, middle aged Bahraini man smoking a cigarette profusely while talking animatedly with two other men. Sara starts to pull her mother's hand to ask a question as usual.

"Mum, why is that man wearing a long dress?" Sara began to giggle.

"Hush, *habibati*, that is not a dress, It is called a kandura. Most men here wear one usually in white. Please don't laugh, it is not polite." Leila too has not seen a man in a traditional Khaleej's outfit for a long time. It was her late father's favourite outfit and he was proud to wear it to work despite his senior position in a local bank.

"*Assalamualeikum*. Can I take you somewhere?" The taxi driver in the long dress politely asked.

"*Wa'aleikumsalam*. I need to go to Mina Salman." Leila responded somewhat overwhelmed by the crowd queuing for taxis outside the airport.

Without much hesitation, the taxi driver carried Leila's bags and put them in the trunk of his white and beige taxi.

"Looks like you are planning to stay a while in Bahrain?" the driver inquired.

Leila was edgy and felt annoyed with all the questions. She just wanted to reach her destination with the hope that all will be well with her family. This was a surprise visit as none of her family members knew of her return. She decided if she is welcomed back into her old home, then she would consider remaining longer in Bahrain. Alternatively, there was always Wisconsin, if she could bear surviving with such painful memories.

The taxi began to cruise on the crowded road approaching Manama. How things have changed in the last ten years. Many places were no longer recognisable to Leila; skyscrapers are all over the island and the city was vibrant with life. Where was the old, quiet, laid-back Bahrain that Leila used to remember? Perhaps lost in the pursuit of development, whatever that word means these days.

The taxi driver eyed both Leila and her daughter curiously. He caught her eye in the rear view mirror.

" My name is Ali. I thought it will be nice if we know each other's names at least. Are you from Bahrain?"

"I am Leila and this is my daughter Sara. I am Bahraini, if you really need to know." Leila answered curtly.

"Looks like you've been away from your country for a long time?" Ali wanted to pursue the conversation.

"Something like that." Leila was beginning to be exasperated by Ali's overt curiosity.

"I left this country once upon a time as well." Ali continued.

Leila was silent, hoping Ali would quit his persistent questions. He continued looking at her from the rear view mirror, perhaps hoping for some response. Instead Leila wound down the window to let the evening air in. Her hand gently stroked her daughter's hair while the child began to fall asleep. Leila was beginning to feel nervous again about her decision to return home. What was the family meeting going to be like, she wondered in her mind? Will her family accept her, like nothing had ever happened between them?

"I went to live in the US for twenty years." Ali continued his story thinking Leila might be interested.

Leila ignored the man and continued looking at the sights as the taxi moved from one part of the city to the next.

"You look sad." Ali commented, much to Leila's annoyance.

"I am just tired, that is all." Leila tried to ignore Ali.

"Don't worry because everything is going to be all right. Wherever you go, there is nothing like returning home. Believe me, I know." Ali tried to convince Leila.

Leila could not help but notice that despite his attempts to annoy her with questions, he was really quite a nice man. Maybe she should just sit back and do some talking anyway, to ease her mind. She needed to keep her worries at bay.

"So tell me, why would a Bahraini man live in the States for twenty years? You must have a good reason, right?" It was Leila's turn to ask the questions.

Ali started to laugh, at the same time a little embarrassed by Leila's question.

"To be honest with you I went to study engineering but dropped out of college to marry my American sweetheart. My parents could not accept my decision. I could not return home with my foreign wife because it would hurt my parents too much. They were traditional people and you just could not change them to accept my ways." Ali was honest about his past.

"But you came back....why?"

Ali was silent for a while. He then changed the subject, describing new buildings in the city.

"Look, there is the Financial Harbour. Bahrain is really attracting foreign investment." Ali kept pointing and describing the background of various buildings they saw on the way to Mina Salman.

"You will make a good tour guide, Mr. Ali." Leila could not help but smile to herself. It was obvious that he was avoiding any further questions about his past life. He continued driving in silence, occasionally changing the radio station.

A traditional Bahraini song came on the air. Ali began humming along enjoying the rhythm of a famous song from the 1970's.

"Do you like local music?" he asked, tapping his fingers on the steering wheel in tune with the song.

"Not really. I have not heard it in a long while." Leila, in reality, could not even relate to Bahraini culture any more. It seemed so alien to her.

"You have been away too long, yes?"

"I guess long enough to forget my origin," Leila admitted.

"No one can forget their origin. Once a Bahraini, always a Bahraini. That's my belief." Ali was affirming himself.

"When you returned after twenty years away, was it easy? Tell me the truth." Leila suddenly wanted to know more about Ali's past adventures.

"Yes, and no." Ali's answer was brief.

"Go on tell me more." Leila insisted.

"Am I helping you if I tell you what happened to me in the US?" Ali queried.

"Yes, and maybe no." Leila too was brief in her response.

"I told you I got married, dropped out of college and had kids with my wife Fatima. We did not have much money but we had a good life. Then one day, it was all gone. Fatima became sick and the next minute, she left me forever." Ali's voice began to quiver with emotion.

"I have two teenage boys that I could not take care on my own, so almost overnight, I made a decision to return back here." Ali made it all sound so simple.

Obvious to Leila, that Ali's life parallels her own. She too had someone she loved taken away from her so suddenly.

"Can I ask you what brought you home?" It was now Ali's turn to ask.

Leila took her time to reply. "I was married too, just like you, to an American. He left home to go to work two years ago and never returned home. It was snowing heavily, when his car skidded and... The police told me what happened but I was not interested to know, well, it doesn't matter, does it, when someone is gone forever?"

They were both quiet, each one lost in the thoughts of their past. What is the possibility of two strangers ending in the same car and sharing a similar experience? Things do happen for a reason, don't they?

"How was it for you?" Leila continued after a long moment of silence.

"You mean the loss, or the return?" Ali was not sure what Leila meant.

"Both. But talk about what you are more comfortable with."

"The loss of Fatima was hard on me and the children, especially my younger boy. To tell you the truth, I still haven't fully recovered. But the return, *Masha'Allah*, I cannot believe how my mother just welcomed me back like I never left. I am her son and will always be. That's a mother's love for you." Ali briefly smiled.

Leila smiled in return. "Actually, I am glad I took your taxi even though it was the oldest and dirtiest one in the queue." They both laughed to lighten the previous serious moment.

The music continued when their conversation came to a halt. It was an old song about fishermen returning home after a long day at sea. Leila felt she had drifted away just like the fishermen in their boats. Like them, she returned again to the shore ready to face another day.

The sign on the highway said 'Mina Salman.' Ali turned to the right and asked Leila the exact location of her family home. How could she possibly tell? The streets were so different and everything seemed to have changed so much. Then she saw it. Her unmistakably familiar family home. The same multicoloured bougainvillea overflowing from the wall to the road. For some unknown reason, the front of the house was brightly lighted with multicoloured lanterns. And then she saw a banner saying "*Marhaba Leila* (Welcome Leila)" How could they possibly know?

As the taxi approached the front gate, a crowd of relatives came to the car. Almost at once, everyone was saying, '"Leila is here! Leila is here!" From among them, stood Umm Ahmed silently. Leila got out of the taxi to embrace practically all of her relatives at once. When Leila came closer to Umm Ahmed, her eyes began to well and tears flowed without her realising it. Without saying a word, Umm Ahmed embraced her tightly. No words were necessary from her mother. Leila knew she was back in her mother's life. Once a daughter, always a daughter.

She returned to the taxi and woke the sleeping Sara. Everyone exclaimed "*MashaAllah* what a beautiful child you have! Let me see her!"

Leila, in her excitement had forgotten to pay the fare to Ali. Ali was waiting and leaning by the taxi door, idly smoking a cigarette. He grinned when he saw Leila approaching.

"Mr. Ali, thank you for the ride home." Leila too had a broad smile.

"I like it that you say 'home.' You know now that all the time you were travelling, it was actually a journey for you to finally come home. Ms. Leila." Ali said philosophically.

Ali gave a final puff on his cigarette, threw it on the ground and crushed it with his feet. He opened the taxi door, switched on his Bahraini traditional music station and drove away, all along his hand waving to the jubilant crowd who could not stop hugging and kissing Leila and Sara.

FROM ANOTHER COUNTRY

by

Zahra Zuhair

From another country,
when I was five,
I came to Bahrain,
young and alive.

Smiling in anticipation
over the life that awaited me,
unaware of all that will come
my way and all I will be.

Met many people,
from many places,
and was welcomed grandly
by many smiling faces.

Today, many, many years later,
without hesitation I say
of this country and all in it,
as I have grown, so have they.

Progressing and growing
amazing the vast globe,
while inviting the world through its doors,
this country is not just a symbol of hope.

With a struggle on its shoulders
like the struggles shared by many a country,
Bahrain has risen
all around me.

I now bear witness
to all good things this country has to offer
and know in my heart,
it's the reluctance of the people to suffer

that has wonderfully bound us all
with the sand that blows through this country,
and the dates that grow in its palms,
it's all of us, including you and me.

MY BEAUTIFUL BAHRAIN, MY BEAUTIFUL ANYWHERE

by

Nadia Muijrers

My opinion when it comes to Bahrain's beauty is not only subjective; it has been quite confused throughout my life. I come from an ethnically mixed background with a Dutch father and Bahraini mother. I grew up in the Netherlands as a child, and then one day my entire childhood existence was uprooted and, at the age of ten, new seeds were planted on my behalf in Bahrain. Naturally any resistance there has less to do with Bahrain than the experience of change itself, but having lived in two very different countries impacts the person I am today. I sometimes wonder what I would be like had I lived my entire life in the Netherlands, or all in Bahrain. My relationship with Bahrain has changed many times though I did come to the realisation that it has been my home for quite a few years now, regardless of where I may have been living at the time. I have now lived in Bahrain longer than I have in any other one country, and I am happy to say we're getting along much better now.

The year 2011 has been quite a tough time for Bahrain in good and bad ways. I would have loved to write this piece had 2011 not been what it is for the country, but the timeliness of this anthology has motivated me even further. Given my historically mixed feelings towards living in the country, I started by looking for inspiration in others who live or have lived in Bahrain. I asked anyone who was willing to briefly answer:

"What is your favourite thing about Bahrain? and if you could, at the snap of your fingers, change/improve one thing about Bahrain, what would that be?"

The responses I received where overwhelmingly positive. People who have experienced Bahrain, love and care for it. Answers varied, but the consistency of how much people cared to tell me their opinion and to stand up for the country – no matter who they were – was truly touching. Given my own personal culture, lifestyle and personality, the group of people asked varied quite a bit. The mix included a cross-section of Bahraini society as well as expatriates who lived here for varying lengths of time. A few friends (somewhat cautiously) enquired why I was asking these questions, and by telling them what I planned to do, one strongly encouraged I write this piece and another was inspired to start a different writing project as a result of me just having asked the questions.

My favourite answer to the first question was "it has you in it" whereas my favourite answer to the second question was "import more good-looking men". So much for the objectivity of my survey! Joking aside, the following sampler of answers from very different people will give you a good idea of how people feel about our little island:

`"I miss the food! I miss the kind people, I miss Mai Tai (bar), I miss brunch on Fridays at Mövenpick, I miss the shopping, I miss the weather, I miss the warm waters! I miss being able to drive amazing cars where gas is cheap! I miss everything! Except the labour conditions for certain people." - Expatriate, lived in Bahrain for a few years and has now moved elsewhere with her job.

"One; our multiculturalism. Two; due to the result of the political situation, I would say I hope for people to love and accept each other once again and more than before." - Bahraini, lives in Bahrain

"Simple. People: Friendly, helpful, educated and hard-working. Cosmopolitan environment yet five minutes drive out of the city and you get a sense of how Bahrain looked like thirty-plus years back." - Bahraini, lives in Bahrain

"For what I would like to change, I would say more acceptance of differences. What I love about it is the fact the people are down to earth and humble - actually most humble in the Middle East." - Middle Eastern expatriate, lives between Saudi Arabia and Bahrain

"I want beaches like Jumeirah (Dubai). We're a damn island. I want to erase 2011 events and make everything go back to normal. I want a better standard of living for the people so that everyone is comfortable. My favourite thing about my island is how humble and friendly the Bahrainis are. This is not what I feel; this how other nationalities feel about us. It's a small island but has a rich culture. A small island, but every neighbourhood is unique and different from the other. Our accent is the best and everyone loves it. There are a lot of favourite things!" - Bahraini, lives in Bahrain

By far the most popular answer to the first question concerned the character of Bahrain's people. Bahrainis are described as most humble, friendly, educated (and so on) in the region. While there is plenty about the Bahraini character I could complain about, I have to agree that there is truth in this stereotype. I grew up being fed information about the goodness of our society's character and as an adult I gladly discovered it myself - definitely so when compared to the region. Qatar may be richer, and Dubai more cosmopolitan and developed, but as a society (and in spite of recent events) Bahrain remains most humble, educated, hard working and friendly - as described. My personal experiences aligned with the answers I received.

Due to recent political events and social unrest, there has been quite a bit of 'hate' going around among Bahrainis which I will not deny. It has caused strains on our social fabric that have been emotionally very difficult to observe and experience. I have always been of the opinion that where development of any kind is concerned, making changes at the economic and political level are easier and more tangible than at a sociological level. Bahrain will need time to heal, but I genuinely hope it does. It would be a shame for coming generations to have this trait of good character be changed for the worse. I think the characteristic of a people is one of the most important features of any country. It is no different from an individual; if a person's underlying character does not suit you or is bad, does the rest really matter? The rest is window dressing. Bahrain's people are far from perfect, but no person or society is. And while a stereotype is but a stereotype, does not evolve out of nothing.

Another positive feature that was repeated was Bahrain's multiculturalism. Historically, Bahrain was central to trade routes meaning various peoples passed through the country. To this day its population is diverse, and the 2010 Bahrain Census shows that non - Bahrainis, comprising fifty-four percent of total population, now outnumber Bahrainis. Non- Bahrainis have been in the majority since 2008. To add another level, amongst Bahrainis themselves there is great diversity based on ethnicity, religion, and even language. In any society - but especially so in cosmopolitan or diverse societies - living together is difficult unless people are respectful to their differences and choose to live together peacefully and as equals. At the time of writing this, Bahrain's ability to do this is currently being tested at a scale I have not yet before experienced in my brief lifetime here. It is difficult to express this point without over exaggerating the situation to war-zone levels, but I also do not want to underestimate the importance of what the country is going through. I only hope that the societal strains heal so that the events of 2011 do not lead to the withering of the country's most beautiful traits.

In discussing the answers to the first question (what people's favourite thing about Bahrain is), one of the main complaints (the consequences of the 2011 political events) has also been highlighted. An additional area which could use improvement, with which I agree, is that our little island does not always feel like one. We are blessed with both desert and sea, and yet looking at the number and quality of our beaches you would not think you lived on an island. I will not delve into each colourful snap-of-the-fingers-request-for-change given, but Bahrain could certainly use more beaches that are public, pleasant and safe. A number of public walkways and parks have been developed recently, and every time I have gone to one it is full of people and families which is wonderful. Given beaches are the topic here and not parks, it may be more difficult to balance the cultures of those who wish to bathe in bikinis with those who do not. I would suggest giving yourself free choice and others respect, but if that worked the world's problems would have been solved already. Nevertheless, Bahrain is an island and an island should have plenty recreational beaches where people can relax, enjoy the warm weather (of which we have plenty), enjoy water sports, and so on.

Going back to my own confused opinions about Bahrain and my feelings towards it, the answer I wish to offer is the one which helped me find beauty in it after many years during which I focused on anything but beauty. A quote by Dr. Wayne Dyer sums it up very simply: *"Heaven on Earth is a choice you must make, not a place you must find."*

To many this may sound awfully cliché but fact of the matter is everything in life exists in duality. This is evident in everyday life. With regards to living in any one country, I have visited and lived in enough countries to know that there are aspects of life in each that I simultaneously love and that I hate, that have the potential to make me exquisitely happy and absolutely miserable. When I say there are things about Bahrain (life here, its people, its culture) that I love and hate, I can just as easily say the same for another country, including my childhood home, the Netherlands. It really is a matter of how you choose to look at your life, wherever you may be based. Should not your mindset define your life rather than what part of the world's earth you happen to stand on?

Globalisation and communication are also making the world increasingly converged. I have found western lifestyles and practices in the East, and eastern lifestyles and practices in the West. A closer look at any societies, cultures and religions will also reveal the basic building blocks to be the same. It may not always seem that way at the surface, and unfortunately it seems the majority of the world's population will not choose to view things this way. Not sufficiently so anyway. The current ripples in our world - the financial crisis, increasing income inequality in the West, the economic rise of China, as well as the Arab Spring - have further pushed the overly simplistic divisions of the world into question. Which country is modern and which is backward? Which is developed and which is undeveloped? In any country, you will find worlds within worlds.

My favourite thing about Bahrain, and the most beautiful thing about it to me, is that it just so happens to be the setting I am finding my own peace in. As I am choosing to live a happy and peaceful life full of creativity, growth and freedom, I am increasingly finding these qualities in my surroundings. Wherever I may live in the future, I hope to take this beauty with me.

"While we may not be able to control all that happens to us, we can control what happens inside us." - Benjamin Franklin

Cultivate beauty from the inside out. It is the only way your life stands a chance to be beautiful, no matter where you find yourself.

MY BEAUTIFUL BAHRAIN

by
DaVonda St.Clair

My Beautiful Bahrain…
Has encouraged my spiritual wisdom and prayer life.
Hearing the call to prayer physically reminds me to always take time out of my day to thank my Heavenly Father…

For myself…for life… for family… for grace… for wisdom…for peace…

Even if I forget my waking prayer or the workday becomes too busy the Adhan (call to prayer) causes me to stop and pray.

Taking time to open my heart, my mouth and my mind for praise, worship, confession, guidance, thankfulness, existence, love…

Not waiting until something drastic, dramatic or devastating to happen in order to call or talk to the Lord.

My Beautiful Bahrain…

Has helped my strength/peace of mind and mental flexibility.

With revelations of increased tolerance, patience, acceptance, self love, self worth, personal development, counselled progression of others and TRUTH.

Elevating my inner strength and inner power.

Conveying internal happiness and bliss to all.

Always comfortably adjusting, switching and blending into changing environments.

Constantly building thinking power by expanding my openness to new and different ideas on a global perspective.

Living… instead of ONLY existing.

{ DAVONDA ST.CLAIR }

My Beautiful Bahrain…

Has radiated a (self) consciousness …an enlightenment … an awakening like no other… a self actualisation.

What more can I accomplish, what additional contributions will I be able to make…toward the immediate community…the global community?

Being more circumstantially aware of what's around me, who's around me (physically / spiritually), what non-verbal/verbal impressions I give, what energies are accepted within my realm…

Not living by emotions, instead, living by intuition, advertence and philosophy.

Living up to my full potential, with a restored focus, increased ambition not giving myself boundaries…..being limitless.

My Beautiful Bahrain…

A country known for its oil and pearls.

Increased my cultural knowledge / awareness / sensitivity…for my own America, the Gulf States, Africa, for all countries around the world, to a more profound level.

Where there is a cultivation of the soul and mind.

Being more in tune with cultural values, beliefs and perceptions.

To distinguish, interpret and evaluate cultures and traditions in different ways.

Mindful that there are multiple ways to reach the same goals and to live life.

My Beautiful Bahrain…

Nurtured the development of my womanhood.

Encouraging a fire for determination on knowing what I want.

Upholding my values for who I am.

Fostering the strength of sisterhood from all my beautiful sisters of every age, race, ethnicity and religion.

Knowing the power I (we as women) possess, having my sisters rallying around one another with united support.

My Beautiful Bahrain…

Has embraced my imperfections while illuminating a vibrant personality.

Manifesting goodness, purity, and selflessness.

honouring myself and all accomplishments.

Reminding me to spoil and pamper myself.

Celebrating life with style, class and opulence.

My Beautiful Bahrain…

Is for love found, love damaged, love lost, love hoped for, love renewed, love soon to come and love meant to be.

In favour of what love has given me.

For all that love has taught me.

Continued wisdom for what love has revealed to me.

All love will bring to me.

Strength for what love has in store for me.

Everything I've given for love.

What I will entirely continue to give for love.

My Beautiful Bahrain…

A place that I miss when I'm away for too long.

MY BEAUTIFUL, LOVELY, EXASPERATING, EXPATRIATE BAHRAIN

by
Rohini Sunderam

Having spent a total of nineteen years in Bahrain, I think I can claim with some degree of certainty that we all develop a dichotomous relationship with the kingdom. We love it, we hate it, and we'll defend living here tooth and nail to outsiders, especially every time we return to our 'home countries'. Yet we miss, or pretend to miss, certain aspects of 'back home' especially when we're in a mixed social group or when life isn't quite going our way, like when 'that yobbo with the Saudi licence plate' cuts us off without so much as signalling. "OMG," I can hear so many people (including myself) say, "Back home the cops would be on him in a flash"… or similar.

And, given Bahrain's history, I have developed the quirky opinion that this love-hate relationship with Bahrain has always existed, even from the time the legendary Gilgamesh first came to Dilmun. Now, I'm guessing that all Bahrain-o-philes have some idea of the Epic of Gilgamesh and his supposed connection with Dilmun – considered by some to have been a name for Bahrain.

For those who don't know it, here's a quick run-down garnered from Wikipedia: The Epic of Gilgamesh is a poem from Mesopotamia and among the earliest known works of literature. Scholars believe that it originated as a series of Sumerian legends and poems about Gilgamesh King of Uruk – which is in present day Iraq.

The story revolves around a relationship between Gilgamesh and his close friend Enkidu, with whom he undertakes many dangerous quests that incur the displeasure of the gods. In one of these quests, the two friends kill the Bull of Heaven and so to punish them, the gods have Enkidu killed. The latter part of the epic focuses on Gilgamesh's distressed reaction to

Enkidu's death, which takes the form of a quest for immortality. In this quest Gilgamesh tries to learn the secret of eternal life by undertaking a long and perilous journey to meet the immortal flood hero, Utnapishtim and his wife, who are among the few survivors of the Great Flood, and the only humans to have been granted immortality by the gods. Gilgamesh comes to the twin peaks of Mt. Mashu at the ends of the earth, through the mountains along the Road of the Sun. He follows it for twelve 'double hours' in complete darkness. Managing to complete the trip before the sun catches up to him, Gilgamesh arrives in a garden paradise full of jewel-laden trees; in another legend this is the place referred to as Dilmun.

Gilgamesh notices that Utnapishtim seems no different from himself, and asks him how he obtained immortality. Utnapishtim tells an ancient story of how the gods decided to send a great flood - very similar to the Flood in the Bible and Noah's Ark. The main point seems to be that Utnapishtim was granted eternal life in unique, never to be repeated circumstances. After instructing his ferryman to wash Gilgamesh and clothe him in royal robes, Utnapishtim prepares to send him back to Uruk. As they are leaving, Utnapishtim's wife asks her husband to offer a parting gift. That's when Utnapishtim tells Gilgamesh of a boxthorn-like plant at the very bottom of the ocean that will make him young again. In some stories it is the pearls that are considered the 'grapes of the sea' that will grant immortality. Gilgamesh obtains the plant by binding stones to his feet (very similar to the early pearl divers of Bahrain) so he can walk on the bottom of the sea. He recovers the plant and plans to test it on an old man when he returns to Uruk. Unfortunately, when Gilgamesh stops to bathe, the plant is stolen by a serpent which sheds its skin as it departs. There is a lot more and it is a far more complex epic than I have placed here.

In the Epic, Gilgamesh returns to Uruk, however, in my imagination, he never really leaves and the following poem draws on several myths around ancient Bahrain, using different names by which it was or supposedly was known – Dilmun, Tilmun, Nidukki, Kur-ni-tuk. Those interested may explore these further through that wonderful resource; the Internet.

THE LAMENT OF GILGAMESH

South, south he rushed
To the midst of the sea
To the place of the rising sun
To the place where some day
A king would live like a fish
Twelve double hours away.

The fifth King of Uruk was Gilgamesh
Descended five times from the time of the flood
And son of the goddess Ninsun.
He sailed for a day
He sailed for a night
He sailed in search of Dilmun.
He wished to eat of the grapes of the sea
Those pearls from its bed would grant him
Eternal bliss and companionship
With the sage King Utnapishtim
In legendary Dilmun
In twice-blessed Dilmun.

Twice blessed by the god of sweet waters
Twice blessed by the god called Enki
So south he rushed, south by south-west
And he met with a following wind
Until he came upon this jewelled isle
(A sad, far cry from Sumer).

Here the date palms stood tall sentinels
Their green arms stretched to the sky
Waving a warning from dusk until dawning
That this idyll would soon pass by
But, he heeded them not brave Gilgamesh
For he had reached the isle of his dreams.

Then Gilgamesh dropped anchor
And entered the waters green
Where betwixt the salt, through the seabed rose
The sweet waters of Bahr ein
With stones on his feet down, down he dived
To the rocks where the pearl beds lay
He closed his eyes against the salt
He pinched his nose with a date palm peg
While he harvested those pearls of rose and grey
Harvested the grapes of eternal day
In the twice-blessed waters of a tiny bay
Off the island of Muharraq near Bahrain
Off the waters green that spread between
Muharraq and Bahrain.

How long he stayed beneath the waves
Neither he nor the sages could tell
But he took many shapes beneath the seas
Once a dugong shy, then a dolphin spry
Then a shark, then a dolphin again.

And he sang a song, a lament forlorn
Of what he saw had been done to Dilmun.
And this was its burden long:

"Ah me Dilmun, Tilmun!
What became of your bearded palm trees green?
What became of your shingled shores?
What became of your soft undulating sands?
Of the burial mounds of your immortal clans?
Who has broken these temples and laid them bare
So that emptied and hollowed and ravaged they stare
At the sky and the taunting sun?
Ah me Nidukki!
Did the oil then come?
As Mesopotamia of old had foretold?
And is it true Kur-ni-tuk
That your pearls you forsook
For the sake of the black, black gold?"

And at night when a full moon is in the sky
And a Sambuk is sailing silently by
Old sailors at their fish traps say;
If you hear the shudder of an oil-tanker
Start up on a night such as this
Emanating from the sea comes a moan and a cry
And the lament of Gilgamesh.

And to what do we owe the changes that came about in Dilmun? As Gilgamesh says in his lament: the discovery of oil. This as we know, changed life forever in Bahrain. The next verse deals with some of the legendary references to Dilmun the land where 'the raven never croaked, and the sheep lay alongside the lion without fear'.

DILMUN

The raven does not croak here
Nor the lion roar
But this today is after
And that was before.
The raven comes disguised now
His croak softened with chalk
The lion is a prancing Peugeot
And though the Jaguar doesn't roar
A Van dan Plas or an XJ6 purr slowly by.
On Fridays the palm-fringed streets
Trill to the sounds of a Suzuki Jeep
A Cougar pounces down the road
Rubbing shoulders with a GMC's load...
And a forgotten nodding donkey
Wearing a hoopoe bird's face
Hangs it head in shamed disgrace.

All that is in the past. And to this day so many of us, who come to Bahrain and stay for more than two years, are mesmerised by the country, the easy life, and some even convert to Islam, often for love. The following is in memory of a person from Scotland who followed the Great Prophet for love and gave up all that had once been second nature to him. I always believed that behind his sad eyes there was a hankering for his early life. I could be wrong, but there is a sixth sense that sometimes picks up on that intangible emotion: wistfulness. I sensed it here, although the individual has stayed on in Bahrain and made this country his home.

NO CUP O' KINDNESS

He came all the way
From a land of grey
Craggy rocks and soft green moss
Where the harshness of the landscape
Was ever mellowed in a mist.
And in his whispered, burry voice
Lingered a memory: 'I wish'
I hadn't heard the words
Of another Prophet calling
I hadn't seen a promised land
Nor learnt of its appealing
Enchantment of another kind
Delusions of the mind
Seeming straightforwardness
Ever twisted in a tangled mess
Severe deprivations of the body
Seducements to the spirit.

Yet, daily
The indulgences to satisfy the flesh
Blew up before his very eyes
And more and more did he disguise
His weariness
With pathetic little gossip
Disparaging the lifestyle
Of what was the right style
Yet tried to seem so flip about himself.
Hiding as best he could
The image of a man he would
In other circumstances, most despise.

He languished.
Near a lake of sand
Beneath a clear blue sky.
He withered
In the promised land
And never more said 'aye'
To an inch of amber in a glass
Nor a rude and honest high
Not e'en that cup o' kindness
That was drunk for 'Auld Lang Syne'.

And then there are so many of us others, who just enjoy the marvellous freedom that tax-free salaries provide. The material delights, the facility with which one can go buy another car, for instance... So this one is dedicated to auto enthusiasts who have their pick of vehicles, makes, models and marques:

WINDOW SHOPPING FOR WHEELS

Ah! The weekend!
Let's enjoy.
And to a car showroom deploy
Our energies. Our fantasies
Because after all some day
The will to go will go away
And perhaps the wherewithal
Will go the way of pleasures all
Down to a might-have-been.

Now, let's see. What shall it be?
The Town Car that's left on the shelf
The latest Taurus, or shall we
Indulge our fantasies and go for
A Lincoln Continental under a self-financing scheme?
Let's to another showroom wander
And check out the newest Honda
BMW's over priced for me
And, though they're nice
I don't care for Land Rover
A Mitsubishi'll do for you
We could get it brand new.
For myself, I can't decide
Perhaps I'll check the classifieds
And exercise a little prudence.
Or shall we in a fit of caprice

For a Cadillac or Bentley place a deposit?
But really when you look at it
The cash one spends upon some cars
Is worth a flat, a home, by far
More likely to appreciate…

But, let's to a showroom anyway
It's how I like to spend Thursday.

Then there are the children who grow up here, who believe that this way life exists everywhere. Their parents wish to caution them, to tell them to study hard, because 'back home' things are different. Either the academics are too hard or daily life – no housemaids, nannies, cooks, or someone to take care of laundry. There's also the inconvenient need to travel by public transport and not be chauffeur driven everywhere or own a car with ease. In addition, here they see that most people are able to enjoy fully paid-for three-week vacations and go wherever one's fancy takes one, in addition to making that obligatory visit 'home'.

Consequently, many of our children grow up not really believing our tales that life isn't quite the happy-go-lucky existence they enjoy here. To them it's another of our fake bogeyman tales, which they think we invent so that they might work a little harder.

WHICH IDEAL

I came here when I was four
The world was still so new to me
The sun rising and full blown
The moon: half, full, or crescent 'C'

MY BEAUTIFUL, LOVELY, EXASPERATING, EXPATRIATE BAHRAIN
{ ROHINI SUNDERAM }

I know no different I cannot see
That this idyll
Is a shell and it's fragile (I've been told).

The blue skies and the palm fronds
Clubs on Fridays
Ramadan dry days
The summer sea a static pond
Of which I have grown fond.
I know no different I cannot see
That this idyll
Is a shell and it's fragile (so they say).

Easy school days, breezy homework
When I grow up I'll be no clerk
Tennis lessons at the club
Tuesdays brass band
Life is swimming
And the so-called real world
Is just a quirk.
I know no different I cannot see
That this idyll
Is a shell and it's fragile (is it really?).

Yet, somewhere a wave beckons
Other horizons call to me
Saying there's a greener, brighter land

Away beyond the sea.
They say it daily drizzles there
The skies are pearly grey
There's an exciting acrid smell
Of happenings in the air.
And the future that it promises
Is clear and bright and fair.
I think perhaps that that too
Is an idyll and a shell.

Ah! The expat who is into everything: we see them in souqs and malls, striding with the latest equipment into a gym or club. He or she enjoys a busy round of social and 'business' entertainment, and lives life to the full. However, even these individuals know deep within their hearts, or at least they always have that nagging suspicion that on a dime it could all suddenly come to an end.

BUSY, BUSY

Tennis: Saturday, Monday, Tuesday.
Golf, I get in early, early Friday.
The Manama Players on Wednesday —
No that's the singers.
Sunday, church of course.
Thursdays we keep for dinner parties
And hobnob with the glitterati
After golf Friday's reserved for the family
Unless of course it's absolutely necessary
Then we might, just might

Ask the housemaid to stay overnight
I take the children to school every day
In the BMW except Wednesday
When I take the Isuzu
For she has bridge and plays till two
Oh, the workload of our workaday week
It isn't easy but it isn't steep
We start at seven thirty in the a.m.
We knock off at half past one
We might go back after three
But the bosses leave it up to me.
The money's good, the sun is bright
And the memory of commuting is a dark, dark, night.

Frequently one comes across the 'wife' who doesn't or can't, for any number of reasons, work outside the home. She is involved in many activities and has an opinion, sadly, often negative, about how people are treated in the workplace, especially her husband. In some cases she may be right, but dear, oh dear, she feels she must express her exasperation... although if the truth were told, she loves it here!

IS THIS HAPPY?

I can't stand it any more!
This daily dreaming
Work that only seems to be, yet, he slogs all day
But doesn't seem to have got far.
His efforts spill into my life.

It's not right.
Are we tied hand and foot?
Are we bound by some Mephistophelean deed?
I've told him, enough! Let's leave.

You call this a school here?
This 'hunky-dory' learn what you will
Without text books or tests
And then they tout abroad that it's the best.
Yet, I must do the teaching one on one.
It's not right.
Will the sins of the parents
Be visited on these so young?
I've told him, enough! Let's leave.

They're a nuisance
These sunny days
All we do is swim and laze
Like salamanders in the sand
We bask and then we hurry.
It's not right
The ease of our existence
Is it rust upon ourselves?
Or a corrosion of the mind that first hits the cells?
I've told him, enough! Let's leave.

This whole sensation is so strange
A circular path of repetition
With no change.
No ambition to fulfil
No hopes to still
No disappointments to fear.
I do believe
That all in all
I am happy here.

The following is dedicated to those of us who revel in this new-found wealth and freedom. Double-income families enjoy the best of the best. They enjoy access to the many delightful services in Bahrain and the low-cost labour helps, put us in an altogether different class. And in honour of them:

APPURTENANCES

But of course, my love, don't you know
My whisky-voice is mature mellow?
I am what I am because I got there
On my own steam — more or less.
It helps. He's in oil.

But, I worked too
And made it... did you?
House mortgage paid up in Lancashire
A Mercedes for him, for me a Daimler.
Single carat diamonds in each ear

And none of your eighteen carat gold, my dear.
Twenty two, it doesn't matter
That gold's gone down or is it up?

We take R & R trips to London town
Sometimes the Seychelles
And perhaps this winter we'll finally go
On that much put-off trip to Mexico.

I'm Joan-Collins slim with a bit more style
The tailors here are so agile.
Weekly facials and hairdos
An oil massage for an hour or two.
I'm berry brown from sunshine haze
While on our yacht on most Fridays.

No, it isn't an exotic lifestyle really
Everyone lives like this, well, nearly.

After spending several years in Bahrain, we begin to notice that we have a disconnection with families and friends in our home countries. That's when our conversion to Bahrain-o-phile is complete, and the idea and acceptance that this has become our 'home' fully dawns on us.

HOME THOUGHTS AT HOME

Every time I visit home
I think, I ask, 'is this my home?'

MY BEAUTIFUL, LOVELY, EXASPERATING, EXPATRIATE BAHRAIN
{ ROHINI SUNDERAM }

The jostling crowds seem louder now
The relations seem more cloying now
And too, with every passing year
Aggression seems the order now.

And should I dare to criticise
My words are met with deep, dark sighs
A ringing 'tut' a look of disdain
You're not unfamiliar with the pain
So what has gotten into you
You once lived much the same as we do.
The neatness, cleanliness and hygiene
They proudly show are edged in grime
And mine the only eyes that see
That first class isn't first, really.

We visit all the top hotels
Sights and sounds I once knew well.
Willingly I pick up tabs of one kind
Having lost the knack of finding tabs in minds.
I am the alien Rip Van Winkle
I've lost the jargon, lost the sparkle.
As they used to say at one time
I'm out of it, I've lost the line.

I see their love across a lens
I see their smiles, I hear their laughter

Across a time-lag slightly after
I see their love I make amends
I kiss, I hold them ever tighter
I kiss, I hold them through a muffler
I hold hands, I make a fuss
A show of love that once we shared
Excitement so intense, we cared.
And yet, today we can't be friends.

Do they sense the gulf between us
The wide Arabian Gulf between us?
Do they feel the air's gone thin?
And though we talk so much more
Can they sense the silence in
Between the words?
We kiss, we hug, we part again
I hurry back to this isolation
This strange cocoon where once I cried
And ached so much to go back home
And now I ask, 'where is my home?'

The following is an observation of a particular kind of expat who has, over the years, taken on an aspect of expatriate behaviour that isn't home grown from his or her native place. They too delight, in their way, in a new-found exuberance for life. They join in the large life and often live beyond their means, racking up credit-card expenses, and often ending up in dire straits. They are what I consider:

LOTOPHAGUS* LEPIDOPTERUS SIMPLUS

Caterpillar

I came with cataracts in my eyes
Half blind
A refugee from tears and sighs
So weary
So weary of my insect life
Kafkaesquely mundane strife
The daily munch, munch, munch of travelling
Leaf to leaf, job-to-job commuting.
The strange thing is
I thought that that was
All that life could offer.

Cocoon

Then wrapped in silken transportation
I arrived here.
At first morose: Is this salvation?
I survived here.
Still I lay and learnt through senses
The breakdown of my old defences.
Learnt that other lives there be
Learnt from those like birds so free
Learnt that one could hope to be
Other than chained to leaf and tree.
Could perhaps beat gravity
And lose and shed solemnity.

While retaining memories
Of the life, as grub I led
Of the moult that I would shed

Butterfly
The moult came off with difficulty
First it cracked
And I crept back
Afraid of losing my identity.
Half in half out, I waited
With beating heart, breath bated.
One antenna, then the other
Sensed in the breeze, what I could gather.
Nectar from this island's flowers.
Some offered disco dancing till the wee hours.
Others were possessions
Brightly hued and plenty.
I could choose from those around me
Soft or bold or gold or glitzy

I stepped out of my cocoon
And in the heady perfume swooned.
And in my swooning I spread my wings.
Why! I could dance most anything:
A sprightly bright fandango
Bee-bop, bump, waltz 'n' tango!
I could alight on any flower

At any time, at any hour.
Gathering rosebuds while I may
I could watch the hours slip fast away

And then, upon a frog-loud pond
Broad leaves with dewdrops I espied
The sacred flowers of the Lotophagi★.
They lured me with their perfumes sweet
And I couldn't leave 'well enough' alone.
So, on anxious wings I soft descended
Knowing that my time was ended
Aware that although such as I
Were truly not Lotophagi.
Now it seems so rich to die.
While I can see the evening in the sky
Spread purple, pink and salmon gold
Knowing I shall not grow old
My head I rest upon a leaf
A perfumed dewdrop brings the sleep
From which I shall not wake for ages
And, though the lotus I've not tasted
On its leaf I lie fake-wasted
And with my dying inward eye
See that butterflies such as I
Are mere imitation Lotophagi.

★ Lotophagus - Lotus eaters with reference to the place in Greek mythology where Odysseus' men eat of the narcotic 'lotus' plant and forget their homes and purpose.

Another aspect of life in Bahrain is the coalescing of our faiths. Some of us may not have been ardent followers of the religions we were born into in our home countries, but here, suddenly faced with the strong convictions of our hosts, we turn back to our religious roots with a fervour not experienced before. And, especially for those of us born into the Christian faith, the proximity of places like Jordan, Babylon and other Biblical sites, being here in Bahrain takes on an extra-special significance. We're so aware, that if not the Messiah perhaps one of his early followers could so easily have visited the very sands we walk on…

THE FISHER FOLK

Here we are in the lands of yore
Not far from where once
He walked.
His footsteps fell on similar sands
His words were heard by similar bands
Of men
Wearing loose garments, heads covered
Ears and eyes shaded
But so many were blind
'Too much heaven on their minds'
And now they choose another's words
They seek the life of another's world
But we from afar
(Blessed are we who believe
And have not seen)
Remain pure
Steadfast in our faith we try

To save the Saviour's one-time lands
We cast out nets
Our hopes are met
On the wrong side of our boats
We draw them up
We wind them up
Our lines and nets are empty
In terms of what we fish for
And what we hope to catch.
Our hopes are threads strong knotted
But our nets have gaps wide-slotted
And their small minds slip through the snare
So pleased, so free, so unaware.
They flounder in the turquoise deep
And floundering know not that they flounder
While we retain our purity
And yet again we scythe the sea
Searching for a harvest of lost souls
Trying to raise their interest in our goals
Hoping that here again
We, renamed in faith may be
Exalted in time as true fishers of men.

I have also seen people – both men and women – who affect a certain urbanity as if they aren't really fazed or impressed by all that they see here in the Middle East, whether Bahrain or Dubai, Abu Dhabi, Kuwait or any other Middle Eastern state. They like to make out that they are accustomed to the level of wealth they see in close proximity or sometimes actually hob-nob with individuals who are, to put it plainly, 'loaded'. These people could come from literally any part of the world and any social status, but they take pains to let those around them know that 'back home' all this was par for the course, when really most of us know quite well that it isn't or wasn't.

SERENITY!

Serenity!
That woman there so self-possessed
Articulate, well groomed and dressed
Cool and distant as a painting
Of a surrealist landscape.

Her every movement's practised right
And too her lips, skin, blush and slight
Bent forward head, speak artifice
As does her languid cigarette.

And yet I know beneath that calm
Exterior beats a timorous heart
Nervously twitching lest all should see
Her fearful inadequacy.

She craves acceptance and respect
Her hands with nervousness are wet
The shell she's built is wafer thin
But hard so others don't get in.

And painted on its smooth surface
That speckled camouflage - her face.
Her head is filled with all the news
She parrots all the proper views.
But behind her deep dark eyes
Throbs a mind that screams, 'lies, lies!'

Yet every night with care she clads
Her wafer shell with flakes of sad
Hard nacreous secretions. So
That through some tiny gaps or holes
The world, nor anyone should see
That though she loves her life of ease
Her body sates to a fine degree
Beneath it all there longs to be
A soaring spirit flying free.
Perhaps not perfect but at least
Divested of her self-possession
She could make a true confession
And declare to all around her
'This child beneath the shell is me.'
But her shell is her protector
Both her shelter and her fetter.

Sometimes the knowledge that this life of ease could perhaps be making us, mentally or spiritually lazy, nags at us. But we try and ignore it. Because we know that if we allow ourselves to think about not stimulating our intellects, or challenging the status quo, we're afraid that all these marvellous comforts that we enjoy here will be lost. The following is dedicated to all of us who every now and then indulge in:

INDOLENCE AT 10AM

On chocolate velvet half slumbering
Cup in hand of Earl Grey tea
A lazy silver teaspoon
Slips easily.
A tiny discordant chink
Against the cadences of a soft violin
On whose wings she is transported
To a land and time far distant
And alien to this present unthinking
Undoing state of dilute comfort and degradation
The knowledge shrieks shrilly in her ears
But the violins take over softly, softly yet again.

Something else I have noticed is nepotism. And when someone from one country is in a position to help another of his or her countrymen and does so, usually by providing a job, then he or she expects unequivocal loyalty. And the person for whom the favour has been done is trapped into a show of support no matter what the dependant actually feels.

ALLEGIANCE OF THE FLY

Caught.
Trapped.
On the silken threads of a gossamer web
Adamantine hard.
Inextricably
Unequivocally
Baited by compatriotism
Ensnared by debits and credits
Caught.
Trapped.
On the sickening threads of a gossamer web
Adamantine hard.
Obligations
Of a nation
Gratitude or its verisimilitude:
Mere thanks
For being allowed to join the ranks
Although an officer not a professor
Caught.
Trapped.
On the sticky threads of a gossamer web
Adamantine hard.
Linked
By bonds of similar losses
Tears and heartaches shared
In spite of all their latter distances
They are well and truly ensnared.

And so, finally I come to people who have stayed beyond their 'best before' date. People who know that perhaps they should have left while they were still marketable, or could have, should have, upgraded their skills but didn't. They have been very happy here, but the writing on the wall says it's time to go. They disagree with some points of life here but are too comfortable in their situations to make a stand, often, sadly they are in a position to be able to make that stand. When the poem was written they couldn't do so, but today there are options and they can stay and make Bahrain their home. The question is, will they?

LAMENT OF THE LOTUS EATERS

A deep slumber
A dream remembered
Once upon a time, we lived
Between birth and death
Suspended like a dewdrop
In the dawn.
And all life
Was a desperate clinging to the leaf.
From each breath
Each ray of sunlight
Each wisp of mist
We extracted every molecule of joy
And now, we wonder why
Struldbrugs
We just wait to die.
Growing old in Shangri-la
Having lost our precious 'wa'

And yet not lost our equilibrium
We wait
Suspended, lives askew
Between don'ts, won'ts, can'ts, I could, I should
And I do.

So there we have it. This is our odd love of Beautiful Bahrain; as typified by the expatriate population that has grown to admire this tiny country. People who have learnt its history, recorded its milestones, and in many cases, like Sir. Charles Belgrave, helped lay down the blueprint for its future. I salute them and smile at them, and hope some day to be considered amongst those who made albeit a tiny difference and left a small footprint in the sands of its times.

LAND OF THE LIVING

by

Omar Ahmed

The soft winds of October arrive,
and the withered leaves follow.
As they caress the palm trees,
brushing their dried eyes below.
The trees now awake from summer sleep,
welcome the winds with open arms.
Uncoiling their roots from the desert sand,
they fall in line and begin to march!
Their long roots sweeping behind,
like a wedding gown of a bride.
They raise their arms, singing in praise,
for today is the telling of a story,
the story of Gilgamesh!

Around five thousand years ago,
when civilisations were but brewing seeds,
there lived an ancient Sumerian King,
between the rivers of Tigris and Euphrates.
Gilgamesh a hero and supreme ruler,
two thirds God, one third man,
tamer of beasts, breaker of mountains,
shifter of seas and leveller of lands!
Superiority and pride fluttered in his mind,

an unfettered power, unchallenged in hand.
His greed ran free and devoured everything,
that roamed on the bosom of his kingdom's sands.
The Gods that heard the people's lament,
Couldn't bear the agonising cries,
of Gilgamesh's exploitation of the men,
and theft of the young virgin brides.
So they created for him an equal being,
uncivilised and covered in hair,
Our King's path with the creature intertwined,
impressed by his strength he grew care.
Fondness made him a companion and friend,
he sought to civilise and tame him,
though in the process and the adventures,
he was filled with disgust to the brim.
He realised his unworthy way of life,
feeling regret and deep sorrow of his crimes.
He found great affection and meaning,
to redeem with his friend all the lost time.
But the thread of every man's life expires,
and death arrived one begotten day,
playing tender tunes on her melancholic flute,
and took his sleeping friend away.

The dawning truth of his mortality,
trembled our King to find an escape.
He thought of himself to live forever,
enjoying the world's spaces and shapes.
It was the King's time too,
death stalked him where darkness lay,
But our King sailed away from Uruk,
to find a place, where death had no say.
"Such a place exists!" cried the oracles of our King!
"Somewhere to the south of Babylonia lies an island,
the land of the living, where the sun rises.
A garden of everlasting life for heroes and kings,
where there is no lamentation, suffering or vices.
There is a plant that grows in the waters of Dilmun,
it has a prickle like a thorn.
Succeed in taking it, and your hands will hold that which,
restores youth to the old."
Gilgamesh sailed to the unique seas,
that of sweetness and salt.
But death was keen to follow him,
and take that which belongs to her.
The tunes of her flute faded,
the closer he approached Dilmun's shores,

{ OMAR AHMED }

The thick layer of darkness cast by her,
began to separate even more.
It was the break of day,
and Gilgamesh searched the land to find,
the plant of immortality in his grasp,
but he realised the vanity of his design.
"The gods give man all pleasures of life,
but also give him his demise,
they hold life, but not human life,
for death is what makes us alive.
Who pants for glory finds but short repose,
A breath revives him, and a breath overthrows"
At this fruition of truth he decided,
to bury underneath the earth, this deadly knife,
And thousands of years later,
a tree grew in its place, alone in the desert,
called the 'Tree of Life'

Writer's notes: From time immemorial, Bahrain has attracted travellers to its shores. Some like Gilgamesh (whose legend was captured in stone), were kings in pursuit of the island's fabled secret of eternal life. It holds the world's largest known prehistoric cemetery with more than one hundred thousand burial mounds covering areas of Bahrain. Pearls have been found alongside other jewels, clay pots and artefacts in excavated grave mounds, indicating a belief that the island possessed the secret of immortality. A land without death and sickness, with an abundance of sweet waters believed to grant eternal life. The Tree of Life is believed by local inhabitants to be the actual location of the garden of Eden, how this tree has survived over the centuries in the middle of a desert is a mystery. And thousands of years after the pursuit of Gilgamesh, Bahrain still boasts to be a melting-pot of nationalities from around the world, renowned for its friendly people and relaxed lifestyle, tax free environment and large investment potential. There is a culture of openness and tolerance to all sects, ethnicities and religions. A mosque, a church and a temple will be found standing near each other. Expatriates enjoy the blessing of celebrating life in a peaceful, secure and quiet Island. It is truly a sanctuary for those who want to live a life of Immortality!

SNAPSHOTS FROM AN ISLAND

by
Steve Royston

I have lived in Bahrain for two years. Not exactly a lifetime, and certainly not as long as many of my fellow expatriates on the island. But in writing about Bahrain, I do have the small advantage over the thirty-year veteran of being able to cast fresh eyes on the country. I have spent many years in the Middle East – most notably in Saudi Arabia – and in that time, for one reason or another, I rarely had occasion to visit Bahrain.

I put that right by moving to the island to start a business in September 2009. Since then I have had many memorable experiences of life in a small but incredibly diverse society. I have made many Bahraini friends, and seen Bahrain move through interesting times. I wrote these snapshots to capture the aspects of Bahrain that I hope will endure.

The Middle East is changing fast. Whatever its recent troubles, Bahrain and its people have qualities similar to those of neighbouring countries, yet different. I hope that these brief vignettes capture some of those unique qualities, and especially the warmth and charm for which Bahrainis are renowned.

THE RESTAURANT

Bahrain is a country of many restaurants. *Time Out Bahrain* lists over a hundred of them, typically in places beloved of expatriates, such as the malls, hotels and areas heavily populated with Westerners - Adliya, Saar and Juffair for example. Go to one of the swish restaurants in Adliya, and you're unlikely to come away without spending 20-25BD per head (50-65USD), sometimes much more.

Make friends with someone who knows the island well, and you can find wonders unknown to readers of *Time Out*. My friend Mohamed, one of the most interesting and likeable people I've met in Bahrain, has a local's knowledge of eating out. We recently got together for dinner, and I mentioned that a colleague from France was coming over for a visit, and that he was a serious lover of fish. So when Fred arrived I contacted Mohamed, and he suggested we meet at Tabreez, a fish restaurant near Adhari Park on the outskirts of Manama. I've never written about eating out before, so forgive the unrestrained superlatives which a gnarled old gourmet like Michael Winner might choke on with mirth. But there's a reason.

Tabreez is not mentioned in the restaurant guides. That's because it serves a Bahraini clientèle, as well as being very popular with Saudis who come across the causeway for the weekend. The interior looks a bit like a British transport 'caff', and there's also an outdoor area with a few tables scattered about. In the autumn, Bahrain starts cooling down from the stifling heat of the summer, so eating outside starts to be a pleasure again. So we took a table in the courtyard. But first we had to choose our fish. Now Fred considers himself an expert on fish. I only know that if the fish stares at you from the ice with rheumy eyes like a ninety-year-old with cataracts, it's best avoided. So Fred inspected the eyes, the scales and the general look of the fish, and pronounced them good.

Mohamed suggested two fish I'd never heard of. One, known locally as yanam, was about eighteen inches long with a wide body. The other, ma'id, was much smaller - a bit like an overgrown sardine. Both, he said, were caught locally and Bahraini favourites. For good measure, he suggested we get some very fat prawns.

We took our table, which the waiter covered with two plastic sheets Arabian-style. We started with hors d'oeuvre, hummus, tabbouleh and a pile of the flat bread which they baked on the premises. Then the fish arrived. The prawns were barbecued with a delicious yoghurt and herb sauce. Then came a plate of ma'id, grilled with little embellishment - very delicate white flesh – flaky and moist. Finally, the yanaan. Cooked as you would a sole, but with a thick crust of spicy vegetables - chunks of flesh coming easily off the bone, similar to sea bass.

Fred, who, being a Breton who caught his first sea bass from the rocky shores of Brittany at the age of eight, is not easily impressed. With his typically lyrical turn of phrase, he commented; "it was as if the enjoyment would never stop - a moment out of time."

After three hours of great conversation and equally great eating, we walked out of Tabreez with a bill that came to a third of what we would have paid in the swish restaurants of downtown Manama. But not before we were shown the bakery in action, and presented with a couple of pieces of bread straight from the furnace - a typically Bahraini touch.

Breakfast in the Souk. Mornings for me usually start with the local newspaper and a sweep through the news sites on the web. On a weekend, it's nice occasionally to taste the joy of small things. My friend Mohamed, despite surely having had enough of Fred's and my company at Tabreez, showed us yet another face of Bahrain. This time we came together for breakfast at a little Bahraini restaurant called Maseela. It's near the entrance to the Manama souk, and consists of a number of tables in the alley outside, as well as an indoor family area.

For those not familiar with Bahrain, I should explain that the weekend is on Friday and Saturday. So this Friday morning was the equivalent of Saturday in the West. Since I arrived in Bahrain I've got into the habit of going to the excellent Friday Brunch at the British Club - in terms of the volume of food, a serious assault that usually requires me to take to my bed for the afternoon to recover.

So Maseela was a welcome change. A traditional Bahraini breakfast consists of a number of small dishes - scrambled egg with tomatoes, chicken liver with potatoes, a runny lentil dish and a spicy mince stew. All eaten with the inevitable flat bread straight from the oven that was blazing away on the other side of the alley.

The restaurant was thronged with families and groups of men meeting for a chat - a truly social occasion. Mohamed is a man with many friends, and every so often an acquaintance would stop by to say hello.

Fred, Mohamed and I were joined by another Fred, who was over for the weekend from Saudi Arabia.

We then set off for a wander round the souk. Fred One was looking to add to his new collection of Afghan seals - beautiful latticed silver objects about two inches across with a stone seal mould (agate, jade and lapis lazuli) as the centrepiece. The seal images are carvings of horses or other animals, or Arabic inscriptions. The same shop sells Islamic coins, which is an interest of mine, and a host of other good stuff.

Having made the necessary purchases, we followed Mohamed to another eating place deeper in the souk. This is a tiny shop which has been open for fifty years. Inside there's room for about five people standing up. Most people eat from there outside in the street. We sampled the food - a plate of potato fritters served with a very tasty chickpea sauce. Apparently, the man who owns the shop has built a sizeable property portfolio, all from the takings of a tiny outlet in a backstreet. A prime example of patience over the instant gratification urge of today's business ethos.

What was originally planned as a breakfast get-together was turning into a full morning's outing. Mohamed's pleasure in showing us his Bahrain was matched by ours at experiencing it. We went on to a shop that sells herbal water - remedies for indigestion, headaches, diabetes and a host of other complaints. The herbs are all locally grown, and the produce is known throughout the Gulf. One of the lesser-known local industries - a throwback to the days when the country had an abundance of spring water and large fields of date palms. Much of that water is gone now, sucked away by the increasing population and the industrial plants that have sprung up on the island over the past thirty years. But the herbal business remains.

Then on to Bahrain Fort, an ancient structure that dates from the Dilmun civilisation that flourished around four thousand years ago. There's a new museum at the Fort, which boasts Sumerian tablets, Dilmun seals, Persian figurines, silver tetradrachm coins from the time of Alexander the Great (who visited the island - then called Tylos - on his way back from Afghanistan), Parthian pottery and artefacts from the days when the

Portuguese established a bridgehead into the region. Next to the museum is a café looking out over the sea - a great place to visit as the sun goes down over the Gulf.

We rounded off the tour with a visit to a couple of old houses - now derelict - which reminded us that before the days of tower blocks and apartments, most people on the island lived a life of simplicity.

A great three hours exploring parts of Bahrain that I'm ashamed I've not taken the time to visit before. All through the generosity of a man who clearly loves his place of birth, and is more than willing to share its delights.

THE ARTISTS

One of my big regrets in life is that I'm not a connoisseur of fine art. I envy the likes of Brian Sewell, who lisps his way through his TV and radio commentaries on art with that curious retro-accent that went out of fashion thirty years ago. I may not be an aesthete, but I am a fan. I lapped up Kenneth Clarke's Civilisation TV series in the seventies. I head for galleries whenever I'm in a city like Florence or Venice. When in London, I pay regular visits to the National Portrait Gallery, because I love portraiture – especially some of the renaissance artists like Durer, who so expertly capture the cunning, the mean and the ruthless spirit of the age. And the Florentines, masters of portraying realpolitik.

One of the joys of living in the Middle East is that there is no shortage of art and artists. Elegant calligraphy, Ottoman miniatures and geometric motifs in the Islamic tradition, a thriving community of Arabic cartoonists, and the figurative and abstract works of present-day local and expatriate artists. Not to mention some magnificent architecture, both new and old.

Here in Bahrain, the Bahrain Arts Society provides a platform for Bahrainis and foreigners alike. Recently they displayed the works of Mohsen Ghareeb and Abdulshaheed Khamdan. Both artists draw on the influences of traditional Islamic art, particularly Arabic calligraphy, to produce striking abstract paintings, and then it was the turn of Meriel Cooper Wallace and Michele Karam. Meriel paints mainly in watercolour and her exhibition portrays the natural world. Michele is a ceramicist who draws heavily on oriental influences. The exhibition was a feast for the eye.

Not being an art critic, I'm unable to wax lyrical on this or that technique. But Bahrain has a long tradition of fine art. If you happen to be in Bahrain for a short trip, and tire of the malls and restaurants, you could do worse than pay a visit to the Society of Arts Gallery in Budaiya, or to one of the other galleries on the island. You're unlikely to be disappointed.

THE GOLF COURSE

I'm one of these sad individuals who look for a golf course wherever he travels. Until about fifteen years ago green courses in the Middle East were a rarity. Saudi Aramco in Dhahran had a brown course, and I remember playing a course on rocky terrain overlooking the Haj Terminal at Jeddah's King Abdulaziz International Airport. The 'browns' were patches of sand rolled with oil, and player would bring a strip of Astroturf on which you would place your ball when teeing off, or playing off the not very fair fairways. These days every self-respecting GCC country has at least one green course. Dubai has several. Riyadh has three, and these days Saudi Aramco's Rolling Hill Country Club boasts not only rolling hills but lush green fairways and greens.

The Royal Golf Club in Bahrain is an interesting addition to the portfolio of Middle Eastern courses. I have played in many odd places. Podybrady in the Czech Republic for example – set in the grounds of a Cold War electronic listening station – the only course I know of, where there are real bunkers, of the concrete variety, scattered around the course. And then there's the course in Belgium surrounded by World War One cemeteries and criss-crossed by shell holes, trenches and military detritus.

But the Bahrain course is the first one I've played on what is obviously an oil field. Apart from the fact that, for a hacker like me, the course is fiendishly difficult – it was designed by Colin Montgomerie, and locals say that he was going through a bad patch in his life and took it out on the course – it has a unique ambience. You pass by nodding donkeys gently extracting oil from a fenced-off well. There are holes where if you miscue you can end up lodged between pipes that hiss as they carry oil and gas to the nearest manifold. Well-manicured fairways slope down to rocky gullies, which can quickly lead you to destroy your expensive clubs in an attempt to return to the green. Some of the greens are so viciously sloped that they can make you weep with frustration.

Not for nothing is it called a championship course, and I'm no champion. So if your handicap is above ten, my advice is to take a preparatory course of Prozac and a set of old clubs. It is an experience though, and worth visiting if you're moving to Bahrain, or just passing through. If you're a fanatical golfer, you can buy one of the spacious new villas dotted around the course which are part of the very plush Riffa Views development. The club house is also very posh, with reasonably-priced catering and regular social events.

As a tourist venue, Bahrain is lagging behind Dubai, but given Dubai's recent financial troubles, Bahrainis would say that this is no bad thing. What is encouraging for a lover of golf is that the game is being taken up by increasing numbers of GCC nationals. Bahrainis, Saudis, Qataris and Emiratis are regular participants and winners in local tournaments, and it can't be long before one of them hits the big time in one of the major tours. So golf in the Middle East is no longer the exclusive preserve of a few Europeans and North Americans. In its own modest way, it's doing its bit to bring people together from all cultures and countries represented in the region.

Long may it continue. I just wish I could stop wrapping my irons round palm trees.

HIGH SOCIETY

Bahrain is a captivating place. Not because of the beaches, because there aren't many. Nor because it has a host of glitzy tourist attractions and ersatz souks like Dubai, because it doesn't. Nor even because it has a pristine desert environment interspersed with charming oases and interesting micro-climates like Oman, because it doesn't have these either.

For me the charm of Bahrain is that of its people, who have a character very distinct from that of their neighbours. Friendly, hospitable, and with a great sense of humour, they have embraced their expatriate community with a tolerance rivalled by no other GCC country. As a maritime trading nation, they have seen immigration throughout their history. Bahrainis have a mixed heritage dating from centuries before the discovery of oil in the 1930s – many trace their origins from the Arabian peninsula, Iran and the Indian subcontinent.

Bahrain is not without its problems: periodic political unrest, infrastructure trying to catch up with population growth, divisions between rich and poor, an education system in need of an overhaul, pollution and inconsistent industrial safety standards. But despite these challenges, the Bahrainis remain welcoming hosts to the expatriate population. It takes time to get to know a country and a culture, even in a small island like Bahrain. Anyone coming here to work would do themselves a favour by buying a book called *The Inshallah Paper*. The author is Andrew Trimbee, who arrived in the early 70s as the editor of the first English language newspaper on the island.

Andrew tells a fascinating tale of mucking through against the odds (similar to my experience in 1980's Jeddah), of outrageous characters within both the expatriate and Bahraini communities, and of the life of a pioneering editor as he totters from cocktail party to royal majlis to factories and refineries in the island's fast-growing industrial sector. What shines through the book is his affection for the civilised nature of Bahraini society.

Even though I'm a latecomer into this society, for me, much of what he describes holds true today. Perhaps everyone's a little less eccentric these days as the corporate sheen envelops the island, but Bahrain is still a country where at many levels there is a greater degree of integration between local and expatriate than in many parts of the Middle East. In some respects, it's similar to Jeddah, which has long been a cultural and ethnic melting pot because of its location as the principal entry point for the multitude of pilgrims visiting Mecca for the annual Haj.

One striking facet of Andrew's legacy is that from the humble beginnings of the *Gulf Mirror*, which started as a weekly newspaper, the Bahrain English-language print media has blossomed to an extraordinary degree. A population of a million, of which fifty percent are expatriates and a small minority are mother tongue English speakers, is served by one daily newspaper, the *Gulf Daily News* and a host of glossy magazines, ranging from business to lifestyle. As a subscriber to the GDN, I get *Gulf Insider, Bahrain Confidential, Woman, Fact Bahrain, The Gulf* and *Bahrain This Month* delivered to my doorstep for free. I can also buy *Time Out Bahrain* and a couple of other magazines devoted to business in the Gulf. They are lavishly produced, packed with ads, and some of them run to two-hundred pages.

I am truly amazed that all seem to survive and prosper, especially in these straitened times. One common aspect of the Daily News and the lifestyle magazines is what *Tatler* would call the social pages. Page upon page of parties, dog shows, charity do's, leaving do's, embassy functions, national days, corporate launches, product launches. Then there are the political and government events: conferences, visits of foreign dignitaries, royal events. I swear there must be people who do nothing but hop from party to party, event to event! And how many photographers must be out there to feed the insatiable appetite for pictures of party goers, business people, dignitaries and associated hangers-on?

One pervasive media star whose picture seemed to appear at least thirty times a month, was the well-respected former British Ambassador, Jamie Bowden. That man was everywhere! Let it never be said that 'Our Man in Bahrain' didn't earn his corn, and eat some of it too – though I feared for his health given the amount of toasts and rubber chickens he must have got through during his working life here. He looked well on it though, so I'd be interested to know his secret. Perhaps it's the Foreign Office training, and a few tips from Her Majesty, who has had to endure sixty years of dodgy catering herself in her long reign. The new British Ambassador Iain Lindsay took over from Jamie in August 2011, I'll be interested to see how long it'll take him to fall into the media spotlight too.

Recently there came a great moment for me: my début photo in the Bahrain media! I was pictured in a golf event lining up with my partners. Unfortunately, the resulting shot made me look more like a sumo wrestler than the (relatively) slim former athlete I always imagined myself to be. The fact that everyone else seemed to be about to throw themselves grunting into sandbox consoled me a little. It must have been the camera – the photos were all squashed. Fat chance. But hey, I've joined the Bahrain elite, so it's all up from here. It must only be a matter of time before I'm granted an audience with His Majesty.

Meanwhile I rejoice. Nicky, Kimon, Dr. Faisal, Professor O'Malley, Fatima, Linda, Dr. Bindu, Ahmad, Hala, Mr Al-Umran, your Highnesses, Excellencies, Sheikhs and all you other movers and shakers on this island – I have arrived, and thank you for welcoming me to the glossy pages of Bahrain's high society!

Oh, and can anyone direct me to the nearest gym?

A NIGHT IN MUHARRAM

As I sit in my balcony enjoying a balmy winter evening, three very different sounds compete for attention. To my left, a raucous party blaring out from a nearby apartment block – Filipina girls having a rare old time singing Christmas carols. In front of me, shouting from a football game at a nearby recreation ground. To my right, the mournful sound of an Ashoura ceremony – drums and cymbals in a slow rhythm, a cleric reciting verses of lamentation in a strong baritone, and a choral response from the faithful. In an island of tolerance, a very Bahraini tableau.

At the time of writing this, we are in Muharram, the first month of the Islamic calendar. The tenth day of Muharram is known as Ashoura – which is Arabic for tenth. For Muslims of all schools of thought it's a special day. For Sunnis, Ashoura marks the day on which Moses (known as Mousa in the Koran) and his people escaped from Egyptian servitude by walking through the Red Sea, parted by divine intervention. For them, it's a day of fasting.

For the Shia, Ashoura and the ten days preceding it are days of lamentation for the death of Husayn, the third Shia Imam and grandson of the Prophet Mohammed. At the Battle of Karbala, Husayn and many members of his family were vastly outnumbered and killed by the forces of the Sunni Caliph, Yazid of Damascus. His fall crystallised the schism between the Shia and the Sunni branches of Islam. This was rooted in a dispute about the legitimacy of competing claims for spiritual and temporal leadership of the Muslim world between Husayn, as a direct descendent of the Prophet, and the line of successors chosen from the Prophet's companions.

Here in Bahrain, communities gather across the island to lament the passing of Husayn. And so I accepted the invitation of a friend, Mohamed, to visit an Islamic Awareness Centre near the Manama souk. Its location next door to the Baptist church is an indication that the faithful of many religions worship in close proximity here in Bahrain – a rarity in this region.

For the first ten nights of Muharram, the Centre is the venue for gatherings to commemorate and explain Ashura and the suffering of Husayn. In a large courtyard there was a tent containing a library of commentaries in many languages explaining the meaning of Shia Islam. At a nearby table, women volunteers offered free refreshments – sandwiches, cakes, tea and coffee. Next door was a sheltered auditorium where a scholar in a white turban and black robes was seated on a podium in front of a few hundred people – men on the right and women on the left.

The scholar was reciting Arabic verses in long, slow incantations. When Mohamed joined me, he explained that the speaker was an American from Colorado with a degree in Physics and a doctorate in Islamic studies. Although the majority of the gathering appeared to be Arabic speakers, the scholar started speaking in English. He surprised me by commenting that great strides have been made in expressing the meaning of Ashoura in English –

most Muslims I have met have emphasised the purity of the language of the Koran, and therefore the impurity of translations into other languages.

He spoke of the Battle of Karbala and the tribulations of the family of Husayn. Karbala, he said was symbolic of the struggles we face in our daily lives when dealing with adversity. As he continued on the theme of breaking through from observance to true acceptance in word, deed and spirit of the message of Islam, I was struck by the underlying mysticism of the faith he was describing. Western perceptions of Islam tend to focus on the observance of ritual and behaviour mandated by the Koran and Hadith. Yet here was a man talking in a language that any mystic would understand – transformation of the inner person and communion with God.

As the scholar's address was coming to an end, my friend took me to a nearby street where we could hear the drums of a procession. At the front was a pick-up truck with loudspeakers. The leader was singing to a slow, rhythmic drumbeat. Following him was a line of around fifty men and boys dressed in black. In time to the rhythm, the followers were brushing their backs with flails made of gold beads. This, and hundreds of other parades around the island, was a precursor to the mass marches on the day of Ashoura, in which many followers beat their chests and often draw blood with real flails. Lamentation and guilt at the failure of their ancestors to prevent the wrong done to Husayn and his family.

I'm not a Muslim. Nor am I a theologian or a mystic. In the two hours I spent listening and watching, I couldn't begin to understand the intricacies of Shia theology. But I was struck by the gentle emotion of the occasion, and by parallels with the Christian observance of Easter. Those who look askance at the ritual self-flagellation practised by some Shia at the height of the Ashoura observance should think also of Easter processions in many devout Catholic communities around the world, some of which involve similar rituals. Themes of guilt, redemption and inner contemplation are common to both faiths. But the raw emotions and seeming harshness of the climactic Shia observance of Ashoura were not in evidence, and I was touched by the warmth of the welcome I received.

During my time in the Middle East, I have mingled both with Sunni and Shia Muslims. Images of Islam reach the West via TV, *YouTube* and the print media – the Haj, Ashura and Ramadan. Historical and current events frame our picture of Islam – the Muslim conquests, the Golden Age, the Crusades, the fall of Constantinople, the Ottoman Court, and today, jihad, terrorism, the Taliban, veiled women, Iran, sectarian strife and Iraq. In the West, we fuel our paranoia by seizing upon messages of hatred rather than love. And that hatred is often reciprocated.

For all the posturing of politicians, propagandists, sheikhs and scholars, I also see millions of members of the human race who wish to live their lives in peace and prosperity without harming others and imposing their beliefs upon them. And when the crises of today pass into history, to be replaced no doubt by others, it will still be the common humanity of people like those I met the other day that will give us hope for the future.

Let's not forget the people of good will.

THE POET

The Arabic language has been a constant, though often distant, companion throughout my years in the Middle East. Mournful intonations from the mosques. Quranic incantations on the radio. Sharp conversations on the street corner. Hectoring broadcasts from leaders and imams.

You could argue that I am utterly unqualified to write about this language of three hundred million people, given my rudimentary familiarity with it. Yet in a way, I feel that I can appreciate Arabic as a means of communication in a way many fluent speakers perhaps cannot.

Just as a person who cannot see compensates for his blindness by hearing what the sighted cannot hear, and by an enhanced sense of taste, touch and smell, it is possible to look beyond the words of a language one cannot understand. The distinctive nuances of facial expression, tone of voice, gesticulation and body language convey a meaning that sometimes transcends those words.

And just as one does not need to understand French to appreciate the beauty of a passage from Edmond Rostand's *Cyrano de Bergerac*, so one can appreciate the beauty of the Quran when spoken or sung. It has often been said that Arabs are more openly emotional than the buttoned-up people of Northern Europe and North America. Listen to Arabs interacting, both in anger and in jest, and you will see the evidence.

I had the pleasure of listening to Hamid Al-Qaed, a prominent Bahraini poet who writes both in English and Arabic. He was speaking at a meeting of the Bahrain Writer's Circle at La Fontaine Cultural Centre – a large villa in the centre of Manama that has been converted by its owner into a arts centre and restaurant drawing from traditional and contemporary architectural styles. Stone pillars, cloisters, fountains and open performance areas.

Hamid has had four books published, and he read a selection of poems in English and Arabic – about love, life, nature and much else. His poems were short and emotional, and I enjoyed listening to him speaking in Arabic as much as his English work.

Most Westerners do not understand the importance of poetry in the Arab world. How many sixteen year-old, Internet- savvy kids in England would admit to their pride in the poems they write, as did a bunch of young people I encountered recently in Saudi Arabia? In the royal courts of the region, especially among the gatherings attended by Bedouin tribespeople, it is still common for guests to stand up and recite odes in praise of the host – and receive a small gift as a reward.

If there is to be one positive outcome from the changes sweeping the Arab world, I hope it will be a renewed flowering of Arabic literature. Free speech liberates creativity, and literature is one of the lasting legacies of a culture.

THE YOUTH

I love Bahrain and its people. It's not the kind of blind and unconditional devotion you might feel for your family. More the clear-sighted love that recognises all the ways in which human beings from time to time fall below accepted standards of behaviour and attitude, fall below their own value systems and do things that in their hearts they might regret. But also the kind of love that looks beyond behaviour and sees essential qualities - in Bahrain's case, generosity of spirit and enthusiasm for life – that transcend the acts and failings of individuals.

Since arriving on this island, my feelings for Bahrain have steadily deepened, thanks mainly to my involvement in a youth program that has been more intensive and uplifting than any in my recent professional life. My colleagues and I have been working with around sixty of the brightest sixteen year-olds in the country. They are candidates for the Crown Prince Scholarship Program. In May 2012, ten of them will be selected for scholarships that will enable them to complete their secondary education in the UK or the USA, study at the best universities in either country, and if they wish, to gain Masters degrees. So my team and these students have been enveloped in a bubble of learning – away from all the bones of contention that have been rattling around the country in recent months. Many of the students met each other for the first time. They came from a variety of backgrounds. Some privileged, other less so. Some girls, some boys. Some painfully shy, others brimming with confidence. They arrived with a uniformly high level of academic achievement. They left with bonds that I suspect might last for a lifetime.

The event started with a series of workshops designed to hone their skills for the big step forward from school to university – time management, communications, project management, teamwork and leadership. Following that, a week-long program specifically about dealing with the pitfalls, terrors and opportunities inherent in leaving home for the first time and travelling thousands of miles to study in what for many will be a totally alien environment.

And they spent their final week creating ideas for the economic development of the country, and presented them to a panel of entrepreneurs and corporate executives.

It was heart-warming to see these young Bahrainis gradually coming out of themselves as the event progressed. Shy ones from the villages who could hardly be persuaded to let out a squeak in the first week, became enthusiastic and assertive team players by the end. Private school kids who had an advantage in social skills and confidence, helping those who hadn't had the benefit of their expensive educations. Role-play acted out with the panache of seasoned performers. And presentations that would put many adults thirty years their senior to shame with their clarity, incisiveness and quality of delivery. All in English, their second language, although some would consider themselves bilingual.

What impressed me also was the maturity of their presentation subjects: reflections on childhood, the ethical issues around genetic engineering, early detection of special needs in children, treatment of cleft palates. When I was sixteen, in my private school bubble, my main preoccupation was the next Beatles album and catching the spot on my forehead before it turned nasty.

These sixteen year-olds have idealism and an absence of cynicism that you would rarely find in a street-wise British or American kid. They really want to succeed, they really want their scholarships, but they also really care about their peers, their families, their country and their environment.

There were times when you forgot that you were dealing with youngsters. But occasionally – such as during a series of team problem-solving exercises - the child would come out whooping and squealing as they raced from one decoding task to the next.

There are many other young people like them in Bahrain. Serious, focused and yet exuberant and fun-loving. They represent the qualities that originally attracted me to Bahrain, and I pray that life doesn't knock too many lumps out of their hopes and plans for the future. They and thousands of others - perhaps not quite so bright but with the same qualities - are the future of their country.

In fact, youngsters like them all over the Middle East are the Arab future. For all the uncertainty across the region, we would do well to remember that the long-term future of the Arab world doesn't lie with the adults who are fighting, arguing, reliving ancient battles and re-igniting old resentments. It lies with the region's abundant and talented youth.

The Crown Prince is to be congratulated for an initiative that has transformed the lives of those who have taken part. His scholars are working in high-profile jobs both in Bahrain and abroad, and have competed on equal terms with some of the brightest students in the Western world. Yes, it's an elite program for a relatively small number of people. But it shows what young Arabs can achieve, and it rides roughshod over the often narrow and ill-informed Western perceptions of the Arab world.

If Bahrain is to be the home of inventors, innovators and creators of wealth, rather than importers of foreign expertise and traders of foreign technology, it needs more initiatives like the Crown Prince's Scholarship Program, and it needs the spirit of his program to inspire the education system across the island. An investment in human infrastructure that will be far longer-lasting than tower blocks and flyovers.

IMAGES OF MY BELOVED BAHRAIN

by

Lillian Mills

Aromas of fresh fruit intensified by the humid air, an orange falls at my feet from the passing cart.

Verdant palm tree fronds shining in the sunlight, celebrating the breeze.

Two old men curled up on a bench, arguing with their worry beads.

Getting lost in the rat maze of the souq, and not caring; enticing sights, sounds and aromas greeting your senses at every turn.

Tiny fishing boats leaving the shore at sunrise, their poles softly lapping in the warm water, nets still curled up in sleep.

A chorus of minarets singing to the sky, briefly suspending time.

Turquoise water making love to the hulls of dhows in the harbour.

A cat waiting patiently in the alley for the fish-seller's left-overs.

The scent of an Arabian boy passing in the street; an enticing combination of cologne and freshly-ironed thobe.

Desert exhaling an ethereal blanket of haze.

The aroma of shwarma grilling in the street, announcing: 'Arabia' unmistakably as it wafts towards you on the warm breeze.

A baby camel nuzzling into my hair while I am stroking the softness of his newly emerging fuzz.

Fish eyes staring at me accusingly from their market baskets.

Alleys winding into each other deep in the souq, frustrating the dappled sunlight attempting to search them.

Arabic men doing business on a street corner, dressed like toy dolls in their costumes.

Rusty pipe-lines shimmering in the desert heat, unaware of their treasure within.

A cargo ship in port, trading arriving and departing pieces of lives changed forever.

A cacophony of calligraphy decorating shop signs in the souq.

Pots belching curry in the dim recesses of an Indian restaurant's kitchen.

A wizened 'Box Man' winding his way through an alley, his cargo threatening to topple at any moment.

Minarets lighting up at dusk like an excerpt from a fairy tale.

Gazing out over the Arabian Gulf at sunset, the evening air warm and humid, knowing it belongs to you, and your heart belongs to it.

The roar of a jet engine taking off, lights of the causeway disappearing beneath the clouds; perhaps they were never really there.

BAHRAIN - ARCHITECTURE AND ENVIRONS

by
Jim Scalise

"Of all the sites we visited, what's your favourite?"
"Maryam, that's not an easy question. I'll have to think about that a while" I replied.

Indeed we had visited some of the most interesting of Bahrain's interesting architecture. It was fall in Bahrain, that refreshing breather between the expected heat and humidity of summer and the unexpected chill of winter. There could not be a more ideal time to enjoy the architectural heritage of this little island-country. We had spent three busy weekends, including an Eid holiday break, on our kingdom-wide adventure.

I was fortunate to have - all in one – my very own personal tour guide, a translator when the right words didn't come, a human GPS, and a never-ending source of historical and cultural background, who pulled it all together and enriched each visit. My good friend Maryam. Every visitor everywhere should have a native friend as enthusiastic and happy to share their culture.

HERITAGE HOMES

Bahrain's heritage homes are a compelling starting point for a journey of exploration around the island for a number of reasons; they are the richest local examples of Arab culture preserved, a ready opportunity for expats to compare differences to their own culture, or for natives to learn and bond further with their own heritage. They are sprinkled throughout the villages, but can be found clustered in convenient groups in the old former capital, the small city of Muharraq, and are one more good reason to visit Muharraq's other charms.

Muharraq's narrow, winding, donkey-cart streets and alleyways of yesteryear are as delightful for walking as they are challenging for driving, so grab the first parking spot and lose yourself in the city's maze. The houses are close, better to shade each other. City planning then was one of harmony with the surrounding environment and climate, and with Islamic culture.

As a bonus you might just wander into the Muharraq's Al Qaysariya Souk, a major bazaar of bargains galore and if you can afford the calories then taste of its many local 'sweets'. Well…even if you can't afford the calories.

An architect, guided by Louis Sullivan's 19th century credo, '*Form follows Function,*' will discover it exemplified here at its most basic level. Whether architect or tourist, one could do little better than to start with a study of Bahrain's heritage homes. To an American they bring to mind similarities to the indigenous adobe construction of American Indians, but are much more sophisticated.

These are handsome, especially as creative responses to the country's early harsh surroundings. Most were built in the beginning of the 20th century. The desert provided severely limited building materials to temper the oppressive heat and humidity, but early builders made good use of what little they had.

Early building materials used here were almost exclusively local, items widely available throughout the island, with some few woods from India and Africa. Coral stone blocks from the shallow sea and limestone from under the saline sands formed the walls, built up to approximately one-meter thick for insulation. The walls were reinforced with overly abundant palm tree trunks, bonded with local gypsum mortar, then plastered with clay. Roofs were made of palm trunks, with ceilings of mangrove poles and bamboo reeds, covered with rush mats and date palm fronds. As low-tech as skills were, and with materials readily available for the taking, houses grew organically rather than overly planned, with everyone their own architect and builder.

The Middle East penchant for privacy, owing to both tradition and to religious family values, plus the hot climate, was a prescription for thick walled exteriors. Perimeter walls were built two to three meters high, relatively unbroken except for monumental double wooden doors exquisitely carved in intricate Islamic geometric patterns. Those distinctive design features continue today. Early homes placed living quarters along the inner perimeter of the exterior walls, in turn creating a family courtyard that also enjoyed the cooling effect of the building's exterior shadows. For the same reasons windows were kept small and high, shuttered, facing the courtyard, or facing the exterior for two-story sections.

The culture of Arabic privacy as a design element is evident in the division of homes into two distinct parts, the majlis and the harim. The majlis is a reception room for male visitors, usually the showroom of the house, near the entrance, with traditional ornamental pillows on the floor lining the walls. The harim is the women's quarters, closed to all men except close family members. That design distinction remains today and accounts for the oversized house typical in the Middle East, as they are essentially two houses in one, compared to Western homes.

With so little rain roofs were flat and so were often used for sleeping in the cooler night air. Elevated wooden sleeping decks were similarly a popular feature in the courtyards.

Badgeers, or Wind Towers, an important design element of the early houses here, are an innovative pre-air conditioning feature, a structure rising above the house to channel the cool prevailing wind down, to force the hotter inside air up and out. These wind catchers are marvellously efficient, in use for thousands of years throughout the desert region, capable even of refrigeration.

Early Bahrainis were decidedly 'green' long before it was keen to be 'green'. Their original sanitary facilities by contrast are disappointingly minimal, essentially little more than holes in the floor of small rooms or on the roof, that drained out to the alley, decidedly worse than in early Rome, though no better or worse than in Medieval Europe. Muharraq's following heritage houses are pleasingly varied despite being limited to such few basic elements:

The lovingly restored **Isa bin Ali** House is a good home to begin the journey into the rich traditions of a past culture. Built in 1800, it is nevertheless one of the best surviving examples of the island's traditional homes and one which set the design standards for Bahrain homes that followed. Fit for a Shaikh, it indeed served as the official residence of Shaikh Isa bin Ali Khalifa, the seventh Al Khalifah ruler, and great grandfather of the present Amir. It is a complex layout, on two floors, with four independent courtyards: for the Sheikh, for his family, for visitors and for servants. And if you are there on a hot day you can regain your cool, luxuriating in the breezes of their unwired, always working, Wind Tower.

The most prominent pearl merchant at the end of the 19th century, and owner of several fine buildings in the area was Ahmed Seyadi. Nearby is his **Beit Seyadi (Siyadi House)**, built in 1905, notable for the spaciousness of its compact design. The exquisite ornamentation on the façade, doors and ceiling were the handiwork of the best craftsmen of the day, featuring fine geometric designs true to Islamic tradition.

With graceful arches framing its lovely courtyard, the **Kurar House** offers up a special treat, the opportunity to watch Bahraini women pass on the art of embroidering unique Kurar fabrics, characterised by their interwoven golden threads.

The **Abdullah Al Zayed House** mesmerises, with its powerful play of light throughout the remarkable airiness of its double-height gallery, with white walls reaching up to a large curved skylight crowning the space, with design accents of colourful stained glass fanlight panes.

From first glance the classical colonnade of the **Bin Mattar** house stands in gentle contrast to the others. Yet its interiors are of the same traditional materials and of the same design principles. It was built in 1905, on reclaimed land, and like many others was encircled then on three sides by the sea. It is now well landlocked, the same fate of the others, as sea reclamation pushed progressively onward and outward without restriction.

A cluster of eighteen buildings in old Muharraq makes up the **Pearling Pathway**, a major restoration project. Homes involved include a few of the above, plus others, plus a special section of the old waterfront. The Pathway revives that golden era of Bahrain's early natural-pearl economic base, now under consideration for the List of World Heritage Sites. The buildings individually, and especially as a group, are outstanding architectural resources reflecting the early marine history of the island.

Buildings either already restored, or targeted, are mostly late 19th century vintage, of traditional Bahrain architectural style and construction. Most of the Pathway buildings, in particular the residences, contain architectural elements noted earlier. The Pearling Heritage Project also includes mosques, souqs, warehouses and public majlis (places for special gatherings). Some will remain as residences; others will be used as a museum, a library, an art gallery, guest rooms, and a multi-media centre, all with a historical pearling focus. Among them are: **Siyadi Mosque, Siyadi Majlis, Siyadi House, Muharradh House, Amat Ali Rashid Fahlia I & II, Fakhro Amarat, Siyadi Shafa, Murad Majlis, Murad House, Fakhro House, Al-Alawi House, Al Jalahma House, Badr Ghulum House, Al Ghus House, Qua' lat Bu Mahir,** and **Bu Mahir Seashore** with its nearby preserved pearl oyster beds, plus the pathway itself between them.

Be sure that you have comfortable walking shoes if you take up the Pathway Challenge. Although the buildings are in the same area, they are a bit scattered, and the path around all is several kilometres long. A great way to mix culture with exercise.

FORTS

There's little argument that forts are Bahrain's most prominent architectural items, with three strategically placed around this once vulnerable little island: **Qal'at al-Bahrain** - the **Fort of Bahrain, Arad Fort,** and **Al Fateh**

Fort in Riffa. They are constructed largely of the same readily available local materials as used in homes: coral stones, limestone and palm tree trunks.

We started off big on our fort exploration - with **Qal'at al-Bahrain** – protector of the ancient harbour and capitol of Dilmun near the island's north-west shore. My first impression of the Fort was its magnificent size.

Looking at it from the deck of the Fort's Museum Pavilion, before we ventured on the kilometre-long approach walk, it seems to stretch from one end of the horizon to another. A walk around it is over three kilometres, more than a mile. The Qal'at occupies one hundred and eighty square meters, or forty-four acres,

The next thing that comes to mind as I walk around it, is the variety of shapes incorporated in the fort. One is left to think that the master builders assembled a variety of wall-building stone craftsmen, one an expert in building curved walls, one expert in perpendicular walls, another expert in angled walls and one each specializing in walls projecting out and the other in walls projecting in, and the masters said, "Now build me a mile-long wall around this site, each wall showing off the best of each of your specialities. And oh, by the way, mix it up randomly just for good show. And give me a bunch of different heights and arches, inside and out while you're at it." The end result – an intriguing shape no less. Actually the great variety of shapes that make up the fort is, in itself, what gives it harmony. It is a variegated mass of coral rock rising randomly from beach sand, but at one with its surroundings.

About one-third of its height extends below the level of the surrounding land to allow for the obligatory moat, wide and stone-lined. The interior is a seemingly random grouping of thick stone walls, of Arabic and earlier arches, all at a variety of levels. Although ruins, it is all exceptionally well restored.

In the early 1500s the Portuguese saw Bahrain as key to protecting their trade routes between India, Africa and Europe. This fortress, already aged when they appropriated it and attendant structures, were strengthened by them, with towers added for their military use.

But the fort is important more as a long term historical site than as just a military monument. It dates back five thousand years, to when parts of it served as the capital of the Dilmun civilisation, with seven successive civilisations of outsiders since. Dilmun has been called the 'land of immortality', the ancestral place of Sumerians, a place where the Gods are said to have met. The earliest known Dilmun burial mounds are traced here, to Qal'at al-Bahrain. Continuous human residency from 2300BC up to 1700AD has been established, notably Dilmun, Tylos, Islamic societies and Portuguese occupying it during different periods. Layers around the fort have revealed military, religious, commercial and residential structures, some of which are of a similar date and style as that of the Barbar Temple.

The area is a reclaimed seafront, and the fort and surroundings are built on a tell, an artificial mound twelve meters high, created by the successive layers of human occupation. Over the centuries it has served as a city, a trading post and a fort.

Excavations reveal a village with modest houses, built with the same materials as recent homes, from rough stone bonded with clay and lime mortar. The houses had plastered floors and were positioned on well laid out streets. They were built around an oasis and functioned as an agricultural community, with cattle, sheep and goats, and with fishing. In 1800BC it appears to have been deserted, and subsequently covered with drift sand from the sea.

In 2005 the area was designated by United Nations Educational, Scientific and Scientific Organisation (UNESCO) as Bahrain's first World Heritage Site.

Sitting on the Museum Pavilion after the long walk to the fort, around the fort, then back again, we were appreciative of the cool fruit juices and iced coffees available at the Pavilion café. From here we could enjoy a last distant view of the fort, with a close view of the falling tide of the Gulf alongside the Pavilion. As a bonus, the sun was setting behind the fort and palm groves, silhouetting them in streaks of purples, blues reds and oranges. Great picture taking time. All the cameras on the Pavilion clicked together – adults' as well as kids'. Three riders on horseback circled round the long sandy fort road in the distance, then galloped straight towards us, turning at the last moment just in front of the deck, racing along and down the water's edge and off into the distance. I watched till they rode out of sight. Then, all of a sudden, the lights of the fort came on, washing over its entirety, illuminating its great length, its towers and turrets, its parapets and battlements. A long flaming orange line it was, straight along the base, broken and crenellated along its top. It was an image projected against the softly darkening purple-ink sky, with enough reds to bring out all the cameras again. Sensory stimulation over, I slipped back to this other world.

Arad Fort was built in the 15th century on the north-east section of the island, overlooking and protecting important sea passages between Muharraq island and the major land mass of Bahrain. Its compact designs a simple square symmetrical plan with four semi-circular sloping walls at its corners, enclosing a large central court. It has a typical crenellated top with upper battlements and is surrounded by a rampart and moat. It is believed that in about 1800 the fort was used by the Omanis during their brief venture into Bahrain.

On several visits to Arad Fort, I had the good fortune of two-for-one. One was the fort itself; the second was the musical and dance performances of the Bahrain Spring Fair which uses the fort as its major venue and a distinctive backdrop and powerful counterpoint to the elaborate performances. The fort is a special treat at night, powerfully illuminated

However the parking is not up to the demands of the Fair. We were buried in hopeless gridlock on leaving my first Fair visit. But my cultural ally, Tony, a scientist, extricated us handily, breaking the gridlock for all by manoeuvring his SUV over a blocking sidewalk. We thereby formulated the 'Law of Parking', applicable for Arad and all Bahrain but really for all gatherings, which states: 'Time Taken to Extricate a Car is Inversely Proportional to Time Taken Earlier to Walk from Car to Venue'. So we spend a little more time parking farther away to save major time when we leave.

The **Sh. Salman bin Ahmed Fort** at Riffa is distinct from the others and from most forts in that it is not on the sea but is landlocked, in the very heart of the island. It is a strategic position nevertheless, built atop a cliff between the then two major Southern Governate cities of eastern and western Riffa. It controlled the extensive flat desert area below from its perch, with a commanding view across the Hunanaiya Valley to the sea on the island's west coast.

The fort was originally built in the 17th century during the reign of Sheikh Al-Gabrey. After accession of power by Sheikh Sulman Bin Ahmed (al Fateh) Al-Khalifa, the present fort was built in 1812 on the ruins of the old fort. It was built primarily for military purpose, but after the frontiers of the island were secured the fort became a seat of government until 1869 and then served as a residence.

The fort is constructed in a square shape with a total area of two thousand five hundred square meters, divided into three separate courtyards surrounded by thirty-five spacious multi-purpose and residential rooms and utility chambers. Even to this day it remains important in terms of the national security of Bahrain.

It allows a spectacular view to the valley below and is one of the best places to enjoy the cooling wind blowing over the desert sand at night. It is Maryam's favourite evening picnic spot, and as we were arriving at dusk and were all hungry we stopped on the way for some takeaway. Although the hamburger and hot dog invasion has waged successful inroads in Bahrain, we treated ourselves to native Middle East takeaway: biryani - rice cooked with various meats, and shawarmas: Turkish inspired, heated meats sliced thinly and rolled in a soft bread cone. Great finger food. The rear deck of the fort and its great view served well for our picnic. With Bahraini Maryam and other close friends; Dr. Ashraf, Egyptian physician, Marissa, his Filipino fiancé whose photographic passion provided helpful later reference, and her Chinese friend XieMie, we relaxed in good company. Such an international smorgasbord of friends is the norm in Bahrain for any occasion. Lights twinkled on across the broad deep valley below, signalling the approaching darkness. Just then we were treated to unexpected entertainment: a group of Eid revellers and an impromptu dance on a level just below us, to the beat of tin and plastic makeshift drums. Dr. Ashraf explained, "This is their traditional folkloric dance, the Tagleedi".

ISLANDS

On to the next adventure. Fall was a perfect time to enjoy roaming through Amwaj Island (Amwaj is Arabic for 'waves'), a grouping of four islands newly formed around a lagoon, joined by bridges, all recently reclaimed from the Arabian Gulf. Amwaj features all the facilities and amenities expected in a small self-contained modern resort city. It is one of five other island masses, either newly created from open sea, or in planning or development stages. Bahrain has been extended often recently dating back generally to 1968, with once seaside buildings now as much as a kilometre away from the sea. Hard to imagine under restrictive property laws of Western countries.

Reclaimed sea has an even longer precedent here, dating back to over four thousand years, back to the Dilmun civilisations development of what is now the Bahrain Fort. Amwaj, as Bahrain's first complete island community, was reclaimed with a vision of returning waterside living to this little country. Bahrain's land mass, though only about one sixth the size of Rhode Island has one hundred and sixty-one kilometres of shoreline, one hundred times the ratio of shoreline to area compared to the US. But prior to Amwaj it had only about thirteen small public and private beaches for its population of about 1.2 million. By comparison, California, USA lists over six times as many major beaches per kilometre, and they are all huge in comparison to Bahrain's.

Amwaj Islands is a start in reversing the great beach oversight here. It offers a complete community for thirty thousand new inhabitants, forming the country's new north-east coast. It was planned by US architects Skidmore, Owens and Merrill as a grouping of mini-islands, each bordering both the Arabian Gulf externally and their own Lagoon internally, with self-styled 'Venice-like' canals and rear-lot mooring interlaced throughout.

It is a small city, with all the facilities expected in a fashionable seaside resort. The central Lagoon amenities are reminiscent of London's Covent Garden and Sydney's Cockle Wharf. Amwaj boasts a hospital, schools, sports, entertainment, five-star hotels and shopping, Marina and Marina Mall, fine restaurants and lounges, health clubs, botanical gardens, condominiums, apartments and beach front villas, in open and gated communities, all surrounded by crystal clear azure waters and golden beaches. Properties are available for freehold purchase by expatriates also. Unfortunately I don't get sales commissions.

The architectural significance of Amwaj Island is that it is emblematic of the emerging new Bahrain, awakening at long last to the pleasures and beauty of its surrounding warm sea. It is the first of many future island communities and small cities in planning and under development. As most of Bahrain's southern half is desert, the islands will no doubt be its architectural showcases.

Other islands of various sizes, newly created or in various stages of planning and development are **Bahrain Bay, Reef Island, Lulu** and **Diyar Al Muharraq,** with the ambitious **Durrat Al Bahrain** its crowning pearl, a tourist resort city on the south-east coast, planned with thirteen interlaced drop-jewel islands in shapes of ornamental fish and sea shells, symbolic of an elaborate Arabesque necklace. The **Financial Harbour** however is a major land extension rather than an island. Development is continuing, though not as furiously as before the global slowdown, further slowed by internal problems. But the fervour is still as strong.

Plans extend beyond these near-shore reclaimed islands, with a visionary network of sea bridges to connect over thirty existing offshore islands or islets (more at low tide).

Sitting on the seaside deck at the Dragon Hotel, this Western expat was sipping a pineapple cooler, appropriate for this tropical setting, while my Bahraini host, Maryam, sipped her tea. A good example of the relaxed friendliness and ready acceptance of cross-culture for which Bahrain is noted and which is duly appreciated by expat visitors and long-term residents.

'Dragon' seemed a strange name for a hotel in this part of the world and I had never heard of such a chain. So I asked the waiters, who had not a clue why it was so named. "Hmm," I thought, "if I worked at such a hotel I would think that would be one of the first things I would want to know". So I posed the question to Maryam. Her answer: "If you look at the island from the air it looks like a dragon head and tail." Well, I had to Google that further to confirm it, and sure enough she didn't disappoint. What I found was the following hyped description by a hotel PR flack who explained it thus: "It (the Dragon Hotel's logo) is designed to reflect its name in the shape of a sleeping dragon with its long neck stretching across the water to form a conical dragon-like head, reminiscent of a majestic giant watching over the waters of the Arabian Gulf. Its distinctive dragon scales prevail over the land - marking the hotel's most unique and iconic architectural feature." Well OK, if you say so... But if you squint, the aerial view of the island complex is really - a dragon head - no less.

We were enjoying a special show in the illuminated sand shallows just below the outdoor dining deck. Little fish darting hither and yon and a tiny crab scurrying about, stirring the sand in its path, for titbits thrown from the tables. A small testament to marine life returning to the reclaimed shallows.

I closed my eyes for a pleasant moment to taste the cool Gulf breezes washing over my face, and opened them to evening lights now flickering on randomly across the bay, dancing on the water against the darkening Gulf sky. Testament to the transplant of human life to the newly planted villas and apartments in the reclaimed sand. Maryam pointed to her villa under construction across the water, and raised concerns referring further to the sparse activity. "Where is the 'community' they advertised?"

I couldn't imagine what more the designers could have done. My reply, "You have Westerners here with their culture mixed with

Middle-Easterners with their culture. Give it time to gel". For certain, a sense of community lifestyle is one reason why Westerners buy into resort developments. Amwaj was designed to offer both an entertainment lifestyle for the young, and a quiet comfortable environment for the retired, targeting native Bahrainis, as well as expats.

The architectural style of the buildings here can be described as 'Modern Arabic Aesthetic' but could be labelled Miami Contemporary as well. High rise buildings are, like everywhere else, glass on steel frame, some with interesting and/or whimsical shapes such as the angular **Marriott Renaissance Hotel,** raked, stepped and folded around its entry focus.

There is Arabic homogeneity in the low-rise buildings, block concrete shapes with large shaded overhangs and large vertical openings. Liberal use is made of Arabic-style arches, as well as a sprinkling of modern tensile tent/sail structures for variety. Low-rise buildings are just about all concrete, due to limited structural wood in the desert climes,

The unanimously favoured colour here as throughout Bahrain is the one which blends best into the surrounding sands: if you like beige there is every shade that you ever could imagine - plus whites galore. And don't plan to paint your building exterior such "garish" colours as green, blue, etc., which are under new building restrictions.

Amwaj was built with considerable attention to its environmental impact. Reclamation of the island was an interesting engineering and environmental feat, using a sophisticated technology which employs recently developed Geotubes as the key feature of the design. Geotubes are sand containment sacks, highly UV stabilised, of heavy woven polypropylene geo-textile fabric, thirteen meters in circumference. They are hydraulically filled with dredged sand, and are dual stacked to form the island perimeter retention dike, for minimum impact of spillage on the marine habitat. The Geotubes are hydraulically filled, then covered with a series of increasingly larger rip-rap stones on their exteriors, then filled in between with sand reclaimed from proposed navigation channels and marinas to further mitigate environmental effects. A turbidity curtain between the tubes and the sea was used during dredging and filling to greatly reduce the siltation and migration of fines to the surrounding area. A breakwater of similar but submerged reef-like structures is used offshore all around the island for tempering of wave surges.

COMMERCIAL BUILDINGS

The country's largest mall is Manama's new world class **City Centre Mall.** This retail and leisure complex includes a dramatic glazed atrium roof, forty meters high, covering and lighting all walkways throughout. The Mall is rectangular with an internal balcony-like rectangular walkway open from floor to ceiling, with clear views throughout the continuous three-level atrium, imparting a grand sense of space. The walkways connect four roundabouts at the corners of the interior rectangle, with major stores on the exterior side of the walkway, and smaller stores on the interior.

The Centre comprises two hundred and seven thousand square meters of retail space, two luxury hotels, an energy centre, a twenty screen cinema, a five thousand five hundred car multi-storey car-park and the Middle East's largest indoor climate controlled water-park. Mott MacDonald Group, UK, served as lead consultant and engineer.

As dramatic is the interior is, the exterior is contrarily drab for such a major building. The public entrance is only through the multi level car park, blocking the entire façade, with no sense of the exterior of the mall except for drive-by views along the highway, and then only of a neutral façade there.

Al A'Ali Mall is a small centre featuring top designer stores, and is notable in blending the look and feel of a traditional open air souk within its modern air-conditioned confines. A glass roof, stores with old-fashioned Arabic wooden doors and carts selling souvenirs all add to the atmosphere.

This selective architectural itinerary will focus a bit on restaurants because seldom can the subtle effects of good architecture on a building's function be so readily appreciated as in a thoughtfully designed restaurant.

And Bahrain has more than its share of well-designed restaurants - with tasty offerings to match. I have happily sampled many, with an architect's eye for the aesthetics as well as the food.

Here's a little-known secret: Four of the most popular and successful restaurants in Bahrain, covering a range of cuisine, owe their design, development and management to one company, Al Ghalia Contracting. In this one company's domain are four local favourites, all award winners, and are all as different from each other as can be, sharing only good food and good design. **Mezzaluna,** elegant and sophisticated dining in a converted traditional Bahrain house with lofty covered courtyard; **Zoe,** an intimate space for seeing and being seen, inspired by New York loft design; **Café Lilou,** decadent treats in a Parisian patisserie with delightful alfresco terrace; and the **Monsoon,** romantic, exotic Asian, inspirit with Buddhist temple design; are all within a short walk from each other in Adliya's core, the locally famed Block 338 restaurant row.

Around the corner from these are two other locally cherished dining spots. **Café Italia,** recipient of this year's Favourite Restaurant 2011, with Italian inspired design elements. Nearby is **TIAN Asian** with its oriental inspired design décor, both sharing similar architectural treatment, i.e. minimalist sleek lines with clean sculpted décor. Nearby, the **Upstairs-Downstairs** is a workable replica of a covered New Orleans jazz club courtyard, on two levels, with the focus of both levels on the downstairs jazz combo.

For design interest, twenty minutes away but near each other on the Seef waterfront, are two other favourites. **Bushido,** is chic and trendy, powerful re-interpretation of Japan in a soaring two-level space surrounded by protective Samurai statues swathed in full traditional armour, Nearby is **Trader Vic's,** Ritz Carlton's showcase restaurant/lounge which does as effective a job of integrating the indoors with their splendid oasis and gulf outdoor views as you will be treated to anywhere.

Amidst all the talk here of fine dining, it's worthwhile mentioning in another breath 'Franchise Alley', a planning anomaly. This 'Las Vegasesque' strip, extending for half a kilometre from the US Naval Base along Shabab Avenue in the Juffair area, is lined on both sides of the street with just about every US fast food franchise outlet imaginable, from Burger King to Starbucks. Originally planned to draw US Sailors from their base into town, it has now surpassed sheesha shops in its popularity with locals.

My favourite restaurant in Bahrain however, and one of my favourites in the world is the Monsoon. Other Bahraini residents agree. It was voted 'Bahrain's Favourite Restaurant' in 2009, and either 'Favourite Restaurant' or 'Favourite Asian or Thai Restaurant' for most years since it opened in 2000. I include it here, not just from personal sentiment but because of its special architectural ambiance, and to make the case for the influence of the architectural environment on the function of a building, and in this case on the success of a commercial enterprise.

You are greeted at the Monsoon entry by a lovely Asian hostess, with the gentle traditional Thai Wai greeting of upward-pointed folded hands and lowered eyes. The design is obviously not a local architectural style, but is decidedly Balinese, a tropical style that seems natural in this tropical-like setting. The main dining area is a 'U' shape; with seating on a raised platform. A moment of reverence seems almost in order in the temple-like grandeur of the soaring wooden ceiling. Surrounded by a polished wood interior, radiating a warm glow, it is an open invitation to relaxed and pleasurable dining.

A decorative moat, a meter wide by a meter deep surrounds the dining area and sets it off. Candles float peacefully throughout the moat, lined with candles all along its edge. You are tempted to wonder if anyone has ever fallen in. I do ask and the hostess smiles and nods yes, and says simply; "several". Then I notice that she has carefully positioned herself between us and the moat as she escorts us to our table. Just in case? I chuckle. But I instinctively walk just a step farther away.

There's a large glass wall across the rear, looking out at one of the restaurant's design features, a traditional Japanese kaiyu-shiki or strolling garden, with lanterns, sculpture, koi pond and island, and chashitsus - open tea gardens for outdoor dining. All are in a formal 17th century-style, a walled and fenced courtyard garden. Stepping stones, raised millimetres above the quiet water, bridge the pond, and I smile to myself crossing it, thinking back to the tale of accidental swimmers in the inside moat. So I tip-toe across with just a little extra caution. The garden is open for dining only during Bahrain's pleasant spring and fall months unfortunately, but is nice for hovering over drinks with friends at other times.

Off to another landmark, **Bab Al Bahrain,** the 'Gateway of Bahrain', originally the waterfront gateway to the city. Hundreds of pigeons scatter flappingly in all directions as we wander through the parking lot across from and seaward of the Bab. All this area, including the InterContinental Regency hotel lot just on our right, plus all the sea-shore extending for a half- kilometre inward toward us from the sea was water not many years ago.

The semi-circular driveway ahead, with a huge ornamental fountain at its focus, leads us into the impressive Gateway, just past the circle of taxis waiting to pounce on fares at non-metered prices. A couple of hundred expats, many construction workers, are just hanging out on the expansive walkway all around the Bab on any night, especially Friday, enjoying the camaraderie.

The monumental building was designed by Sir Charles Belgrave in 1945 to house government offices. The monument got a facelift in 1986 which added architectural features of the Islamic style. Today, the building houses the tourist information office and a handicrafts and souvenir shop. The design features a two storey arch in the centre formerly a drive-through, now the pedestrian entrance to the famed **Manama Souq.** An extensive and lively marketplace, Bahrain's major souq wanders through the narrow labyrinthine back-streets, with a wide variety of souvenirs, fabrics, spices, handicrafts, kaftans, nuts and dry fruits, and just about anything one can think of, all at bargain prices. Most of the shopkeepers are residents of Bahrain. But there are traders from Bangladesh, Pakistan, India, Egypt and other neighbouring Gulf countries displaying assorted odds and ends. If you are in search of pure hallmarked gold, here you can find 18carat to 25carat gold items, typically 21carat, respected for its quality. Or natural Bahraini pearls famous all over the world.

There are restoration efforts under way here as in Muhrarraq and in selected villages or 'towns'. Still called 'villages' or towns, they have developed and merged into what would be considered 'subdivisions' elsewhere,

MANAMA HIGH-RISE

In Bahrain, there is increasingly less left of the old Manama. Older buildings have either been left to gradually deteriorate by owners indifferent to preventive maintenance, or they have just given up, making way for the wave of new high-rise offices, apartments, condos, and hotels. From a boat looking shoreward, a new skyline rises higher day-by-day from old Manama, some towers are glinting flashes of sun off their shiny glass skin, covering a variety of shapes, some, still dark, are still only partly completed concrete skeletons. The skeleton shapes are crowned by construction cranes, looking like flocks of alien birds perched atop their favourite rookery, some searching for prey, restlessly moving, some silenced for the time being by the economic slowdown. Bahrain's skyline looks more and more like the changing skylines of other thriving modern cities.

The **Bahrain World Trade Centre (BWTC)** is the most recognisable landmark on the horizon. A stunning design by the multi-national architectural firm W.S. Atkins of the U.K., It features twin fifty storey sail-shaped towers dynamically twisting skywards together, ending in a dramatic two pointed star.

Built in 2008, it is the first skyscraper in the world to integrate wind turbines, for which it has received numerous design awards for energy sustainability. The twin towers are designed to funnel and accelerate wind through their gap to three turbines. The turbines are linked via three sky-bridges, each holding a three bladed propeller turbine aligned north to capture breezes from the nearby Arabian Gulf.

They are designed to provide up to fifteen percent of the towers' total power consumption.

Its awards include the '2006 LEAF Award for Best Use of Technology within a Large Scheme', the 'Arab Construction World Award for Sustainable Design', The 'NOVA Award' in 2009, and the prestigious 'Palme Award' in 2010, among others. Atkins has also designed the spectacular Burj Al Arab in Dubai. A wise man can quickly orient himself on Bahrain's meandering roads with just a glance at the BWTC twin star points, a ready reference throughout Manama.

The **Bahrain Financial Harbour (BFH)** is a large-scale integrated waterfront development in the centre of Manama on reclaimed land, under development as a complete financial city, a self contained community of office space and luxury residential together with retail, hotel, leisure and entertainment properties. It was designed by Bahraini Architect Ahmed Janahi, and is being developed in multiple construction phases.

Major components of the Financial Centre include the Harbour Towers, the Harbour Mall and the Harbour House. The twin Harbour Towers, Commercial East and Commercial West, mark completion of the first phase and stand as the two tallest towers in Bahrain at fifty-four floors each. They feature state-of-the-art intelligent building systems throughout. Their interesting architectural shapes, featuring steep 'ski slope' shaped façades on each building, are the latest easily recognisable landmark for the area. The BFH financial community landmark was named 'Best Mixed-Use Development Project' at the Arab Investment Summit in Dubai in 2011.

Zamil Towers stands as a second Gateway to the centre of Manama, incorporating a drive-through arched tunnel in the building's centre, reminiscent of Bab Bahrain. It is a modern twenty-two story building with façade and interior on the lower part crafted in the Islamic style, with upper part incorporating modern architectural elements. It is is an excellent example of Islamic traditionalist arched entrances and interior materials and motif coexisting with modernism. It was designed as a gateway from modern Bahrain to the traditional Souk area, another step in the ongoing regeneration of Bahrain's traditional bazaar. The two-tower building was designed by Ahmed Bucheery, Bahrain Architect, and received the Aga Khan Award.

The National Bank of Bahrain (NBB) is an elegant study in sophisticated simplicity. It was designed by Abbey, Hanson, Rowe & Partners, Architects, UK, with concave glass surfaces on two façades, and convex glass surfaces on the other two opposing sides. As conceived by the architects, the special glazing acts as a giant curved mirror reflecting the predominant blue skies of Bahrain. At twenty-seven floors high, it houses the bank's main offices, in the centre of Manama, another landmark on the city's skyline.

The **Abraj Al Lulu** is an impressive major residential development in the very centre of Manama packed with all the amenities a discriminating urban dweller could possibly want and close to everything one would need. It consists of three large towers, nostalgically named Gold Pearl, Silver Pearl and Black Pearl, each fifty, fifty and forty floors high, with awe-inspiring views and a parking garage for over one thousand cars - a luxury in Bahrain. It is available for purchase freehold by expatriates. Al Lulu's design is by association of Architects Jafar Tukan, Jordan, Aga Khan Award recipient; Cowi Al Moayed, UAE and Habib Mudara, Bahrain.

MOSQUES

The **Al Khamis Mosque** is notable as the very first mosque in the country and the most ancient monument of Islam in the vicinity. The foundation probably dates back as far as 692AD, however inscriptions indicate more recent construction around the 11th century with addition of the present minarets during the 14th and 15th centuries. The ruins include standing stone walls and columns, and surprisingly the two minarets, presumably the most vulnerable parts of the structure. On my visit the site was closed, probably due to Eid holidays, but I did manage to get a glimpse through the gates.

Al Fateh Grand Mosque in Bahrain is the largest mosque of the country, constructed in 1990. Though not architecturally ground-breaking, it is truly grand in its ability to accommodate about seven thousand worshippers at a time. It is an imposing monument and good example of current mosque design. It is notable for its Islamic décor and its sixty tonne dome – of fibreglass. If you have wondered at the design or workings of mosques this would be well worth a visit, as excellent guided tours for non-Muslims are available throughout the day, except during any of the five prayer times.

ARCHITECTURAL VERNACULAR

The **University of Bahrain,** which was designed by Architect Kenzo Tange, Japan, a 'Pritzker Prize' winner, established the first School of Architecture in 1990. Prior to then architecture by locals was practised by Civil Engineers and Architects who had completed their studies abroad. Bahrain now enjoys the beginnings of a flourishing architectural community, with expectations of a building boom, an outgrowth of the mega projects now in the planning and early development stages, in particular the offshore resort complexes. Much of the large-scale contemporary architecture in Bahrain is now practised by international firms, with increasing collaboration by Bahrain Engineers and Architects.

Architects seem to enjoy extracting order from the variety of building styles and their influences over the years. Such is the following short summary of Bahrain Architect Ahmad Bucheery's insightful study, *Contemporary Architecture* in Bahrain. He divides the island's recent architecture into five periods:

I Traditional - 1800-1945: Adherence to Islamic values and Arab customs, with local technologies and materials dominant.

II Transitional - 1946-1970: Change from pearling to oil based economy, with the consequent expansion of government infrastructure.

III Modern - 1971-1979: Meteoric development due to the booming oil revenue abetted by new western construction technologies of steel and pre-cast concrete structures.

IV Post-Modern - 1980-1989: Nationalistic quickening, spurring major municipal projects.

V Revivalism - 1990-1999: Flocking Saudi Causeway visitors prompt new hotels, apartments, restaurants, etc., bringing hefty investment capital with them.

I would add a sixth:

VI Future City – 2000 and beyond: I might also call this the Mega Project Period. Here Bahrain turns from development of only individual buildings, to planning and implementing large scale community re-development, and even creation of entire new cities. Its effects will be a renaissance of dynamic architectural mega projects from developers and architects worldwide. At the same time the country must make major changes to its already overtaxed infrastructure, most notably its dysfunctional traffic and road system. Bahrain has come far – quickly. The country has great future dreams and they will be realised, but only if the country continues to work with that unified goal.

Arabic Architecture, or more specifically **Islamic Architecture,** is worth discussing both for its pervasive influence in Bahrain as well as throughout this entire part of the world, while its rich contributions to the architectural vocabulary are largely overlooked in the West.

Arabic design springs from the rich and ornate architecture of its early mosques and is interwoven in the complex fabric of Islam itself. The use of human and animal statues and pictures are haram (forbidden) in Islam, so Muslim architects turned their design talents to redefining spaces as extensions of Islamic ideals, to broadening the simple forms of domes, cupolas, arches columns, piers, niches , colonnades, and decorative elements of the earlier Byzantine. Arabic design strives to be different and succeeds stunningly, with visual rhythm and harmony throughout Islamic structures. Islamic architecture's more elaborate elements are balanced always with its traditions.

Islamic architecture has taken simple Roman arches and formed them into an elegant variety of graceful new shapes. Their Pointed Arch is a transformation of the traditional rounded crown, bending it into a more fanciful pointed top. Their Ogee Arch takes the Pointed Arch a sensual step further by shaping the arch sides in an 'S' shape on the right and a reverse 'S' on the left. Arabic architects developed the Horseshoe Arch, a regular rounded top but with the bottom sides curving inward as in a horseshoe. Their more decorative and whimsical arches include the Scalloped Arch, composed of a continuous series of generally five intersecting mini-arches forming the arch sides and top, and the purely decorative Stalactite – a series of arches alongside and above and below others to form patterned ornamentation. Examples adorn Bahrain's heritage buildings but can be seen as well as icons in contemporary buildings recalling the romantic symbols of their past.

Arabesque Art is an integral part of Islamic architecture. It is an ornate repetition of geometric patterns, or decorative elements derivative of plants, of fractal geometry in radiating curved lattice patterns. Their fanciful arches and other architectural shapes are an outgrowth of their skill in geometric art. Their motif is considered spiritualistic, based as it is on an Islamic world view of patterns extending beyond the visible material world to symbolise the infinite and therefore un- centralised nature of the creation of the one God ('Allah').

An added distinctive feature of Arabesque art is **Calligraphy,** which for the Muslim is also a visible expression of spiritual concepts. Calligraphy is a venerated art form, as it provides a link between the languages of the Muslims and the religion of Islam.

There is a new awakening of Islamic values in architecture and the arts, with a number of recent international conferences throughout the Middle East devoted solely to their study and implementation.

ARCHAEOLOGY AND ARCHITECTURE

On one of our jaunts Maryam headed to the Barbar village, on the west coast, wherein the historic **Barbar Temple** excavation remains after five thousand years. It took a few turns to find the site, as there are few highway and street signs, a common omission in travels round the island.

The site is worthy of both archaeological and architectural study. The standing ruins are of the most recent of three temples erected on the same site, approximately five hundred years apart, as each in turn was demolished. This most recent temple is from approximately 2000BC, the earlier from approximately 2500BC, established through Radio Carbon Dating, with the earliest from 3000BC.

Excavation extends from subterranean cellars to above ground ruins of various shaped walls: ovals, rectangles, circles, etc., each at various interconnected levels, with wall remains from one-half to one and one-half meter high. All three temples were made of limestone, and an elaborate plan is evident, with well preserved stone steps leading a wanderer throughout the ruins.

On the way back from the Al Khamis Mosque, Maryam took a slight detour through the village of El Ali and its early historic **Dilmun Burial Mounds.** "I know you're interested in the ancient burial grounds," she offered, "and this area has some of the best preserved examples." These are the major remains of the once mighty Dilmun civilisation that flourished here during the Bronze Age of 3000BC.

Architecturally, the Burial Mounds are rare structures worth a note, primitive as some are, stone chambers lined with plaster, into which bodies in wooden coffins were placed, with the structure then covered over with earthen mounds. The stone chambers however vary from simple rectangular boxes to more complex intricate networks of adjoining chambers for later burial of several family members.

The mounds are further important for the sheer extent of their physical coverage of Bahrain. In those primitive times this necropolis covered the central two-thirds of the entire island, literally a 'country of the dead.' Most mounds have simply been overbuilt, but a preservation effort is underway, enclosing large burial areas with security walls. This burial ensemble is on the list for inclusion as a World Heritage site.

LOOKING AHEAD

Major city planning projects which will impact the island's architecture include new restoration efforts focusing on entire villages in addition to individual buildings.

Architecturally, the planned **Bahrain Museum of Contemporary Art** is awaited with breathless anticipation, a free flowing fantasy as can only be dreamed of and delivered by Zaha Hadid, Architect, U.K. Her international projects and awards are far too numerous to mention. The museum is designed as a complex of curving arcs that lift slowly and then soar horizontally, twisting and turning fluidly in unexpectedly delightful ways and shapes. It is described as mystically floating above the coastal landscape, gracefully soaring along the waterfront, focusing light on the exhibits, then gently curving to a cantilever over the water.

Major infrastructure plans include a bridge far, forty kilometres across the sea to Qatar. This **'Friendship Bridge'** is under design by US engineering firm KBR and UK firm Halcrow. It will be the seventh longest bridge in the world. Given the unprecedented boom brought by the Saudi Causeway, Bahrain will have to grow its entire infrastructure just to accommodate the influx of this one ambitious undertaking.

With pearling washed away and its oil drained, Bahrain is of necessity reinventing itself, both as a financial centre for the Gulf area, and more broadly as a tourist recreational magnet. Recent cruise ship interest is a case in point. For tourism, forward thinkers are looking increasingly to regenerate Bahrain's past cultural assets for future interests, for the enchantment of travellers hungry to soak in Bahrain's special heritage while enjoying its sunny clime and its flurry of cultural activities.

And so I return to Maryam's opening question; "of all the sites we visited, what's your favourite?"

I admit to having to punt on this one. My favourite, architecturally, is one we haven't visited, Zaha Hadid's Museum of Contemporary Art, coming soon to a waterfront in Muharraq. Architecture by Hadid is music for the eyes. Of those we visited however. I will return often to Amwaj, and could happily retire there to enjoy the lifestyle and amenities created by its designers. It is also obvious that I will be returning often to Monsoon, an aesthetic as well as a dining delight. And, like antique lovers everywhere, my visits to Bahrain's splendid heritage homes have further enriched my appreciation for the endurance of good art and its influences far beyond its time.

In Bahrain there is a varied architectural menu to savour, whatever your palate.

NEW BEGINNINGS

by

Bron Vanzino

I struggled with the decision to pack up and leave,
There were so many unknowns.
I signed up for a year only:
I might not like it.

I found good housing,
Good food,
But the job was disappointing
And my husband faced his own challenges.

Slowly I began to make friends,
I got used to the traffic,
But I put on weight
And stopped being active.

I started to travel to exotic places.
The regional culture offered colour,
Ancient history, spiritual depth,
Accessible luxury and polite mannered service.

The job improved
But my husband's health was dire.
I became homesick for my own family and country.
Still I signed up for another year.

I visited many places of interest
Museums, craft centres, historical buildings and sites.
I met the Tree of Life:
A tolerant, kindly creature who shared his patience with me.

A shift came towards the end of the second year.
I began to enjoy living and working with the people around me
My husband's health improved
And I went to the gym.

I changed, I let go and took wings.
There were no certainties but now I did not mind.
Bahrain supported me even though I was not always happy there.
I left Bahrain and moved on to a new place, confident that it too would support me.

BAHRAIN - A CULINARY OASIS

by

Anita Menon and Namit Bhatia

Living an expat's life in Bahrain for the last two years has been the most enchanting one. Every single day, I get a new cultural insight that leaves me enriched with life's lessons. Having spent a lot of time living in various countries, I found it relatively easy to settle in Bahrain because, all at once, it gave me the essence of all those places that I had lived in before. Initially I had reservations about adjusting to the Middle Eastern culture, but I was proved wrong in no time by the openness and the warmth of the people of Bahrain. But this education, that some of the cultural differences are only skin deep, was more through accumulation of little bursts of realisation than moments of epiphany.

Bahrain, with its salubrious climate and sagacious clans, occupies a very prominent place amongst the countries in the Gulf. Bahrain's Arabic name 'al-Bahrayn' means 'The Two Seas', but which also symbolically stands for Compassion and Love; the true Islamic spirit. Since time immemorial, Bahrain has been a trade port and a region of vast natural resources. If her sands could speak, they would unravel mysteries of age-old traditions and tell tales that have slowly faded over time.

George Bernard Shaw said; *"There is no love more sincere than the love of food"*, and it could not be any truer. Food is a great leveller and great food much more so, as it transcends culture, race and geographies. Societies are more accepting of foreign influence on food than on any other aspect of life. History is replete with witnesses of societies who have amalgamated different influences in food and created a new and unique blend to call their own. The Bahraini cuisine today is influenced by all the cultures that have settled in this country over the centuries such as Indian, Persian, Sri Lankan, and Palestinian. In the course of my culinary adventures, it dawned pretty soon that it was only in Bahrain that the aroma of Indian food merges seamlessly with the waft of Mediterranean cooking methods, interspersed with Arabic ingredients making it a heady concoction and a true 'foodie's' delight. From simple aromatic cuisine and local markets, to snazzy restaurants and sizzling grills, Bahrain pleases and teases with the variety of food it has to offer.

Being a connoisseur of good food, bordering on gluttonous, I found that Bahrain was nothing short of a 'Culinary Oasis' that offers an unimaginable array of food options. Having a food blog helped, as it became a valid excuse to eat through Bahrain, literally! Sampling my way through more than fifty to sixty restaurants and local eating joints with family and friends has been by far the tastiest endeavour I might have ever undertaken in my life.

FOR THE LOCAVORE

If you want to understand the essence of the Bahraini food culture, all you need to do is to follow my lead and pull up in a car to the tiny aluminium window at any of the bustling roadside grills and raise a hand to order a tikka. While you wait, sipping on a chilled cola or fresh fruit juice, and making idle conversations with your friends, a server would have by then set about preparing a lip-smacking wrap that can be eaten in the comfort of your own car. Tikka, or cutlets (usually lamb or chicken), are savoury pieces of meat usually herbed and spiced, marinated, char-grilled to perfection, and accompanied with a salad of fresh vegetables. Remember to chew it well, savouring the gorgeous texture of the chunky meat and wash it down with a cold drink. Ordering seconds is very common because these grills are known to churn out the most delicious pieces of meat eaten on their own or with pita bread / khuboos (Middle Eastern flat breads) as a wrap called the shawarma which is similar to the Australian gyro.

From the juicy meat pieces, we head towards the famed bread making khuboos shops of Bahrain. It is fascinating to watch a queue build up by nightfall outside these traditional bakeries. A burning clay hearth and experienced pairs of hands slap the dough to make khuboos, the most popular flatbread that the country eats every single day of its life. This hearty bread forms the base for almost all the food that is served at homes and in restaurants. A freshly baked khuboos emanates an aroma that tantalises the senses with its simplicity and flavour. Khuboos comes in a lot of sizes, shapes and flavours including sesame, melted cheese and honey brushed. My personal favourite is the plain khuboos that I love devouring bit by bit with some vegetables and hummus (chickpea dip).

These days tremendous stress is being laid on eating in harmony with the seasons, and eating locally produced food. Unfortunately for Bahrain, only one percent of the land is arable, and so the country is unable to produce enough food for its population and relies almost entirely on imports. But it is heartening to note that the Central Market, sprawling in the heart of Manama, sells fresh vegetables, fruits, seafood and meat which are either locally produced or imported. One can find an abundance of fresh fruits like dates, bananas, citrus fruits, mangoes, pomegranates, tomatoes and cucumbers that are cultivated in the region. Central Market also caters to the fresh meat and fish requirements of the populace.

There is a wide variety of fish in Bahrain, but none as prized as the hammour. The hammour is a member of the grouper family, but unlike many other groupers it can grow to two meters long, making it an outstanding sport fish. Prized for its firm white meat, there is no end to the various methods by which Bahrainis prepare this delicious fish. The meat absorbs the traditional spices perfectly and combines to create some remarkable and very memorable dishes.

Oysters are another staple that the local populace eats with great gusto. Ninety-nine percent of oysters do not have a pearl in them. Fortunately, they do have a luscious lump of flesh, meaning all is not lost when you crack one open and don't find a gem. Finding my way around the Central Market was reminiscent of the busy bazaars of India and haggling over crates of fresh produce gave me a high, like no other.

Once you have your meat and vegetables, all you need is the spices to cook them into finger-licking fare. For this, one has to visit the souq to experience the traditional way to go grocery shopping. The souq, the traditional market-place, is replete with mystique and a very enigmatic you-never-know-what-you-will-find charm. Upon entering the souq, one is welcomed by chatty shopkeepers trying their best to sell their resplendent wares. It would also be difficult to miss the aroma in the air, redolent of spices and herbs that seem to lead me to my chosen destination. Black lemons, saffron, cardamom, cloves, dried rose petals, turmeric, and sumac are some of the exotic spices that make their way into the aromatic Bahraini cuisine, and lend it the wonderful depth of flavour.

Souqs of Manama and Muharraq are equally popular, and both of them do their bid in narrating stories of the past with great panache. I took an afternoon stroll through the colourful winding alleys of Manama and the Muharraq souq, which would go down as one of my most memorable walkabout in the city. I love visiting the country's old capital, Muharraq which is a city rife with history and culture. It is one of the few areas in Bahrain that still maintains its authentic feel and true spirit, where a visit to its winding streets always brings with it deep sense of nostalgia and pride in the old city's heritage.

The mention about seasonal foods would not be complete if I were not to mention the special occasion of Ramadan and the glorious food consumed during the Holy Month. It is a religious month when many Muslims fast between dawn and sunset. They only eat twice a day; suhoor, a meal eaten before the sun rises and iftar, the meal that breaks the fast at sunset. Traditionally, Muslims who fast, break it by consuming some date fruit at sunset before they go for their evening prayers. Dates are known to be the food that Prophet Muhammad, (Peace Be Upon Him), ate when he broke his fast. Dates are an excellent source of fibre, sugar, magnesium, potassium, and have carbohydrates which aid the body in maintaining health. The carbohydrates found in dates also make the fruit a slower digesting food.

For Bahrain, the date or ritaab is nothing short of the 'jewel' of the nation and is a staple in Bahraini cuisine. A variety of dates are produced in abundance each year such as mawajji, shbeed, khlaas (the most popular), hatmi, and khwaja. It is a spectacular sight to see these varieties arranged in round wooden baskets on display at all the local stores and supermarkets. The dates are a source of national pride that provide nourishment to the body and heighten the flavour of any dish.

When Ramadan ends, celebration is in the air and Eid Al Fitr is celebrated with great excitement and furore with feasts in every home. Welcoming guests with sweets is customary during this time and halwa features most prominently amongst all others, in Bahrain. The halwa, a special concoction of cornstarch, saffron, sugar, nuts, ghee and rose water, is the harbinger of all things that mark a special occasion. It is jelly-like in texture, colourful, sweet and full of nutty goodness. Stored in large aluminium and steel containers, halwa is a decadent dessert that you would find on all special occasions such as weddings. The Showaiter name is synonymous with halwa in Bahrain and boasts of the most interesting colours, ingredients and tastes.

Bahrain's traditional food includes fish, meat, rice and dates. One of the traditional dishes is machboos which is made up of meat or fish served with rice. Another known food is muhammar which is sweet rice served with dates or sugar. Bahrainis also eat other Arabic food such as falafel; fried balls of chickpeas served in bread. Traditional snacks include samboosa and pastry. Another delicacy is qoozi (ghoozi), which is grilled lamb stuffed with rice, boiled eggs, onions and spices. It is a Bahraini custom where a plate is shared between several (or all) members of a family / party.

With seven months of summer, it can get pretty hot in Bahrain and on a sultry day, however weird it may sound, I would gladly settle for a chai haleeb (tea). A local favourite, the tea with milk is a staple in Bahraini cuisine and diet. This aromatic infusion of tea, cardamom and milk is consumed from beautifully decorated slim glass cups called istikanah or the more casual glaas. This concoction awakens the senses gradually and as you drink it, it cascades down the back of your throat lending the much needed warmth required in the early hours of the morning. As simple as it sounds, it becomes indulgent when special herbs and condiments such as saffron, black lime, fresh mint leaves, and cloves find their way into this humble chai.

Also, if you are hanging around with some hospitable Bahrainis, there's a high probability that they would usher you to an Arabic coffee house (or known as gahwa shops locally) for some drinks. The lanes of Bahrain are dotted with these coffee houses and manage to hold their own among the Starbucks and Costa Coffees of today. These coffee shops provide the conversational gambit and socialising opportunities for the youth and the elderly gents alike. They spend time playing a game of carrom, dominoes or watching a live football match of their favourite team on television, whilst sipping on their stimulating beverage. Serving gahwa to guests is considered a part of the traditional welcome in Bahrain. It is usually poured into a coffee-pot, which is called dalla and served in a small cup made for coffee, called finjan, which is only half-filled. The term gahwa was originally applied to wine and gahwa was known as the 'Wine of Islam'. Originally, the un-roasted beans were ground and brewed to be used as a stimulant to prevent sleeping during ceremonies. The Persians are responsible for adding the roasting process later on. It took an embarrassing episode to orient me into the Bahraini coffee drinking culture when I found that my cup was being refilled again and again without my insisting to do so. I will forever remember that I need to shake the cup indicating that I have finished and wouldn't want any more coffee. I was told later that it is considered good manners for the guest to restrict themselves to three servings of coffee and, to my dismay, I had surpassed that limit of servings. But the large hearted Bahrainis often overlook first time blunders and we still have a hearty laugh recalling that instance.

Most of the times, a coffee is most enjoyed in the accompaniment of sheesha. The traditional sheesha (hookah), containing sweetened, and often flavoured, tobacco is smoked by many Bahrainis. The sheesha is served in most open-air coffee shops, where both locals and expatriates can be seen whiling away time enjoying the sheesha, and sharing a conversation.

FOR THE GLOBAVORE

Bahrain offers all sorts of cuisines to cater to all price segments and palettes, from neighbourhood take-out joints and food courts to exquisite fine dining and speciality restaurants. A staggering diversity of global cuisines from the common Indian and Middle Eastern to the rarer ones like Polynesian, can leave you spell bound. So there is no reason for any expat or tourist to feel homesick because in all probability they would be able to savour their country's food in many restaurants in Bahrain.

Like any expat, I spent the first few months devouring the gourmand delights at the restaurants in Adliya, to the point that it inspired me to start an un- sponsored Restaurant Review Project on my blog. Each restaurant snazzier than the other and I happily coined Adilya the sophisticated celebration of urban Bahrain. The district offers a choice of high class restaurants that are bold and eager to innovate and to please the evolving palates of their customers. So if you have the cash to splash and a penchant for elegant food, this dining scene is for you. Some of my personal favourites are Camelot, Upstairs Downstairs, Café Lilou and Jim's. Having said that, it would be unpardonable not to mention the other restaurant districts in Juffair, Seef and Budaiya. These culinary districts offer a fantastic range of different cuisines in well-designed outlets. Many of these restaurants are old houses converted into very nice restaurants and lounges and it's near impossible to find a table on the weekends.

I also find myself heading to Seef more often than not in search of more varied experiences in eating out. Seef is a cosmopolitan area with a high concentration of internationally renowned restaurants offering every conceivable cuisine including American, Japanese, Lebanese, Indian, Chinese and French; even the odd chocolatier can be found. Bahrain hasn't remained unaffected by the organic foods trend that has taken the rest of the World over by a storm. In Seef, you would find organic foods being sold in outlets and cafés.

Some of the other popular restaurants in Bahrain that serve great international fare include the restaurants at the Ritz-Carlton Hotel and at the Regency Intercontinental, Fish Market Seafood restaurant at Al Bander resort, La Pergola at Gulf Hotel and Kei in Golden Tulip. Some of these hotel restaurants even run theme buffets which are interesting, seasonal and they serve all twenty-four hours and seven days of the week. The tipping etiquette requires that in addition to the ten-fifteen percent rule, it is generally acceptable to round up the bill amount and consider the change involved as tip.

The other distinctive feature of this tiny island's eating habits is that fast food joints are ubiquitous in every nook and corner of Bahrain. Jasmi's is a home grown fast food brand of Bahrain and very popular among the locals and expats alike.

For writing inspiration, I often find myself heading to Starbucks or Caribou Coffee in the American Alley in Juffair. Nothing stokes my imagination more than a hot cup of cappuccino prepared perfectly by smiling servers at these coffee joints. American Alley is named so because it predominantly burgeoned to cater to the American Naval Base in its vicinity. This sparkly street is a 'foodie's' paradise and wonderful on a day when you feel like hanging out with your friends and having a hearty meal that is also light on your wallet.

The newest sensation to watch out for in Bahrain would be the waterfront pioneering project in Amwaj Islands. It has some of the most ultra modern, classy restaurants and cafés precinct and each day keeps adding more glamorous outlets to its repertoire. Bahrain's insatiable appetite for growth is developing this tiny, historic island into one of the Gulf's most dynamic food hubs.

I don't think any account of the Bahrain would be worth reading if it didn't at least in part, try to explain the warmth and kindness of the Bahraini people. '*Ahlan wa sahlan!*' means "Welcome' in Arabic and it is so much a part of the Bahraini life that they even cast the words in brass and hang them over the front door for all to see. Hospitality is a source of pride with the Bahraini people; there are few places in the world where will you be made to feel so welcome. So I hold in very high regard their generosity of spirit and enthusiasm for life which translates into their cuisine and food habits. The food of Bahrain inspired me to start a food blog which I so enjoy writing, eating, cooking, baking and creating for. With every bite I feel I am given the opportunity to discover attitudes, practices, and rituals surrounding the food culture in Bahrain. Attempting to understand Bahrain through its food is a journey that I have undertaken with great passion and the experiences have been nothing less than spectacular.

PEARLS

by

Aaron Maree

The turquoise seas of the Arabian Gulf glistened in the morning brilliance of yet another summers heat wave. The breeze enjoyed in most corners of the world where sea met land, non existent in these parts. A stifling atmosphere, dense in humidity, thick with sweat.

The pearling dhows of Bahrain's waters motored from their offshore anchors toward shore. Like dinosaurs of an age long past, dhows were the traditional boats of Arabic Seas. Cumbersome in look, they were not the agile speed-boats of a modern age, but the slow moving carriers of dates, fish, equipment and animals, along the coastal regions. Today they are used for fishing, pearling and the one thing that does bring in money; tourism.

Another day of diving yet to begin, riches awaiting the lucky, or not. Cleaning, washing of rigging and equipment, the days chores began on deck as the dhows slowly motored to waiting jetties for crew, supplies and tourists.

Khalid Achami, dhow Captain, had pearled these waters around the island nation of Bahrain for several years. His looks defied his title; most dhow captains looked as beaten as the weather which lashed their vessels. Dressed and smelt as rough as their catches, but Khalid Achami was none of these. He had come to pearling late in life. A life of success and riches, lost to an era simply coined the Global Financial Crisis. Today he sought freedom of mind and spirit somewhere between captaining his dhow in the vast Gulf waters, and the silence he enjoyed diving for its treasures; pearls.

Pearling had become his life. It offered solitude and peace; time to think, deep beneath the normalities of regular life. It was the edginess, the risk, the choices he loved. As a free diver, it was his choice for how long to dive; his choice about how much pain he suffered by allowing his lungs to burn with each and every dive. The tightening and constriction, his body begging to draw a gasp of fresh air, at any cost. It was this intensity, this choice, he adored. He often wondered what it would be like never return to the surface, to hold the breathe just that few seconds longer than in-built sensibilities instructed. This was no suicidal tendency, just an inquisitive one. He found knowledge within his thoughts. Life in the working world had brought with it different types of pain and anguish, these ones where by choice. Pain of loss he knew well. Loss of everything, cash, cars, concubines. That was pain. Holding your breathe and the feel of burning lungs, pure exhilaration. Bahrain and its waters offered freedom, choices and a lifestyle of his own choosing. This was his paradise.

Pearling, like most loves, did not pay the Captain's mounting bills. Once a prized and honourable trade, pearling had suffered in Bahrain's waters, as with much of the Gulf region. Land reclamation, abuse of the waters from the oil companies, modern life and its decimating ways of natural resources, had all taken their toll on the pearling industry.

Today, as with most, Khalid Achami paid bills with tourist dollars. Eager to dive, eager to pearl, to try their luck seeking riches beneath the seas. This was a legal form of gambling in the Islamic world. Risk versus reward. Which would win, with each single dive?

Tourists were easy cash for the Captain, finding a pearl or not, they were happy to sit waterside, sun bake and be fed, to find a pearl was just a bonus on their vacation.

Today the pier was all but empty. A solitary traveller stood by as the dhow moored dockside, not the usual dozen tourists. The Middle Eastern heat of this time of year, making hotel pools more desirable than anything on the tourism map.

"Khalid Achami, Dhow Captain, pleased to make your acquaintance," he stretched his hand, to shake that of the young man.

"Hey, cool dude, yeh, I want to find a pearl," the young man shook the hand stretched before him.

"No, not dude, son," Khalid was used to these troubled lost teens who thought everything was 'cool', everyone a 'dude'. They needed to be taught respect. He held the young man's hand tight, pulling him closer.

"I worked hard to become a captain of this dhow. My dhow! I would be pleased to welcome you aboard. But, My dhow! My rules! Respect that! " he pushed the young man backward.

Still holding the outstretched hand he stated again," Khalid Achami, dhow Captain, pleased to make you acquaintance."

Visibly shaken the boy fumbled words, "Yes Sir, me too Captain, pleased to make it, your acquaintance that is, Sir."

Happy at the response, the Captain ushered him aboard, "Welcome aboard, lets find a pearl then, shall we?"

A strong sun overhead toyed with the waters stretched before them. The dhow glided effortlessly through the still waters as the Captain spoke of the history of the pearling trade, of Bahrain, to his young adventurer, "Bahraini pearls are believed to be the best in the world. It is said that the beauty comes from the special forces of the two seas, fresh water and salt. That's where Bah-rain also gets its name; "two seas" in Arabic. Bahrain pearls have been renowned since the Dilmun empire – thousands of years."

"Come on Captain! Enough with the history lesson, Lets get to the cash bank," the young man stood, impatiently pacing the deck.

"This can either be a very long day for you or an enjoyably enriching one. Either way I'm already paid for your excursion. I don't care which. Why don't you just sit, calm down and learn something on our way to the pearling banks," speaking as he motioned for the boy to sit. "Why are you so scared to learn something! So in a hurry for the prize but not willing to endure the work before it?" asked the Captain.

The young boy sat, rolling his eyes. "Okay enough! You sound like my parents. Continue, I'll listen."

"For nearly one hundred years, from the mid 1800's until the depression of the 1930's, thousands of divers pearled these waters searching for a white gem more valuable than diamonds. What the depression did not kill, oil discoveries did. Oil was easier than free-diving for a small white gem, and pearling never again found the same lustre in the eyes of either the buyers or the divers. Today there is less than a dozen oyster beds that haven't been commercially harvested. Cultivated pearls are illegal so it is still possible to find great pearls, just no-one really wants to. Modern life has made things far easier than pearling ever was." Achami, adjusted the rigging as he spoke.

"Excellent! But are we there yet," the amateur pearl diver professed as he now strode the dhows decks again, growing impatient with his history lesson.

"Yes we are, welcome to Umm al Layaal, or Mother of the Families, the best pearl bed there is," the Captain yelled, turning off the motor, pulling in the rigging and preparing to anchor the dhow.

Stripped of his shirt and sporting only his bathing shorts, the young adventurer stood at the dhows edge keen to start the adventure for riches.

"Impatient aren't you son? Wait till I anchor," proclaimed the Captain. "Before we dive let me give you a quote …" He was cut off.

"Oh God, enough with the schooling, this is my vacation. Time to find a pearl… please," he yelled, leaping into the clear waters shimmering below.

As he surfaced he heard the Captain yell above him, "….a quote of Balzac; "'in diving to the bottom of pleasure we bring up more gravel than pearls'."

He dove again, silence beckoned, so too did the adventure of the treasures below.

It had become part of the pearling tourism ritual for those seeking the adventure to also spend time learning about the industry. This was not merely eco-tourism by nature for wealthy tourists seeking to feel good about themselves, this was a way the Bahrain people could teach respect, history and culture for those who sought the adventure. This was true ecological tourism. Meant for those with respect for nature, not a trendy bi-product of corporate tourism. For two days before the boy had dove, he spent time ashore attending classes; history of the natural pearl, and on ecology, biology and conservation.

The boy understood why but this was the reason he had had enough of the verbal side of this equation. The course was mandatory for those who sought to pearl dive, part ecological part informative. It prevented mass tourists from simply destroying the pearling beds while at the same time teaching tourists how to select an oyster, how to open one and to know where to find the pearl inside it.

For hours, the Captain and student held their breath, dove and scoured the pearl beds for likely homes of the prized gems the boy sought.

By afternoon's end the boy boarded the dhow breathless and disillusioned. Of thirty potential oysters plucked from the ocean bed, he had found nothing larger than a blister pearl, a tiny lump worth nowhere near the dollars he had thought he would make.

"You brought me to a stupid pearl bed, there aren't any here," he yelled at the Captain as he too boarded the vessel.

"You did not listen to me did you before we dove. I told you...in diving to the bottom of pleasure we bring up more gravel than pearls."

The Captain tossed the boy a towel. "If this was so easy, everyone would be out here earning their fortune. Like striking oil, panning for gold or winning the lottery, its just not as easy as dreamers would believe."

"Here," the Captain held out his hand a handed the boy an oyster. "Open it."

The boy took it from the Captain's hand and threw it with all his force into the sea.

"Why did you do that?" the Captain screamed. "That was the one."

"Whatever! I opened dozens of oysters and nothing. That would have been the same!"

"You miss the point to life kid. It's not about the pot of gold, it's about the adventure on the way there. Enjoy the trip. Let me say this in a way you might understand in Star Trek terms; 'it's not the destination but the journey that matters'. In your case; if you search for the pot of gold you may end up finding exactly what you wanted, but it may be worthless."

The Captain stood before the boy. "Before we left the jetty on shore you told me you wanted to find a pearl. You found it, probably several blister pearls right?"

"Yes, but..." he was cut short.

"You did not ask to find a real natural pearl or a pearl worth a million dollars you just said you wanted to find a pearl. You travelled to Bahrain because it was filled with pearl divers and you wanted to be one of them. Congratulations son, you are one of them. You found a pearl. A calciferous concretion. Worthless in the eyes of a gem buyers, but the value that you have received by travelling to the shores of this island, the time you have enjoyed here, the people you have met, the adventure of it all, the diving, the hunt, the find. That's where the value lay, son."

The Captain continued towelling himself dry. "Riches do not always come with monetary value, my young learned friend. Riches come from life. I'm sure you feel a little cheated."

"A little? You think old man." The young student scuffed his feet and threw the blister pearl into the Gulf waters. "I dove for five hours for a worthless piece of concrete."

"If that's what you think son, then you have learnt nothing here." The Captain threw his towel, turned to the motor, keying its ignition. "What you should have seen in that white pearl, worthless or not, was what you had learnt over the past few hours. The freedom you enjoy in the water today, the time by yourself. Many people would pay thousands of dollar to live this life. You see no value in it, but that's where you are wrong."

He cranked the throttle on the motor bringing the dhow to life. "Life is not about being the richest, the best, the biggest, or the even the most respected or well-known. It is about fulfilling your own dreams and being whatever you want to be; but being the best at it that you can. That is what makes a man rich. If you seek money in everything that you do, you will end up poor. Poor of heart, mind and soul. But if you seek to do things for the enjoyment, for the passion, the love and the experience, then young Sir, you will reap the rewards of life, the riches. The true pearls that life can send your way. One pearl of wisdom can truly make you a richer person than any strand of pearls ever could. Remember that throughout your life son. Open your eyes and you heart my young friend, let the realities of life inside and stop this 'dude', 'cool' and 'sick' garbage that you speak. Be a real person and speak from knowledge, not from jargon learnt on the internet or school-yard. Be worthy of acquaintances that you make, leave a lasting impression on people that you meet and make them say 'wow', that was some kind of guy, when they depart your company. Seeking riches by diving for a singular pearl to get you out of debt will never make you happy, nor satisfy you for life. You can be worth a million dollars and you can have a million dollars. Both quite different. I'd prefer to meet a poor man who was worth a million dollars than to meet a rich man 'with a million dollars'. The first would be an interesting conversation and an intriguing discussion, the other would be an arrogant bore." As he stopped speaking the dhow pulled alongside the jetty.

The pair shook hands to say goodbye, the young tourist eyes welling with what looked like tears. "Thank you Captain for everything," he said, shaking hands.

"Your welcome my friend, I have enjoyed your company and I hope you remember just some of what I have spoken. " He pulled the boy closer and gave him a manly hug, "feel free to call me Khalid."

The young adventurer held tight to his teacher, "No Sir, you are right, you have taught me so much more in a day than I think I have learnt so far in my short life. You have my respect sir, for always, thank you Captain."

"Okay enough with the lessons, but one final pearl of wisdom for you my friend something for you to reflect upon on your life's journey. Something that only pearl diving can make you truly understand; life is not measured by the number of breaths we take, but by the moments that take our breath away." The Captain grasped the young sailor's hand, pressing a firm white ball into its palm. "Here you have earned this. Don't throw this one away though."

The two parted company, the Captain boarded his dhow, setting sail for his home port. As he watched his friend sail away the young boy looked at the pearl held tightly in the palm of his hand. He waved as his teacher sailed away not knowing if he saw him or even looked back. He had come to the island nation of Bahrain seeking an experience in the search of pearls. At its culmination, he stood on the pier with more pearls than he could have imagined. One worth a small fortune, and many pearls of wisdom from his friend the learned Captain. Pearls worth not forgetting.

"What a country, what a vacation, what a gift," he thought.

Both types of pearl had come from the turquoise seas surrounding Bahrain's shores, a land truly of two seas, wealth and wisdom.

EAST, WEST, NORTH AND SOUTH

by

Zahra Zuhair

Walking to the store,
needed some milk and dates.
I looked to my right, saw a little Indian boy;
looked left and saw a Brit with his mates.

Went to the cashier, a nice Asian woman smiled.
I walked through the street,
passed by a Lankan fruit seller in a sarong,
calling out to whoever his eyes meet.

Took a turn through the park,
saw a little dark haired Bahraini boy play with a little Filipino girl,
their mums chattering away.
Kept walking, came across a depiction of Bahrain's pearl.

Almost home. Pretty couple on the bench,
white girl in a black shawl, handsome dark skinned guy.
Warm wind blew through my white shawl
like it blew past the Arab businessman's tie.

Where was he going? I wondered.
With his pin strip suit and briefcase.
Towards the park, towards the children, gives the little children some candy
as he went by. "Hello", he says.

It was nice being home.
Could smell mummy's pastries,
and the Arabic sweets the neighbours brought.
I'd like one please.

Friends come over,
one in jeans, one in a shalwar kameez, two in black abayas.
We go see a friend, recently married
to an African who sells cars.

If you go to the mall,
you can see them all;
from the east, the west, the south and the north.
They're all there.

THE LITTLE PEARL MERCHANT

by

Catherine Purchase Dedicated to Dr. Beth Olsen

"Tell me a story," Khalid implored his mother.

"Once upon a time, in a land far, far away," she began as Khalid nestled safely against her, and together they were transported from Khalid's bedroom to a mystical land where anything was possible. As she read, his mother's eyes changed from marine to sky blue with the twists and turns of the story. On a gold chain around her neck, she wore a round white pearl, a gift from his father; it shone like the moon in the night sky.

As Khalid listened, he imagined his father as the hero who sailed the seven seas battling jealous gods, pirates, gigantic whales, and two-headed monsters. He dreamed that one day he too would sail the world like his father and bring home such a treasure.

His father, Sheikh Ebrahim, was a Tâjir, a Bahraini pearl merchant of immense wealth, who appeared and disappeared from across the sea. He had married Khalid's mother, an Anglo-Indian beauty, on one of his trips to Bombay. She and Khalid lived alone together near the recently completed Gateway of India. Except when his father would return with his gold-trimmed chest filled with pearls.

When his father was there, a steady stream of merchants and traders arrived at their home. His father would take them to his office where he weighed his pearls on a bronze scale. On one side he would place a weight, on the other, the pearls. One tray was perforated so that any pearl not large enough would fall through. Khalid watched intently hoping to catch a pearl when one dropped. But he never caught even one, for his father knew exactly the size of each and could instantly balance the two trays. Transaction completed, his father stood up, shook hands, and the buyer left clutching a satchel of pearls.

His mother tried to encourage Khalid to greet his father when he arrived, but Khalid stayed hidden behind her. Khalid was scared of his father with his flowing white robes, his head concealed by red-stitched fabric held in place by a black cord twisted like a snake. In one hand, he carried a stick, its ornate handle embedded with pearls. In the other, a string of pearl prayer beads that he ran through his fingers or whipped through the air. "There is no reason to be frightened, my little hero," his mother assured him as she tried to pry his arms from around her legs. But by the time Khalid felt comfortable enough to approach his father, the ornate chest would be empty once more and his father would have disappeared back across the sea.

That night, before his mother finished the story, Khalid had already fallen asleep, dreaming of the high seas.

"And so they lived happily ever after," his mother whispered as she closed the book and kissed him softly on the forehead.

A year later, when Khalid turned six, his mother told him that by the time his father returned, he would have a new baby brother or sister. But Khalid's father was never to return to their home near the Gateway. His mother died before the baby was born and their home was closed up; everything, including Khalid's gold embossed Treasury of *Bedtime Stories*, packed and taken away.

Khalid was woken early one morning and put on a boat. But it was nothing like he had imagined. It rocked from side to side. The waves made him feel woozy. He couldn't get the world to stay still. It kept moving up and down and up and down and up and down all around him. He sat down on a board that was nailed across the stern of the deck but felt the cold dampness of the wood spread through his clothes.

There were no men swinging from ropes. No parrots or peg-legs. No other children with whom he could climb up the mast and be the first to spot land. The scrawny, hungry crew in their dirty rags reminded Khalid of the men who begged in the crowded streets near his home. Even the captain looked no more exotic than their servant Pradeep, who used to bring the fish home each day from market.

The other few passengers on board did nothing more than sit around eat. A woman with three children smaller than Khalid offered him some of their naan bread, hummus and rice. Afraid he might cry if he answered, Khalid shook his head and crossed to the bow of the boat where he stared out at the empty horizon.

There were no fabled lands with gods and goddesses. No winged horses. No brave heroes or treasure. Just endless waves of gloomy water.

By the time they arrived on land again, it was already dark and Khalid could not see anything. He was taken past stretches of empty desert through twisting alleys until finally they came to a stop in front of an imposing wooden door, bolted shut. His father's house.

Inside, Khalid learned that he already had many brothers and sisters. That his father had three other wives, each with several children of their own. The others Khalid noticed called his father Abu Faisal. No one had ever called him Abu Khalid.

He wanted nothing more than to go back home.

He was greeted by his father's eldest son Faisal. Named after their grandfather, he was almost a grown man with a trimmed beard. Faisal boasted that by greeting his father's visitors from around the world he had learned many languages. He spoke a few words in French, Arabic, Persian, and English before finishing in Urdu assuming it would be the only language Khalid would understand. On his wrist, Faisal wore a silver watch with gold rivets. "A present from Jacques Cartier," he told Khalid, "you wouldn't know him, but he's a famous jeweller who travelled all the way from Paris to see my father."

"He's my father too," Khalid mumbled.

"He is taking me with him on his next trip to Europe," Faisal said to make his position clear to this scrap of a boy who thought he was his brother. It was the eldest son who was the most important, not the youngest. And Faisal considered it his duty to make sure Khalid understood.

Khalid had no idea where Europe was, but pretended not to be impressed. "He sailed the world to find the perfect pearl for my mother," he replied, trying to assert his and his mother's importance in this place he had never known existed.

"Father doesn't have to go anywhere to get pearls," Faisal said. "They are brought to him."

"They are not," Khalid replied, ready to defend his father's honour. Faisal laughed dismissively.

That night in his new bed, Khalid lay alone in the darkness before falling into a dreamless sleep.

A few weeks after his arrival, a wedding was held at his father's house and his father's new bride Zara came to live with them. As she showed off the intricate swirling design that had been hennaed on her hands to the younger girls, Khalid realised she was wearing the white pearl that had been his mother's. Perfectly round and luminous in its translucence, it had been removed from its gold chain and made into a ring. But Khalid could recognise its singular beauty anywhere.

Khalid stole close and tried to yank it off her finger.

Zara screamed so loudly her voice carried through the lattice screens of the women's area across the courtyard, its fountains gurgling with water, to the opposite wing where his father was hosting guests from the former Ottoman Empire, now the Turkish Republic.

Before Khalid could try again, someone rapped him across the head. He was dragged to his room by one of the servants who tossed him inside and then locked the door.

Khalid had no idea how long he had been there when the door opened abruptly and Faisal announced with a smug grin that his father was waiting for Khalid in his office.

His father, having ordered Khalid to stand in front of his desk, said he would never have welcomed him into his home if he had known he would be nothing more than an ungrateful thief.

"But it was my mother's pearl," Khalid insisted.

"Nothing in this life is forever," his father said, running his fingers through his pearl prayer beads. "You're old enough to know that by now."

Faisal, who still stood in the doorway, spoke to his father. "See, I told you he would be nothing but trouble."

When his father's first wife Dana found him hidden under the fountain in the courtyard, Khalid was trying to stifle the sobs he had so furiously held back in front of Faisal and his father. She was barely taller than Khalid and, after eight children, all her weight had collected in the middle making her as warm and round as the desert sun.

"Nothing in this world belongs to us anyway," she told him as she helped him stand up. She dug inside her black abaaya and filled Khalid's hand with dates.

"The world is full of pearls, *habibi,*" she said. "Some day you will find your own."

Early the next day, the carved wooden door to the courtyard was unbolted and a man with a tousled beard and battered boots entered. Drenched in the brisk smell of the sea, his clothing was bleached by salt. He was as tall and sturdy as a mast, his skin as weathered and deeply grooved as the planks of a boat. A curved Khanjar knife hung from his waist.

Before Faisal could appear and take over, Khalid stepped forward and greeted him, "*Assalamu'alaykum*".

"*Wa'alayka-salam*. And where did you come from?" The captain asked putting his hands on his hips and looking straight down at him.

"From across the sea," Khalid answered.

The captain laughed. "Then you'll have seen plenty of these," he said as he unravelled a pouch tied to his belt. Deep inside pearls lined the dark fabric like tiny stars in the night sky. Could this be one of the men from his mother's stories?

"Do you know where these come from?" the man asked.

"From a land far, far away," Khalid answered, "but you need a treasure map to find it."

The captain's laugh rose from deep inside his belly. "You won't find anything as rare as these on land. Pearls come from the sea."

Khalid's eyes narrowed suspiciously. He had peered into the sea as he sailed from home, but saw nothing there but darkness. "I didn't see any pearls floating in the water."

This made the captain laugh so hard his shirt billowed like a sail.

"From the bottom of the sea," he said rolling the fabric back up, the pearls disappearing back into the black folds. "You have to dive below the surface to find them."

Khalid imagined the bottom of the sea as a treasure chest, like his father's wooden box, filled with gold coins and pearls.

Staring up at the man, dusted with the salty remains of the sea, Khalid realised that if the pearls really were from the bottom of the sea, then what Faisal had said must be true. It wasn't his father who found the pearls; he just kept them locked up in his chest.

Before the captain had reached his father's office, Khalid caught up with him. "Will you take me with you so I can find a pearl of my own?"

"That is up to the Tâjir to decide," the captain replied.

From the doorway of his father's office, Khalid watched impatiently as the captain gave his father the pouch of pearls. His father examined them one by one, rolling each pearl between his fingers, inspecting the surface and then weighing it on the same perforated tray he had used in Bombay. After scrutinising each one, his father scribbled a few notes in a thick ledger that sat on his desk. Khalid tried his best to stand quietly but it was as though they had forgotten he was there.

He tiptoed forward until he was standing beside the captain.

The captain, who had been silent, conveyed the boy's wish in a few brief words. His father glanced down at Khalid and frowned, annoyed at being interrupted. Without a word, he continued until he had completed the same procedure for all the pearls.

When he was finished, he removed the pearls from the captain's black cloth and placed them carefully in the wooden chest Khalid recognised so well.

Locking the chest, his father finally answered. "He's not old enough to go out on a boat yet."

The captain nodded as he stuffed the empty fabric back into his pocket. "When you're older, Insh'Allah," he said, placing his hand on Khalid's head before turning to leave.

"But I came here on a boat," Khalid said, trying to stand taller.

His father rose from his desk. After studying Khalid for a few moments, as though considering what he might want for the first time, his father responded, "You understand, you will have to leave now and you won't return here for many days? You understand, you will be on a boat the whole time and you cannot get off, no matter what happens."

Khalid nodded, though he hadn't realised at all. But he did not want them thinking he was just a child, so he thrust out his chest as far as he could and said of course he understood.

"Then it's time to let him find out for himself what it's really like out there," his father said dismissing them both as he returned to his ledger.

The captain lifted Khalid onto his horse and they rode back through the tangled alleys of Muharraq, past the empty desert to a row of wooden boats moored on the shoreline. Dozens of men hung around smoking and relaxing. Before the captain and Khalid reached them, they had flung their cigarettes away and returned to work preparing the captain's baqâra for launch.

These were the men from his mother's stories, Khalid was certain. Tall, and muscular, some were bronzed so deeply, they looked as though they had been dipped in the sun. Others were old and wizened, shrivelled by the sea, as knotted and twisted as the gnarled rope they pulled. Men of the sea.

Boys, barely older than Khalid, raced back and forth between the baqâra and shore. Apprentices who dreamed of becoming pearl divers or captains themselves one day. Khalid, uncertain what to do, felt like a child in comparison.

The crew was mostly made up of Bahrainis, filled out for the pearling season by an assortment of Bedouin and wayfarers from the deserts of Saudi Arabia, Yemen and the surrounding Gulf who arrived for the pearling season and left at the end enriched by their share.

The captain immediately named Khalid, Sagiir Tâjir, the 'Little Pearl Merchant'.

When they were ready to launch, the last man ashore pushed the baqâra out into the sea, running alongside it through the water until he was pulled up on deck by the others. The men took up their oars and rowed the baqâra out of the harbour. The Naham, an elderly man, settled at the prow and sang to set the rhythm. He was missing two fingers, which he told Khalid he had lost to a shark when pearl diving years ago.

Khalid watched the shore recede behind them. Out ahead, nothing but the sea.

"Sails up!" ordered the captain and the Naham told a story, as the wind blew them swiftly across the sea, the canvas flapping and fluttering above Khalid's head like a flock of birds.

It was an ancient tale about a hero named Gilgamesh who, after his companion Enkidu died, sailed thousands of miles in search of the white flower of eternity off the shores of Bahrain.

"But just as Gilgamesh was about to seize the white flower," the Naham said, "a serpent lying in wait snatched it away."

"Lower sails!" the captain yelled, bringing Khalid back to the baqâra with a jolt. Above his head the sails flew down in one fell swoosh and the men furled them against the mast.

"But what happened next?" Khalid asked the Naham.

"*Yallah,*" the Naham replied. "There is work to be done."

"Drop anchor!" the captain yelled and the baqâra dipped with a sudden jolt. Khalid went flying across the deck.

"It would appear Sagiir Tâhir doesn't have his sea legs yet," the Naham observed dryly and the rest of the crew laughed. The captain caught Khalid with one hand and steadied him.

"The best pearls in the world are right here," the captain said.

Khalid scanned around the boat but saw nothing but water. He peered over the edge. Squinting, he could see right to the bottom, its sandy floor rippled like the waves above. "Right where?" he asked.

"Where the two seas meet, there will be pearls," the captain replied.

"But where is the other sea?" Khalid asked.

"Fresh water and salt water," the captain explained.

"'He has released the two seas and they meet,'" the Naham recited from the Quran by heart. "'There comes forth from both of them the pearl and coral stone.'"

The setting sun cast its net of pink and purple across the sky as the crew shared a dinner of rice and fresh hammour, which the men scooped up with their hands or torn strips of bread.

When Khalid finally fell asleep, he dreamed of finding the perfect pearl when he dove into the sea. He woke shivering in the darkness. Thinking of the Naham, he quickly checked that all his fingers and toes were still there.

When Khalid awoke again the men were already up, eating dates, smoking and chewing tobacco as they waited for the sun to rise. When faint orange streaks coloured the eastern sky, the men turned in the opposite direction to pray. Kneeling on the deck, they performed their Al-Fajr prayers finishing just as day roused the night fully awake.

Prayers finished, the men prepared to dive. Wanting to help but, unlike the other boys, just getting in the way, Khalid was told to sit at the prow with the Naham. From there he watched as divers plunged from all sides of the baqâra. Holding stone weights in their hands, they descended quickly to the bottom. Moments later, the baqâra started to shake, and Khalid thought that a whale or shark might be under the boat trying to topple them all into the sea.

Seeing his fear, the Naham laughed, "It is just the divers tugging on their ropes to be pulled back up." He paused, "unless, of course, the shark that took my two fingers has come back for the rest," he said waving his three-fingered hand to scare Khalid.

Seconds later, the divers emerged from below like dolphins leaping out of the water. They lifted their baskets full of oysters from around their necks and the boys on deck emptied the shells into a pile. The shells were grimy with sand and Khalid could not believe there could be pearls inside.

The next day, Khalid was given a leather nose-clip softened with sesame oil, cotton buds to stuff in his ears, a loosely woven basket to collect shells and leather finger guards to protect his hands as he combed the sand and coral of the sea floor.

The captain told him once he reached the bottom, to sit down and collect as many oysters as he could. Then, before he ran out of breath, he was to tug the rope and the captain himself would pull him back to the surface.

His first dive, Khalid didn't even reach the bottom. As he plunged down, the nose clip that had pinched so painfully in the air slipped and water streamed into his nose and mouth. He choked and gasped for air. The captain, seeing the flurry of air bubbles rushing to the surface, quickly hoisted Khalid back up.

His next dive, Khalid made it to the bottom, but then panicked. With the salt water stinging his eyes he could not see anything in the murky water and imagined a shark or serpent swimming straight towards him. He tugged the rope hard. The captain pulled him back up and saw his basket was still empty.

"*Halas,*" the captain said before crossing to the other side of the baqâra and leaving Khalid to pull himself back aboard.

"So much for the Sagiir Tâhir," the Naham laughed. "Seems he can't find even one pearl."

The pearl divers laughed and the other boys chanted "No pearls for Sagiir Tâhir," as the divers plunged back down to collect more oysters. Shivering and wet amongst the slippery shells, Khalid returned once more to sit at the prow beside the Naham.

"No pearls for Sagiir Tâhir," the Naham teased him. "How can you be the little pearl merchant when you have no pearls?"

"Why didn't Gilgamesh get his white flower?" Khalid asked the Naham.

"Because it wasn't his destiny."

"Is it my destiny to find a pearl?"

"What would you do with a pearl anyway, Sagiir Tâhir?" the Naham asked Khalid. "Your father already has more pearls than you could ever imagine."

As the pile of oysters in the middle of the baqâra rapidly swelled, Khalid told the Naham about his mother and how, when she told him a story, her eyes would change from the fathomless deep blue of the sea to the transparent light of the sky, and about the perfect white pearl she wore round her neck.

"A pearl starts as nothing more than a grain of sand that the oyster transforms into something precious and beautiful," the Naham told him. "Just like a story."

The next day, Khalid was allowed to dive one more time, though it was the Naham, not the captain, who held the rope for him this time. "It is the only way you will know if it is your destiny to find the perfect pearl, Sagiir Tâhir. You must be brave if you want to be the hero of your own story."

Khalid held the weight firmly in his hands and sank quickly to the bottom of the sea. He sat on the weight and reached his arms out into the unknown. Scouring the seabed, he collected as many oyster shells as he could before running out of air. He tugged the rope and was pulled back up. Gasping when he hit the air, he desperately tried to catch his breath.

He lifted the basket over his neck, and the crew chanted "Sagiir Tâhir," as the captain took the shells and placed them in separate pile. The other boys watched in silence.

That evening, before the sun set, the men gathered together on deck to pry open their shells. Each time they discovered a pearl inside, cries of "*Alhamdulillah!*" and "*Bismillah!*" rose up to the sky.

But even after days of filling the deck with oyster shells, in the end the crew retrieved no more than a handful of pearls that the captain carefully wrapped in his black velvet pouch. Most were so tiny they would be strung together on necklaces. Some of the pearls were round, some oval, others pitted or irregular in shape. There were only a few that were large enough to be of any real value. Of those, one was tinted rose, another as transparent as water, and the last, ink black.

Khalid nervously pried open his first oyster, careful not to cut himself with the knife. To his disappointment, there was nothing inside but grey, slimy mucous. Not even one tiny pearl.

He went on to the next oyster from his small pile, and then to the next, and the next until he was surrounded by empty shells with only one closed oyster left.

The Naham and the rest of the crew watched as he pried open his last oyster shell. Inside there was nothing but a few grains of sand. In time they might have become pearls, but now they were nothing more than pieces of grit.

"No pearls for Sagiir Tâhir," the boys chanted, relieved that the son of the Tâhir had not achieved what they still could only dream of accomplishing themselves. "No pearls for Sagiir Tâhir."

The captain silenced them. "Sajiir Tâhir doesn't need to dive for pearls. One day, just like his father, he will be a Tâhir himself and it will be him who buys the pearls from us."

***

A few years later, when Khalid had been sent off to boarding school in England, he told the other boys the ancient tale of Gilgamesh, King of Uruk, just as the Naham had taught him. He told them how Gilgamesh with his companion Enkidu journeyed to the Cedar Forest and slayed the monster Humbaba before the death of Enkidu sent Gilgamesh on a quest for eternal life. When Khalid reached the end, he enacted the scene when the serpent snatches away the white flower just as Gilgamesh is about to grasp immortality.

He was no longer Sagiir Tâhir. He had been given a new nickname by the other students at his school. He was now called, 'The Storyteller'. Khalid was proud of this name. For on that night, years earlier, after he had failed in his quest to find the perfect white pearl, the Naham had shared with him his most precious secret. In the story Gilgamesh would forever fail in his quest. He was destined to never pick the white flower of eternity. But, Gilgamesh had been immortalised in his epic poem. And although the story was written thousands of years ago, Gilgamesh, the Naham assured Khalid, would go on living as long as his story was told.

Khalid kept the Naham's secret. But whenever he told the story of Gilgamesh to the other boys at his boarding school on the rain-sodden banks of the River Exe, he always added that he himself had dived into the exact same waters as Gilgamesh. He himself had tried to find the perfect white pearl where the two seas meet off the shores of Bahrain.

It would be many years before Khalid was ready to tell the story that was the most precious to him. By that time his father, the Tâhir, had long been retired, the pearling industry in Bahrain eclipsed by the introduction of cultured pearls into the world market. And, Faisal, his father's eldest son, had become a wealthy oil sheikh. For the story Khalid most wanted to tell was a fantastical tale of diving for pearls in a land, far, far away where the two seas meet. It was a story about a young boy and his beautiful mother who read him stories about pirates and treasure maps and the Naham with two missing fingers who showed him where the real buried treasure was to be found.

This is his story.

THIS LAND IS MINE

by
David Hollywood

This land is mine,
But I'm not born,
To own it just for you.
I must ensure,
As you are here,
That I shall pass it through,
For you to have,
Along with who?
When reconciling birth,
Tween separate lives on earth.
And knowing that,
We all were wrong,
To think that he or she or me,
Could own it all along,
Because fore long,
We'll all be gone,
And then what is it worth?

VISITING OLD BAHRAIN

by

Shauna Nearing Loej

According to archaeologists and researchers, Bahrain has a vast cultural history spanning over seven thousand years. In more recent history, over the past forty years, Bahrain has sought ways to safeguard this history while uncovering and preserving its cultural relics. These progressive initiatives are revealed when you walk through the doors of the island's pre-eminent museums, stroll through the old bazaars and can be seen throughout the natural surroundings from the ancient forts to the burial mounds. Preserved for the people and future generations, a look at these cultural treasures is a time well spent.

MUSEUMS

The Bahrain National Museum is located on the waterfront facing Al-Fatih Highway and is home to the most comprehensive archaeological evidence of the country's rich past spanning thousands of years. The museum was purposefully built to house the country's burgeoning collection of cultural artefacts and to preserve cultural heritage. Inside the expansive two-storey building that opened in 1988, are six themed halls housing its permanent collection, featuring the island's most important collection of archaeological artefacts unearthed in digs over the past fifty years. Coins, seals, pottery, jewellery and historical documents are some of the artefacts which piece together Bahrain's ancient history. Even reconstructed ancient burial mounds are on display, complete with skeletal remains and an array of grave-site artefacts. The popular tableau exhibits brings us to more recent history highlighting local customs and traditions still maintained throughout generations of Bahrainis.

Nestled in the narrow walking streets of the old capital of Muharraq is a truly fine example of bringing Bahrain's history to life. The Shaikh

Ebrahim bin Mohammed Al-Khalifa Centre For Culture and Research has restored the traditional homes of some of Bahrain's most significant cultural figures of the past such as namesake, Shaikh Ebrahim, a prominent figure in the fields of education, culture and the social sciences. Opened in 2002, the centre consists of ten distinctive houses dedicated to their past residents who were leaders in music, journalism, poetry and pearl trading. Other houses feature artisans at work with traditional handicrafts, a children's library and a café all within walking distance of each other, except for the Poetry House which is located in Manama. Traditional Bahraini architecture from wooden shutters and stained glass windows to benches and doorways are revived to magnificent form. Each house does an exceptional job of capturing the life and times of its great cultural dwellers and furthering their legacies through the extensive array of activities the centre offers.

The pristinely restored Shaikh Isa Bin Ali House located in central Muharraq is an excellent model of traditional local architecture from the nineteenth century. Home of the longest serving ruler of the country, Shaikh Isa bin Ali Al Khalifa from 1869 to 1932, the structure is characterised by a still functional traditional wind tower and massively thick walls designed to keep its inhabitants cool. Small wooden doors and intricate archways open to courtyards, and to the many rooms regally decorated with wall carvings.

Situated in the Diplomatic district, Beit Al Qu'ran offers insight into Bahrain's religious heritage through a distinguished collection of the Qur'an from around the world. The outside of the building is intricately engraved with Quranic verses and a distinctive Minaret decorate Beit Al Qur'an or the Qur'an House. Inside is an impressive cultural museum showcasing a rare and notable collection of the Qur'an and other Islamic manuscripts. The entrance hall is marked with high ceilings and a small mosque with a remarkable circular stained glass ceiling. The museum also features a lecture hall, a library as well as the Kanoo School for Quranic Studies.

The most recent initiative to promote Bahrain's cultural heritage is the Bahrain National Charter Monument located in Sakhir. Built in honour of the 2001 National Action Charter where the majority of voters pledged support for the King, the museum focuses on past and present achievements of the country. The names of the two hundred and twenty thousand voters are carved on the exterior of the museum. Inside the state-of-the-art circular style museum is an interactive experience exploring recent history and culture. Although unveiled by His Majesty in 2010, the museum is not yet open to the general public.

PRESERVING HISTORY

In addition to the great archaeological digs of the 1960s, Bahrain has gone to great lengths in recent years to restore its cultural relics including its forts, temples, mosques and protecting the burial mounds.

In 2005, the Bahrain Fort on the northern shore near Karranah became a UNESCO World Heritage Site and stands as the island's most significant archaeological finding for the amount of history it covers. The fort was built in the fourteenth century by the Portuguese, however archaeologists found layers of continuous human occupation of the site from the Dilmun, Tylos and Islamic civilisations from around 2300BC up to the Portuguese occupation. The recent addition of a museum enlightens visitors about the fort and its history.

The Arad Fort located in Muharraq is a 15th century fort, built in Islamic style was a strategic defensive fortress. Extensive restorations in the 1980s used traditional materials such as coral stones, lime, gypsum and date palm trunks to maintain the authenticity of the original structure. What we see today is an impressive model of how to bring the past into the present, as the fort is often used as the backdrop for many of the island's cultural events.

Perched on a cliff overlooking east Riffa, the nineteenth century Shaikh Salman Bin Ahmed Al Fateh Fort is an architectural splendour representing Islamic military and local building methods of the area at the time. Compared to other local forts, the Riffa Fort was wholly built by local Bahrainis using local materials such as desert stone, lime, gypsum, clay, palm trunks and mangrove poles. Wooden chamber doors are intricately carved while typical local-style benches decorate the three main courtyards. Although built for military purposes as the battlements reveal, after securing the island the fort was primarily used as a residence for the royal family. In the late 1980s, restoration work began on the fort until late 1993 when the fort opened to the public.

Al Khamis Mosque in the northern area of Manama is one of the oldest mosques in the Gulf region believed to have been built over one thousand three hundred years ago during the Ummayad caliphate. Inscriptions found at the site indicate the foundation was laid in the 11th century. Standing gracefully with its characteristic twenty-five meter high twin minarets, the mosque is believed to have been rebuilt twice over the 14th and 15th centuries with only one wall remaining of the earliest mosque. Another noteworthy historical mosque on the island is the Siyadi Mosque in Muharraq built in the nineteenth century. The mosque's unique minaret towers over the restored Siyadi House from the same period and home of former pearl merchant Ahmed Bin Qassem Siyadi.

The Barbar Temple in Barbar Village, like the Bahrain Fort, provides interesting insight into ancient civilisation in Bahrain. Excavations by Danish archaeologists during the 1960s revealed three temples built on top of one another at varying intervals in time, with the first temple believed to have been built around 2000BC. The artefacts found at the site such as the seals from the Dilmun period, are housed in the Bahrain National Museum. Ancient temples have also been found in Saar and Diraz.

Ancient burial mounds dating from the Dilmun period are believed to be the largest prehistoric cemetery in the world and have provided invaluable historical insight from the artefacts found in and around the graves. Over seventeen thousand burial mounds have been discovered, although many have been destroyed over the years. The burial mounds are found in many villages around the island from Saar and Shakura to Janabaiya and Hamad Town. Those dotted throughout Al A'ali village in particular are excellent examples of preserved mounds and also include royal burial mounds.

TREASURED SOUQS

Bahrain's traditional bazaars or souqs are also steeped in a rich cultural history. From its origins, souqs were more than just a place to buy goods from merchants - going to the souq was a social event. Today, there are many souqs scattered throughout towns and villages on the island from the century-old souq in Muharraq to the tourist drawn Manama souq. Take time to visit these landmarks and witness Bahrain's vibrant culture at its best. Amidst the hustle and bustle there is something for everyone; from clothing, perfume and jewellery to spices, fabric and furniture. Each souq is definitely different from the next so take time to visit them all.

The Muharraq souq or the Al Qaisariya souq as it is known locally, is low-key compared to the larger Manama and Isa Town markets but you will soon discover, this is exactly the reason to visit. You will be struck by its old world charm, friendly folks and interesting architecture of a bygone era. The detailed craftsmanship of the old doors and shutters on warehouses and stores may be in rough shape but you can get an idea of how this area used to look. Small streets are lined with Arab coffee pots, textiles, pottery and fresh produce. Without the typical tourist knick-knacks in sight, you can take advantage of the quaintness of the Muharraq souq. Enjoy peering down the streets lined with barber shops and tea rooms featuring traditional Bahrain-style wooden benches. Given the relentless summer heat, shopkeepers would be forgiven for assembling a makeshift aluminium roof covering. A planned facelift therefore, will hopefully take the best of the old and leave the scrap metal behind.

If you get hungry, a quick stop at one of the small restaurants on the main road for an inexpensive and tasty veggie samosa should stave off the hunger until you can make your way to the sweet shops for a halwa and Arabic coffee - this is really what makes the Muharraq souq famous. Halwa - rich, gooey and oh so sweet, is a traditional Arabic dessert eaten at any time of the year for any occasion. Festively coloured from burnt orange to green due to ingredients like saffron and cardamom, halwa is jelly-like in form and is often laced with nuts such as pistachios or cashews. Halwa comes in a few different varieties and is best enjoyed fresh, warm and with traditional Arabic coffee.

The busiest of the island's souqs is undoubtedly the Manama souq. The souq consists of smaller souqs or quarters known as the Gold Souq, Fabric Bazaar, the Spice Souq and a mélange of tourist shops, electronic stores, perfume stalls, tailors and restaurants. Starting at Bab Al Bahrain which before land reclamation, stood on the waters' edge as the gateway to the island. The seventy year-old landmark is also slated for a refurbishment in time for the island's celebration as the Cultural Capital of Arab World 2012. After passing though Bab Al Bahrain, the main street into the souq begins with regular shops selling electronics and sporting goods, then the street then transitions into tourist-trap stores selling gaudy but fun mosque alarm clocks, musical camels, fake designer handbags and watches. Make your way past these shops and turn down one of the small streets off the main road where you are likely to see shops selling inexpensive clothing, towels and toys.

Like the Muharraq Souq, one should not overlook the food offerings, especially when you Indian food is on offer. Catering to local shopkeepers, businessmen and workers in the area, you can nosh on chapatti, chana masala and samosas with tea for less than one Bahraini Dinar, or visit one of the many juice bars dotting the streets.

Haggling, bargaining, negotiating, call it what you like but when you come to the souq, you want a deal. And a deal is what you will get – if you ask. Unlike the big malls, bargaining is not only expected by most merchants, it is often built into the asking price sometimes by up to fifty percent or more. Go ahead ask for a discount and then like any good haggler, be prepared to walk away. Walking away is sometimes a good way to bring on a better discount. It's worth the gamble and its fun. Some things are less negotiable than others. Tourist items like the infamous musical camel and mosque alarm are always negotiable even down to half the asking price. Tailoring is negotiable within a couple of dinars. At the Gold souq you can always work with your jeweller for a favourable price within your budget. Have courage and bargain away.

The Fabric Bazaar is a souq within the Manama souq and a cluster of fabric shops found mostly on the right side off the main road although you will find some tailor shops scattered throughout the souq selling their own fabric. Start with the popular Mohammed Jamal whose souq location prices are often cheaper than their other locations. After, take a right and then the first left that takes you to a small street filled with fabric shops. A must, is a stop at the sewing accessories store Tarradah on the left side simply to marvel at the drawers upon drawers of buttons and snaps, as well as rolls of colourful ribbons and thread. You can't beat the prices and selection in the fabric souq. A metre of cotton will cost you about a dinar or less if you bargain for it. After you have selected some fabric there is no need to run to the pricier men's and ladies tailors out of town when some of the most inexpensive and very decent ones can be found here. A ladies dress made in the souq starts around 7BD compared to out of town tailors who will make the same dress for you for 10BD or more. To have a men's suit made prices usually start at 22BD without fabric or 40BD with fabric included. Expect to pay the paltry sum of 3BD to have a men's shirt tailored.

When you feel the air thick with a nutty haze, or you catch a whiff of cinnamon, you have hit the spice souq. The spice souq is really a cosy street made up of small shops selling spices and dried goods. The beauty of the spice souq is that you can choose whatever amount of fresh spices, nuts or other dried goods instead of the supermarket's pre-determined size. And you won't pay much for it. For 600fils you can get a half kilo of black peppercorns and 400fils for a 1/4 kilo of coriander powder. In this area you will undoubtedly stumble across shops that have been around for many years and passed on from generation to generation.

The gold souq is housed in a three storey building and is less charming than its street level counterparts. But don't dismiss the gold souq for how it looks – it's what's inside that counts! Inside you will find a glittering array of shop selling their best gold, gems and the coveted and exquisite Bahraini natural pearls. Ultimately, you'll find the best part of the gold souq is not what is on display, but what you can have made.

Customers, who are often expats looking for a better deal then what they can get back home, tend to bring in their own ideas and designs to have made. Jewellers will work with customers from each stage of the design process so that the product can be developed together. Some jewellers will even work over email to design a piece of jewellery. Gold in the souq tends to be 18carat or 21carat. Those favouring a higher carat should also check out the shops at street level around the corner from the gold souq.

On your way out of the gold souq, stop at the ground floor café and for a dinar enjoy a fresh pressed juice or a soft drink cocktail or try their best-selling Oreo Madness Milkshake also for a dinar.

At the Isa Town Local Market or the souq al Haraj, there really is something for everyone from carpets to furniture, fresh produce to dry goods and fishing gear, to live animals. Go on a Saturday morning for the flea market atmosphere when the locals are out scurrying from shop to shop to fill their cupboards and closets. But get there early to avoid parking chaos. The local market will certainly awaken your senses. You will not smell anything like it when you catch a whiff of perfumes and oils mixed with the neighbouring animal bazaar. Cages, tanks, baskets and even car trunks are full of birds, frogs, turtles, rabbits and fish line this area of the market. One dinar will get you a small budgie bird or four small fish or a small turtle while small frogs go for a mere 400fils.

The Isa Town market is also known as the Iranian market for its carpets. You will have your pick of carpet shops carrying contemporary to Persian-style carpets. As you make your way through the small pedestrian streets you will witness a treasure trove of second-hand furniture and clothing shops. Dig deep for that treasure however, as everything is usually heaped up high. If picking through a pile of used furniture and clothing is not your thing, that there are plenty of new furniture and clothing shops throughout the market.

Times are changing for the souqs however, reflecting both a need to update the infrastructure and buildings and perhaps most importantly, to bring people back into what used to be the heart and soul of towns and villages. The most recent result of revitalisation is the covered area of the Manama souq. Visitors to the area can now stroll through an indoor souq with shops and cafés, all within air-conditioning comfort, which is most welcome on hot desert days. Other areas of the Manama souq remain however as they were. Plans are in the works to modernise the Muharraq souq and the Isa Town local market. Catch a glimpse of the past, experience the new and really feel the vibrant souqs of Bahrain. Opening hours are generally between 8am till 1pm, and 3:30pm till 9pm most days with shorter opening hours on Friday.

THE BAKER OF MANAMA

by

Ana Corradini Boreland

I first met the baker at MegaMart, a grocery store close to our home in Juffair. Every Sunday, when we went shopping, there he was. Big white moustache and wearing a little white cap, mixing chocolate chips, macadamia nuts and minuscule marshmallows to make the best cookies in the world – or at least in Bahrain. So every Sunday we bought a box of cookies, which didn't last very long.

One day I just had to ask him if he was indeed the creator of that risk factor responsible for the circumferential menace in which my belly was being transformed into. He just nodded and, as any good bakery groupie would, I reached out my hand to congratulate him. My husband laughed, but I managed to get a free cookie, still warm from the oven.

Another day, driving by 'American Alley', we ran into the baker and his little white cap, riding his bike (an old one), with a plastic bag from MegaMart on the handlebar – and on the wrong side of the road, of course. I felt sorry for the baker in all his humility and wondered what he was taking in that bag. Recipes? A couple hundred fills? Moustache dye? When my husband said it could have been the broken cookies from that day's work, my heart crumbled like a biscuit hitting the floor.

I would rather think that the little bag enclosed the good will to mix the dough, the wisdom to sweeten the mixture, the adventure to test the oven's temperature, the laughter to sprinkle chocolate chips. The bag was not very big, so he must have carried strictly necessary items only. A few, but special ingredients that make up the recipe of a good baker.

THE TWO SEAS

by
Fatima Dincsoy

Amidst the two seas
Is where I found her
Amidst the two seas
I fell and floundered

Amidst the two seas
Is where I loved her
It's where I thought
Everything of her

Amidst the two seas
A perfect romance
Under the palm trees
We... and we danced

And amidst the two seas
I still remember
We had a marvellous time
All through December

For amongst the two seas
I like to recall
Love emerged and enveloped
One and us all

ALI AND THE HUMMER

by

Eva L. Burns

Ali lifted his head and rubbed the sore spot on his forehead. He had been lying there so long, the desk's edge made an indentation over his eyebrows. He glanced at the clock - 1.16pm - less than fifteen minutes left of this torture. He laid his hand back down into his curled elbow and closed his eyes.

It didn't matter if he slept. To help the government achieve full employment, the phone company staffed the customer service department with twice as many people as it needed. As the associates wiled away their seven-hour shifts flirting and smoking; the calls were automatically routed so every employee received at least fifteen calls a day. Today only fourteen service calls came across Ali's desk. After working for nearly a year and a half, Ali knew the answer to about ninety percent of the questions. Most days the callers asked routine inquiries such as:

"How do I install my sim card?"

"How many minutes do I have left this month?"

"Can I text photos to my mother with my plan?"

Ali could almost, but not quite, answer them in his sleep. He tried but his supervisor said customers didn't like it when the operators sounded too sleepy. When morale was at a particularly low point, a highly paid foreign consultant was brought in. He recommended every service associate, as they became known, keep a daily log to track the phone calls received. Now the supervisor had a documented reason to breathe down his neck each day. Ali dreaded the mornings and dreamed of the day's end when he could take a nap then hang out with his friends.

His knee jiggled as he began counting down to his next cigarette. To Ali, work wasn't much different than high school. He still had to be somewhere he didn't want to although he at least now got paid for getting up in the morning. It wasn't much, but as long as he continued to live with his parents and put off marriage, the money he made kept him from picketing the Ministry of Labour for a job and helped buy gas and pay for watching football at the sheesha café.

1.28pm. Ali pushed the call-forward button and grabbed his tally sheet. The supervisor, his eyelids heavy with the same bored expression Ali had two minutes before, slowly plucked time-sheets from the mass of waving hands. Ali pushed to the front of the mob encircling the supervisor and waved his time-card.

As he rushed outside his sunglasses fogged up. He didn't bother to wipe them. He parked in the same spot in the empty lot every day. Ali put out his left arm to stop the traffic and blindly walked across the street. Waiting for his glasses to clear, he stood next to his Toyota lighting a cigarette. Since his A/C didn't work, there was no reason to get in his car and turn on the engine. Toyota quit manufacturing 1997 Cressida parts, but his mechanic pulled them out of thin air, if it was an absolute necessity. While some considered air conditioning in 112° heat a necessity Ali with his meagre salary, felt the situation wasn't critical.

"Ali, *shlow nik*, another day done," called Hashim sauntering over to Ali. As long-time friends did, the two men embraced, kissed on the first cheek, switched, then kiss, kiss, pause, kiss, and kiss.

"*Al Humdillilah.* Thank Allah it is over, man," said Ali standing with his hand on Hashim's shoulder.

Formalities finished, Hashim let go of Ali's right hand. But Ali's left hand remained frozen on his shoulder. A strange look came over Ali's face. Hashim heard a door crash open then he felt the wind sucked backwards towards the building behind him. Ali slid his sunglasses down his nose to see better. Hashim jerked around to see the lone woman clad from head to toe in black, leave the Citibank building. Crystals sparkled where her eyes should have been.

"Man, look at her," came Ali's whisper.

Oversized Bulgari sunglasses covered from her cheekbones to her hairline. Her lace veil covered her nose, then was swept up to billow over her beehive up-do like a flamenco dancer's.

"*Masha'Allah.* She is hot," agreed Hashim barely able to move his lips.

"Her father must be miserable," said Ali thinking about his own sisters.

Only a daughter still living in her father's house could get away with wearing her outfit. From her neck to her fingertips, she was completely covered in black...leather. Technically she conformed to local customs. It was the percussion instruments following her that attracted the attention.

Bling-cha BOOM, Bling-cha BOOM went her hips as her skirt swished left and right sweeping a trail behind her.

Mae West in abaya.

She sauntered towards the parked cars.

The men gathered under the palm trees' shade smoking cigarettes forgot to exhale. Smoke wafted out of their nostrils and ears.

The woman reached into her black Chloe bag and lifted out her keys. The keys slipped from her fingers and fell on the burning side-walk. Cha-Ching. She halted.

Then slooowly she bent over to pick them up. SNAP she popped back up. Her bottom quivered underneath the floor length skirt. Chaaaa – BOOM!

A red Camry ran up the sidewalk into a palm tree at the parking lot entrance.

Ali's mouth went dry. He looked at the speechless Hashim.

The woman pointed her keys – chirp, chirp. A pink Hummer's tail-lights flashed twice. She walked to the passenger's side, opened the door and placed her bag on the seat. She slammed the door shut and walked along the rear gate, the chorus following her. She paused at the HUMMER logo bedazzled with Swarovski crystals and used her manicured index finger to give the H a polish. Sparkles filled the air, blinding the men as she climbed into the driver's seat. One of the smokers fell coughing to his hands and knees. None of his colleagues moved to help him.

"She's out of my league," said Hashim giving up before she even turned on the engine.

Ali looked around the parking lot. There were several BMWs, a couple of Mercedes and an Audi but they were driven by Indian drivers or middle aged Arabs.

Ali compared himself to the men with round bellies wearing white thobes. "You never know. My sister tells me her friends think I'm handsome."

"Yes you are," Hashim agreed. "but he has dough." Hashim was pointing towards a tall man in an elegant white thobe hurrying from the Platinum customer entrance towards the VIP parking lot.

"Maybe she'll feel sorry for me," Ali declared throwing down his cigarette. He slipped the Cressida's roof. "I must try. Inshallah," he shouted.

His hands shaking, Ali unlocked the door with his key. By the time he'd folded his legs inside, the woman had thrown the Hummer into reverse forcing the parking guard to jump out of the way. She drove over the sidewalk to avoid the cars queued at the exit. Arms hanging at his side, the guard watched her leave.

Hashim watched Ali's competition slide into a Mercedes McLaren with Saudi license plate. "At least you're Bahraini," shouted Hashim.

Ali gunned his engine, screeched out of the parking lot, covering Hashim in grey dust and over the curb scraping the bottom of his Corolla. Ouch. He glanced towards the VIP parking. The ice-blue McLaren revved its engine as it waited for the automatic gates' arm to rise. Ali prayed he would not crash through it.

The 'Side-Kick Pink' Hummer didn't slow at the next speed bump. The front wheels pounded it further into the ground. The Hummer swung around the corner forcing a Bengali-filled lorry to swerve left. She accelerated. The tires squealed. Ali followed. He heard the Mercedes supercharged V8 engine hit 100 kilometres in 3.4 seconds. The hunt was on.

In his rear view mirror Ali saw the Mercedes careen into the traffic, swerving into the left lane. The Hummer reached the light as it turned green and took the right hand turn fast but smoothly. The Saudi started to overtake him but Ali pressed his accelerator to the floor. Squealing around the corner he nearly dovetailed into the Mercedes coming up on his left side. Straightening out, the Mercedes easily overtook the battered Corolla and sped after the Hummer.

Too late, Ali thought letting up on the accelerator. His heart was racing. He felt alive for the first time that day. He passed through the next light and approached the four-lane Pearl roundabout lighting a cigarette. In the far right lane the pink Hummer sat stopped by the stream of rush hour cars. The Mercedes inched forward and kissed her bumper.

Throwing his cigarette out of the window, Ali took a hard left and drove up beside her. The Corolla was so minuscule next to the Hummer he only saw pink. He leaned across the passenger seat and called out to the woman.

"*Yallah Habibi!*"

The woman turned her head. Not seeing anyone she looked down and there was Ali, his brown eyes sparkling. The corners of her mouth curled upwards and she accelerated.

The Hummer flew into the roundabout forcing five cars to break. The Saudi honked hard to clear his path and raced into the circle. A TATA van screeched, nearly clipping the Mercedes' tail-light. The Pakistani van driver was pale.

Ali swerved left and drove around the Toyota Sunny stopped front of him.

In the far right lane it looked as if the Hummer was going to drive straight down King Faisal Highway. "I'm not going to reach her," thought Ali.

As unflinching as Simon Cowell, the woman recognised flash for talent. She careened left across two lanes and eliminated the McLaren from the competition. Ali watched as the Mercedes, forced to continue straight with the down-town Manama traffic, lose her.

Spurred by his competitor's defeat, Ali swung around the traffic circle for a second time when the Hummer purred up right next to him. The woman's hand shot out and flicked a small paper towards the open window. Her phone number! Ali lunged across the passenger seat to catch it. The wind caught the note and flung it over the roof into the window of the Nissan Tiida behind him. "OH NO," Ali shouted as the paper hit the windshield then sailed off higher to bounce off a truck. Involuntarily Ali braked. The car honked behind him and Ali turned right. Another car beeped as Ali swerved, then accelerated trying to get out of the way. As he focused on the road in front of him, he saw the pink Hummer fly out of the roundabout towards the City Centre Mall. Ali tried to turn right but it was too late. He started around the circle for the third time as the woman took the exit and disappeared onto the causeway.

Giving up on chasing her, Ali slowed down to find her note. Three cars honked at him before he noticed the flashing blue lights behind him. While the policeman wrote up a ticket, Ali tried to explain that the whole incident was the Saudi's fault.

"But I'm Bahraini," he kept repeating to the officer who acted as if he didn't understand Arabic.

For reckless speeding and his seven other unpaid tickets, Ali's car was impounded. To get the Corolla back, he had to plead his case in front of a traffic court judge. Ali's consolation was that at least the Corolla got to ride in style on a tow truck. Usually it had to suffer the indignity of his neighbour's donkey to pulling it to the garage.

Without a ride, Hashim offered to drive him to work. However after five days of listening to the same story, Hashim recruited some other friends to chauffeur Ali and sympathise over his lost opportunity. After ten days of listening to Ali end each rendition with, "she waved at me, I know she wanted me," they took turns slapping his head.

On the day of his court appearance, Hashim drove Ali to the Ministry of Traffic. The guards wearing their olive pants stopped Hashim and pointed to the new sign taped onto the building's entrance. 'STOP. ALL KNEES MUST BE COVERED. NO SHORT PANTS ALLOWED.'

"Sorry my friend," Hashim said. "You'll have to do this alone."

The guard eyed Ali's hairy lower calf but since he couldn't see his knees, he let Ali pass. In the waiting area, at least twenty men sat holding red tickets. Ali approached the reception desk.

"What is your case number?" the clerk asked.

"3459830-32"

The clerk typed in his number and squinted at the screen. Over the top of his glasses, he peered at Ali before pressing the print button. The clerk leaned back in his chair with his hands behind his head. The printer carriage slid right, then left, right, then left, line-by-line across three pages.

"Your turn," the clerk said tearing off the defamatory document and gave him a knowing look. He handed Ali a red ticket.

"Good luck. The judge is in a bad mood today."

Each offence was listed with its fine for a grand total of 165BD. One hundred and sixty-five dinar, thought Ali. How can that be? It was nearly a half-month's salary. He shuffled over to an empty seat. Forty minutes later Ali's number appeared on the board and Ali approached the judge.

"*Asalam a laykum,*" he greeted him.

"*Alaykum a salam,*" replied the judge as he held out his hand for the list. Ali handed it to him. The judge read the paper and raised his eyebrows.

"Do you know what disturbs me the most about your offences?"

"No sir" answered Ali.

"This last one." His smoke stained finger poked the bottom of the page. "Reckless and fast driving through the Pearl roundabout. After seven other tickets? How many tickets will you get before you learn to drive safely?"

"But you honour," started Ali. "There is a reason - for that last one."

"I'd be interested to hear this reason." The judge's eyebrows remained raised. "I cannot think of a good excuse for putting so many people's lives at risk. Here show me," he said as pulling a paper from the file. He held up a photo, taken at fast speed from an outdoor traffic camera. The Corolla and its license plate were clearly visible. Ali peered closer. In front of his car was the pink Hummer.

"Your Sheikh, you see, I was driving calmly when this Saudi in a Mercedes pushed me off the road."

"A Saudi, I see." The judge's mouth turned into a disappointed frown. "A Saudi visitor in this country pushed you off the road. Why would he do that?"

"There was this woman."

"A woman? All of this speed for a WOMAN?"

"Yes your honour, I'm sorry but she was not an ordinary woman. It was this woman here," Ali pointed to the picture and caught the sparkle of her bracelet. Her hand hung out of the window. The photo was blurry but Ali could tell she was waving.

"Ordinary? All women are ordinary," started the judge. "You are not supposed to take notice of women. You are supposed to be thinking about Allah and your driving."

"Yes Excellency, I know. But look, look here. Here's proof. She's waving at me. She is the kind of woman put on earth to tempt us, to make sure we are saying our prayers. The kind of woman who makes men divorce their wives. The kind of woman…." Ali watched the judge's face pale and go slack.

He's having a heart attack Ali thought. Allah the Merciful he's having a heart attack right now in front of me. Ali turned around.

"Help me he's..." He stopped as the silence in the room swept over him.

Crash went the cymbals.

Bling-cha Boom, bling-cha Boom went the bass.

The woman passed all the men waiting in their chairs.

Bling-cha Boom.

The few women in the room pulled their veils tighter and hissed their disapproval.

Bling-cha Boom.

She stopped in front of the judge, four steps from Ali. Her JOY perfume alighted on his skin and gave him goose bumps. Knowing how much trouble he was already in, Ali stepped left to escape the intoxicating scent. The ceilings fans whirled the air around the judge who inhaled. He closed his eyes.

"Sir, that's the woman I was following." Ali whispered. "She was driving this Hummer," he said tapping the photo.

The judge opened his eyes and rubbed them as if he was seeing his first jinn. Ali knew any future he had with this woman rested on this moment. With barely a metre between them, Ali could have reached out and touched her, but he didn't. He realised his telephone company salary could never afford her. She was out of his class. He had better save himself.

"That woman was driving?" the judge's voice was hoarse. He cleared his throat and without taking his eyes from the woman and whispered to Ali, "That's the woman who tempted you?"

"Yes sir. Now do you understand why I was driving so fast?"

"Yes my brother." The judge sounded sorrowful. Eyes straight-ahead, unblinking, he pawed at his desk trying to locate his pen.

The woman lifted off her sunglasses. Her eyes were green.

"Oh Allah, *Al Wali,* save me," Ali groaned.

"*A salam a laykum* Sheikh. *Low sa mat,*" she sang. "Could you kindly help me with this problem? There seems to be a mistake." Her words were polite but her eyes demanded satisfaction.

The judge cleared his throat. "*A laykum a salam.* One moment - please." He called sweetly to her.

"That is the woman?" he asked Ali again in a low tone.

"Yes your Sheikh. She is certainly the one."

The judge looked down quickly, unable to take his eyes off the black leather for longer than an instant, and found his pen.

"I understand. You are not responsible for this one." He took his pen and scratched out the last ticket. "She is. She is the one who will pay," he announced loudly handing the sheet back to Ali. "There I've taken it off, but you must pay the others. And let me warn you, I do not want to hear about this again."

"Yes kind Sheikh. Your most supreme Excellency. Thank you, thank you, thank you." Ali looked down. The incident was cancelled. Twenty-five dinars less in fines. That's all? He decided not to argue the point.

"Thank you your most gracious honour. You are most kind." Ali made a small bow and backed up.

Cha-Boom! The woman zipped in front of the judge. There was no red ticket in her fingers. She didn't need one.

Ali skipped the fine payment window and rushed outside to wait for her to come out. He was breathing heavily. Did she know who he was? Would she remember waving to him?

Four long minutes passed before the door flung open. The woman exited followed by a parade of traffic department employees who suddenly noticed it was lunchtime. She didn't have far to walk. Her pink Hummer sat displayed on the Ministry's sidewalk next to the 'NO PARKING' sign. She lifted her keys from her purse and clicked the doors open.

I'm going to lose her. *Wallah.* What should I say? This is my final chance, Ali thought. He took a half dozen skips towards her then hesitated as she opened the car door.

That's it? He wondered. What else can I do?

The woman wadded up a piece of paper and lifted herself up on the running board. She pirouetted and tossed the ball in the direction of the trash bin. It landed next to Ali's feet. She slid into the car and slammed the door shut. The engine roared as she drove over the curb scattering the men before bumping onto the asphalt and speeding away.

Ali watched her go then picked up the crumpled paper. He unfolded it carefully, smoothing it on his leg.

It was her ticket.

Hashim was walking towards him, shouting something while pointing in the direction of the Hummer. Ali started jumping up and down holding the paper next to his heart.

"Hashim," he screamed, waving the paper above his head. "I won! I won."

"The judge let you off?" Hashim raced over. "Did he cancel your fines?"

"I won! I won!" Ali screamed over and over.

"You won? What are you saying? Let me see your ticket. Come on give it to me." Hashim reached for the ticket in Ali's hand, but Ali pulled his ticket from his pants pocket and handed it to Hashim. Hashim read through it.

"You didn't get off. You can't afford this. Why are you so happy?"

"Not that ticket, this ticket!" Ali shouted kissing his fist. "Her ticket!"

"Let me see that," Hashim said snatching the paper from Ali's grasp. He focused on the black marks. "All the offences are crossed out. The judge certified the balance due is zero. This is her ticket? You owe one hundred and twenty-five dinars and she owes nothing! How can that be fair?"

"Can you believe it? This is my lucky day. Thank you Allah."

"Did you look at this?" Hashim waved his hand in front of the dancing Ali.

"Yes, right here." Ali said stabbing the paper. On the first two lines was the woman's name and mobile number.

"She gave you her mobile number. You did win! By Allah's mercy, you won!" Hashim grabbed Ali's arms and together they danced in a circle while the envious men turned away.

"We will get your car. Then today we celebrate," declared Hashim.

"Of course. But first we must go to the mosque to thank Allah for his blessings."

BEAUTIFUL BAHRAIN

by

Fahad Ali

A spray of cool air, spiced with salt,
Washes over speeding dhows,
And brings cool to the sweltering heat.
The adept sailor looks out,
Wondering at what the day will reap:
Hordes of fish, perhaps a pearl.
His life and future based upon
The many spoils of the sea.

A stream of cool air, sweet scented,
Passes between the date palms,
And refreshes the shade beneath.
The eager student looks down,
Reading over his notes for the day:
Pages scrawled over with words.
His life and future based upon
The equations in his books.

A rush of cool air, blowing strong,
Wraps around the building tops,

And dances from cranes to concrete.
The skilled engineer looks up,
Envisioning future projects:
Mind-altering skyscrapers.
Our lives and futures based upon
The blueprints he helps design.

A breath of cool air, filled with life,
Sidles around street corners,
And waves the flags of red and white.
The lithe children look around,
Laughing cheerfully as they play:
The ball flies, the children run.
Their lives and futures based upon
Now and then, both past and present.

This is Bahrain.
Diverse, charming, bustling Bahrain.
This is Bahrain.
Delightful, colourful, beautiful Bahrain.

PROTECTION

by

Joanne Jones

The February day was getting steamy despite the fact that it was still winter in Bahrain. I had just collected the hire car from the airport, tentatively driving through whizzing traffic along the Al Fateh Highway.

This day was a watershed for me. Since arriving in Bahrain I had watched my other less anxious colleagues at the Polytechnic hire cars from day one, and fearlessly taking on the terrifying roundabouts. Particularly gut-wrenching was the chaotic roundabout at Isa Town, where there seemed to be no common understanding of rules and it was every man and woman for themselves. Whilst some of my colleagues did admit to sweaty palms and panic attacks as they approached the Roundabout, the more dashing types saw it as all in a normal days' work. For a middle-aged woman from orderly Canberra, Australia, this was very daunting.

By February I had decided that I had to bite the bullet and discover the warrior driver in me. Otherwise I would be constantly at the mercy of my charming but, nonetheless, over committed driver who sometimes found it hard to say no to last minute driving requests. Being an all or nothing person, I decided to also move to Isa Town on that same day so that I would be closer to work and thereby able to avoid a lot of driving.

I negotiated my way as far as the stunning grand mosque. This beautiful building stands alone as an eloquent reminder of the spiritual aspirations of Bahrain in the otherwise seemingly secular suburb of Juffair. The hotels, the modern apartment buildings, the clubs and the take-away area affectionately called 'Cholesterol Alley' by the expats, seemed more like an American miniature city frequented by US service men and women stationed at the Fifth Fleet Base nearby, than a residential area in the Middle East. The mosque and the library behind it with their architectural integrity, tower above the other buildings, if not in size at least in character and substance.

The real Juffair of older style, crumbling houses inhabited by Bahraini families cannot be seen from the highway, but I had often enjoyed walks from Adliya down to the water and back along past the original Bahraini area. An elderly taxi driver explained to me once that when he was a boy, this area was idyllic. He and his father had fished under the date palm trees and watched the sunset. He seemed saddened by the rampant growth of high rise buildings on reclaimed land that now, despite the glitz and ever present sense of affluent expat lifestyles, had none of the charm of the original Bahrain.

The symbolism of the mosque and the contrast of the two Bahrains was lost on me today however, as a sense of bravado over my driving welled up inside. What a fool I had been not to do this months ago I berated myself. I was already planning the weekend excursions I would undertake and relished the sense of freedom engendered by being able to drive again.

I rounded past Al Mahooz and rejoiced that I was now on the straight run that was the Saudi Causeway. I calculated that it would only be one more veer to the right across a flyover bridge and then I would be in Isa Town. Even better I had been told about a route that would allow me to avoid the dreaded Isa Town Roundabout.

My fun was only fleeting. As I glided past rather impressive looking Arabic style villas in New Zinj the sickening thud of a flat tyre was matched by my groan of despair. Like a fast-forwarding movie, I visualised all the implications; stranded on a busy highway, cars screeching at me to get out of the way, lost in an unfamiliar area and, worst of all, derailed in the heat without even a bottle of water or a shop within sight.

I was immediately regretting all of those occasions on country roads in Australia when I had allowed my husband of many years to change flat tyres whilst I sat in the car unconcerned, knowing that I was in capable hands. I had never even hired a car before in my life, so did not realise that a quick phone call to the hire company would have rescued me. As I looked despairingly across the road at the seemingly deserted landscape of imposing villas and contemplated my next move, I noticed a man in a uniform approaching me from inside one of the villas. There was a sign on the villa which seemed to indicate that it was a government office which had something to do with caring for children. The man, thick set and tall, was a security guard. He was the only person within sight, the building being empty of other employees on weekends.

His security role and his physical proportions contrasted with his gentle demeanour. As he approached me he smiled but did not say anything and I soon realised that he could not speak much English. With simple reassuring gestures he pointed to the boot of my car and indicated that he would fix the problem. My response was a mixture of relief and surprise and I pondered whether the heat had made me delusional.

With a simple, no fuss approach and a complete absence of ego, while I sat in the car this stranger got down on the ground and proceeded to sort out my problem. I had thought sitting in the car would be inappropriate while a stranger attended to my tyre so I initially stood behind him feigning that I knew something about the process. He graciously pointed to the car suggesting that I remain there out of the sun. He worked away meticulously and determinedly and within twenty minutes the car was roadworthy again.

By the time he had finished, trickles of sweat were pouring off his forehead. I clumsily attempted to convey to him how grateful I was. He dismissed his efforts with a hand gesture and smiling, started to walk off. I was unsure what his nationality was, although he did look Bahraini. I agonised for a few moments over whether I should tip him but then decided that whatever his nationality he probably would not be earning much as a security guard. So setting aside concerns about appearing patronising, I offered him 20BD. He refused it, shaking his head a number of times so that finally I held it out again and suggested that if he couldn't use it then perhaps his children might enjoy some sweets. That settled the matter and he took the money.

That night in my new apartment in Isa Town I kept mulling over the day's events. I could not at first understand my fascination with the incident. After all, blokes in the West sometimes did similar kind-hearted tasks for stranded women. Why did this time seem somehow different and more special? Perhaps I just felt more vulnerable in a strange country and therefore, like a hostage who falls in love with her captor, I was more grateful to this man than I would have been had it occurred at home. I ruminated on this complexity for several days without finding any real answer.

Many weeks later my female students at the Polytechnic commented on the fact that I was now driving. They wanted to know why I had taken so long to hire a car. When I described my nervousness and alluded to fears of breaking down, they laughed and said that I need not have worried. They explained that they never worry about such things because in Bahrain there is always someone who will help out. Their final words resonated with me; "Men in Bahrain always help women. That's part of our culture." In the students' light-hearted comments there was a gravity that had eluded me for weeks. Yet it was also stunning in its simplicity. I was captivated by a community culture that recognised values such as protection of others as a given rather than as a choice.

I walked away remembering with delight the symmetry of that hot and frustrating afternoon with an enhanced understanding of why I so liked Bahrain.

BAHRAIN IS THE BEST

by

Heera Nawaz

Having lived for two eventful years in beautiful Bahrain, I now grow nostalgic and dreamy over memories of the island...

Yes, I certainly miss the island and I carry sweet thoughts
of television and videos showing a suspenseful movie,
for in Bahrain, entertainment - especially visual -
has always been quite sensational and groovy!

I used to love the latest movies and comedy serials,
telecast from the wild, wild west,
especially soaps, like; Dynasty, Knots Landing,
The Bold and Beautiful and Falcon Crest!

I fondly remember the hotels and the famous Indian night,
which gives a full rein to the appetite with every tasty bite,
Due to the humidity and sultry heat, I got so used to the A/C,
especially when travelling in Mitsubishi and cars that are racy.

I reminisce over Arabic sandwiches, halwa, fruits, fish and dates,
And food brought from all over the world in heavy brown crates,
I won't forget all the gold-decorated stalls in the bustling souq,
and my winning of a Radio Bahrain sticker - but that was a fluke!

I can't forget the dhow, the handicrafts, the delicacies and pearls,
well embellished and glittering forth from the neck of Bahraini girls,
Of tourist resorts are the museum, the mosques, and the burial grounds,
the forts silhouetting history and so, too, the historical graveyard mounds,

I especially miss auspicious Friday and not Sunday as the day of rest,
For logically speaking, don't you think that of all islands, Bahrain is the best?

HIJAB AND TRADITIONAL DRESS

by
Mary Coons

Many Westerners are bewildered by the unfamiliar sight of Arab Muslim women garbed in black. Frown lines form and heads shake in disbelief at the sight of a woman in niqab (full-face covering). It seems strange. Why on earth would a woman dress like that?

It's a well-known assumption in the Arab world that Arab men by nature are jealous creatures. According to Nofa al Sulaiti, many of the reasons a woman would wear hijab (headscarf) are due to the way Arab men were raised. "Men were raised to believe that women should cover up. The new generation is trying to change that, and men are not as jealous as they were before. The men today are more open-minded," she reported. "The generation of men now lets the whole family travel, go into restaurants and public places and sit and eat together. In the early days, no man was allowed to look at another's wife. She should cover up, even her face. Why? He was raised that way. When he was a young boy, he could not look at girls, even his cousins, because he might marry one of them some day. But as a young teen, he looked at girls and thought they were pretty or nice. So when he grew up and married, he didn't want other men looking at his wife and thinking of her as he used to think when he looked at girls."

WESTERN GENERALISATION

'WOMEN WHO VEIL THEMSELVES ARE FORCED TO AND ARE OPPRESSED.'

Is it that they are in black that Westerners think they look scary? Something reminiscent of a funeral? Is it the fear of the unknown or merely curiosity about what is beneath the abaya? Or is it that we can't see their faces or hair? Are they covering themselves because of a self-esteem problem? Do their husbands and/or family force them to dress like this?

Many questions and scenarios tug at Western minds. It is a simple case of genuine ignorance. We simply do not know.

Of course, if one reverts back into history, just about all religions at some point had women wearing some type of veil. Mary, the mother of Jesus, is usually depicted in Christian art with her head covered. By the Middle Ages, Jewish women largely conformed to the custom of hair covering. Until the 1960s, it was obligatory for Catholic girls and women to cover their heads in church. Catholic nuns for centuries wore floor length black habits and had their hair covered. I grew up Catholic and attended Catholic schools, so I didn't find nuns scary looking. However, nuns in full black habits were indeed scary looking to many of my non-Catholic friends.

Traditional Hindu women still cover their heads and at least partly obscure their faces around unrelated adult males. A large number of African women wear headscarves, as do many Russian women.

"Some women are forced to wear hijab," admitted Wafaa Ashoor. "Not the majority of them, but some are still forced. Some fathers force their daughters to wear niqab even today. For hijab, I think the father should insist because this is for his daughter's benefit. Now or later she will know it was the right thing to do and thank him. But to cover her entire face? No, this is not general practice. But there are still some men who force it."

Rania Noor contended that hijab is a statement of a Muslim woman's identity, and that "anyone who sees her will know she is a Muslim and has a good moral character. Many Muslim women who cover are filled with dignity and self-esteem; they are pleased to be identified as Muslim women. As a chaste, modest, pure woman, she does not want her sexuality to enter into interactions with men in even the smallest degree. A woman who covers herself is concealing her sexuality, but allowing her femininity to be revealed. Hijab is not merely a covering, but more importantly, it is behaviour, manners, speech, and appearance in public. Dress is only one facet of the total being."

"The hijab is a very difficult issue for us," said Maryam al Sheroogi. "For many, they believe if they removed their hijab, hell would come to them."

"But many girls now know why they have to wear it," added Wafaa Ashoor. "We must explain to our daughters not only why they should wear hijab, but also tell them they have to put it on. It's not that hard. When I was growing up, people knew it was in the Book about wearing hijab, but they didn't know why women were supposed to wear it. But everybody knows now what is in the Book. It's in our nature to want to do what's in the Book, so we are returning to the Book."

Twenty-one-year-old Nofa al Sulaiti does not wear hijab, although her mother does. I asked her if that presented any tensions between mother and daughter. "Every single day before I go to the university, my mother says something. It's a very difficult decision to make. The hijab is a commitment for me. So if I wear it, I will cover all of my hair and all of my body. Some of the girls in Bahrain – especially the Bedouin girls – do this not for the religion and not for God, but for their reputation and their family. Example; I'm doing this for my family; I'm doing this for my mother; I'm doing this because of my family name; the women in my family always wore hijab. This is what is happening right now."

"If I wear hijab, I will wear it the right way like I'm supposed to wear it, not like the girls do with their hair showing. If I decide to wear hijab, I will wear it for God and not for people. But I have to think carefully about it, because if I put it on and I'm not confident enough, I might take it off. And this is not good. People might have a bad impression of me and say 'Yeah, she used to wear it and now she doesn't. What's going on?' I won't wear it because my mother told me to or because I have to for my family name."

Naseem, Nofa's mother, said she realises that she cannot force her daughter to cover. "She'll go out and take it off, and I don't want that. But I think that here in Bahrain wearing hijab is more tradition than religion."

What if you were married and your husband forced you to wear it, I asked Nofa. "Actually, this is not the point," she answered. "Before we marry, we would discuss it. If I like this person and want him as my husband, and he told me after we were married, would you please do this as an honour for my family and for me, of course, I would. But if after we were married he decided he wanted me to wear it, then that's a big problem. Then it's like he is forcing me, and I won't like that. I'm actually planning to wear hijab whenever I do get married."

"You know, some women who wear hijab look sexier than the ladies who don't," Salah Al Shuroogi told me. "There are some beautiful eyes. And yes, some people think they do look scary. We are no longer a small village; Muslim people travel the world just as American and Europeans do. I would ask the Western people to accept and live with hijabbed women and not to harass women they might see like this."

Nofa also weighs in on the make-up issue as she herself wears make-up and has beautifully highlighted eyes: "Girls and women can wear make-up, but on limited areas. For example, black eyeliner is halal, which means okay. This is a cultural thing, not a religious thing. Prophet Muhammad said this was the culture before Islam, but that women should not wear too much of it. It was the Bedouin culture to wear eyeliner. They also had a herb that women wore, called dorim, that made your lips brownish orange. In the Arab world specifically, because of the way we dress (wearing an abaya) and covering our hair, what's the part of your body that is seen the most? The face. So girls want to highlight that as best they can to show off. Yeah, it's a contradiction within our culture because when we put on the hijab the main idea of wearing it is to prevent men from staring at us. So when we wear make-up … well then, the point is - why are you wearing hijab in the first place?"

Apparently Arab Muslims know Westerners well, as this generalisation popped up on their list, too, about Westerners.

ARAB GENERALISATION

'Westerners believe that Muslim women who cover themselves are backward.'

To most Westerners, it seems as though women in hijab or niqab and those wearing an abaya appear to be more subservient when covered.

"I am a Muslim Bahraini wife and mother," Eman wrote, "And I dress the way I feel I want to dress. Allah will judge me for my behaviour, my good deeds, and my clean heart and mind."

Yet another Muslim woman, who wished to remain anonymous, said, "According to Islam, women should be covered from head to toe if they are in front of any men. This helps protect a woman's body parts from men. It is a shield that protects a woman from evil thinking or the stares of men. Allah almighty has ordered women to cover themselves; so who has the right to say what is wrong and what is right? Furthermore, covering oneself doesn't mean that we Muslims are not modern or 'backward' as many Europeans and Americans think."

In addition, Westerners I interviewed felt the hijabbed Arab Muslim women had a limited education (the mandatory grades until high school graduation) and then were pressured into marrying and immediately starting a family.

The Bahraini Muslim women – at least those in their twenties – that I interviewed are well educated with jobs and career aspirations. Many Westerners think the majority of these women are uneducated and at home caring for their family and husband, and that's the extent of their life.

"I really think Americans have the misconception that Arab women are not that highly educated, and for some reason seeing them in scarves and an abaya contributes to that misperception," said Joan Corey.

"That's an interesting concept about women," remarked Lee Ann Fleetwood after reading the two generalisations. "Americans may think that Arab women are oppressed because they wear hijab. But then Arab Muslims feel that American women are repressed because they have to use their bodies in every aspect of their lives. It depends on which side of the coin you are looking at. Personally, if I had to choose between walking around half-naked and walking around covered, I'd prefer the covered. I don't believe in the extreme form of covering, but at the same time, I find it disgusting that every advertisement in America from socks to cars has a half naked woman in it."

To wear or not wear hijab is a hotly contested issue in this Arab country with no apparent right or wrong reason. There are extreme opinions waged against the more liberal viewpoints, and degrees of everything in between. Again, it comes down to religion versus culture.

What follows are theological opinions, broad generalisations, Muslim women making impassioned pleas to their 'sisters' to wear hijab and abayas, and even some men weighing in on the topic. It is becoming more obvious that the Islamic dress code is not rigidly defined; rather the emphasis seems to be on women dressing modestly – and how can that be a black and white decision?

CULTURE OR RELIGION?

"I believe the Quran says to cover that which you consider private," ventured Nader Shaheen. "And in some references it's translated as covering your breasts as well. At the time it wasn't uncommon for women to be topless, which nowadays – even in the West – is too much. But it's culture and not religion. Cover your head, cover your face, cover your hands – completely black out – no one could point that out in the Quran. No one can show you where it says completely cover yourself from head to toe in black, because it doesn't exist. Therefore, this is culture. It is not about religion. It is a sprout seed that has gone to seed, and something that someone has run with and just kept going. It is not against our secular law to go out with your hair showing, wearing jeans, and a t-shirt. You cannot be arrested for that in Bahrain.

"Christianity and other religions are practised in a hundred different ways around the world. Where the culture will affect it, it manifests itself in wearing the veil. To my understanding, it is not a pre-requisite for being a good Muslim. There are basic and decent things about culture that are vastly more important than whether or not you expose your hair. Do you donate to charity? Do you try to do good works for the poor? Don't steal, don't lie – the basic things – those are much more important."

Lee Ann Fleetwood offered some background history: "Muslims back in the day were being harassed by those intent on keeping Islam from spreading. Muslim women were especially harassed as they were seen as the weaker gender. Arabia in those days was barbaric and very open concerning sexuality. It is well known that women walked around with their chests exposed and nobody thought too much about it. In general, the dress of the time was fairly casual.

"Women wore a cloth that draped over their heads because of the arid, hot conditions of the region. It had nothing to do with religion. It was not held securely around the body or used to cover the hair; most often it hung loosely down and provided protection from the elements.

"Slave women in those days were considered fair game to anyone. Non-Muslims used that as an excuse to avoid blame when they harassed Muslim women, claiming that they couldn't tell Muslim from non-Muslim or slaves. Muslim women appealed to the Prophet to find a solution fearing the harassment would intensify. He prayed to Allah for guidance and the message was that Allah wants the Muslim women to cover their chests and dress modestly so that aggressors to Islam will have no further excuse for causing harm.

"Allah tells them to use the same cloth that they've always used and just bring it over their chests in a more modest fashion. The ultimate aim was to distinguish Muslim women from non-Muslim and slaves. You have to wonder that nowadays its hijabbed and veiled women that are most likely to be harassed because of the distinction, so maybe the opposite holds true now.

"There are Muslims now and from the past who sincerely believe that Allah never ordered hijab to be worn, and so it is a choice for them to wear it or not, and they believe they will not be punished for it. It should not be considered a deficiency in their religion just because others believe it is ordered.

"Allah orders modest dress, modest behaviour, and justice to be done between us. We know that covering ourselves from head to toe in black has no magical effect on men who are intent to cause harm. What we need to do is raise our Muslim sons to have 'hijab' of the heart and mind concerning women, and then the two genders could coexist in a true Islamic society in which women are free to expose their hair without the burden of being seen as deficient or fair game, but still queens and due equal respect as hijabis.

"The Quran does not tell women to wear the hijab and to cover their heads and hair. It's just not there. Hijab for women did not even become a widespread practice until more than two hundred years after the Prophet's death. And it was a cultural practice new converts to Islam used to show the difference between rich women and poor. If it was a direct order from God, then for sure all Muslim women alive at the time of the Prophet would have practised it without a second thought, and so would Muslim women forever after that. But it wasn't and it isn't."

Fatima Ali and Rugayah Sharif discussed the philosophy in their respective Shia families that they experienced as to wearing hijab when they were younger.

"My mother said, 'I will not tell you to wear the scarf'," began Rugayah. "'I want you to come and tell me that you want to wear it.' If I want to wear the scarf, then I have to wear it and never remove it. It was a hard decision at first. But once a girl wears it, she becomes attached to it and doesn't think of removing it. People will ask me - aren't you hot wearing it? Well the thing is, I sometimes forget I'm wearing it; it has become part of my body."

"I feel weird sometimes if I don't wear it," Fatima admitted. "You either always wear it or never wear it. It's an attitude, a way of living. The scarf is not just a piece of clothing that you occasionally wear. Sometimes I'll see a woman not wearing one and she respects herself; I can tell by her pose and the way she carries herself. Then there's a girl wearing a scarf because she was told to, and my God, it is obvious that there is no respect!

"A lot depends on the upbringing as to whether you wear it or not. Some parents are very open and others are very strict. For some it's more of a negotiation; don't go out without one because of a, b, and/or c, and they try to convince their child like that. I will not wear something that I am not convinced of. If my mother tells me that I have to wear the scarf, I won't necessarily because my mother is not here with me this very minute. I can take it off whenever I want. And that's what happens, I think, for most girls if they've been forced into wearing it. You cannot force things upon people, but if I'm convinced about the reasons for wearing it, then why not? It all depends on your upbringing."

"I know families who are very restrictive with their daughters," Rugayah added. "At home they are told to wear the scarf, not use the mobile; they can't go outside with their friends, but as soon as they go off to the university, they rebel. Off comes the scarf."

"I believe that our religion says women must cover their hair," she continued. "I want to protect myself. Here in Bahrain they say that the hair is the cause of evil thoughts. So when you see a girl with long hair, you know guys are looking at her. We may be innocent, but we are not naïve."

When I asked what's so bad about looking at a girl's hair, Rugayah's answer was short and succinct: "A guy's blood runs in only two directions. Wearing a scarf is a cultural thing. If I see a woman not wearing one, and she is respecting herself by the way she acts or dresses, I'm not going to judge her or say she's a bad Muslim because she's not wearing a scarf."

In Bahrain if a Shia girl is going to wear hijab, it usually happens around age nine, but Fatima and Rugayah were eleven and Naeema, Fatima's younger sister, was twelve years old. They explained that their parents did not want to push them.

Although these three young adults do not customarily wear an abaya, they sometimes will. Fatima usually wears it when she goes to the souq, while Rugayah sheepishly admitted she wears one when she's running late for work.

"Women who wear an abaya can remove it whenever they want, but they're used to it. They feel that if they are not wearing one, it's like they are walking around naked. In some families, girls are not allowed to remove their abayas. And they really aren't that hot in the summer; they have some material that is really quite light like the material in a pair of shorts."

"I am a Bahraini Muslim girl," wrote Maha, "And have been wearing a hijab and abaya since I was a teenager. I swear I really feel safe and valuable each time I wear them. I have beautiful hair with a healthy body that strictly should not be seen by strangers, because it is a gift from Allah and a part of respecting His holy instructions. You know that a girl is like a diamond that must always be covered with a veil of silk to protect it. It is important to mention here that not only Islam urges women to cover their hair; the Bible also does. To sum up, I feel like a princess under the umbrella of Islam and its teachings to wear hijab."

Najiya, who chose not to disclose her last name, said that Islam is more cultural than religious. "When it comes to practising faith, we have to follow the rules laid down in the Quran and Hadith. It is from the very authentic Hadith that we get our dress code. We wear the abaya as a shapeless black garment so that it hides the very shapely us. We don't want any non-mahrem (non-related) men seeing how we look."

Another Muslim woman, Maria, noted that all religions, including Christianity and Judaism, value the modest and chaste nature of the woman. "Muslim women everywhere are proud to wear their beautiful and modest Islamic dress, both as a way of identifying themselves as Muslims and as a shield against envious or lustful glances."

"The hijab has an indispensable function in the life of a Muslim woman," offered Ameena Ali. "That is protection and preservation of her honour and chastity. This means that a woman who wears the hijab does not do this to declare her religion or distinguish herself. Rather, she wears it out of obedience to her Lord."

An anonymous male offered his opinion to the hijab debate: "Being a man, I must say that we actually have more respect for women who do cover up properly rather than those who do not. Men generally try to flirt with those who expose themselves. We don't want the risk of being embarrassed by flirting with a woman who is covering herself; she might actually be a respectful, true Muslim who is probably married."

Rasool Hassan, married with three children, has never suggested to his wife that she wear or not wear hijab or an abaya. "Because she grew up in a family where they wanted her to wear one, it became part of her life. Sometimes she only wears a scarf to cover her hair. It's her decision. But to be very honest with you, as a Muslim man, I prefer that she wear both an abaya and a scarf. I think it's nice to see that. Islam does not have a problem with women not wearing an abaya, as long as she is wearing good clothing – nothing tight or short – that respects her and others. I have no problem with that. I have seen midriff tops and low-cut tops on eighteen- and twenty-year-old girls out at the mall – really unbelievable – and because of the way they dress, this could lead to problems. I'm not saying they should be wearing an abaya or scarf to protect themselves from men staring. Whether one wears an abaya or a tent, you'll not stop a man from staring."

Jemma, an Arab Muslim, said, "Muslim women see their mode of dress as a form of freedom from the unrelenting form of obsession and objectification of the female body. It stresses the profound worth of the inner person and reduces the fixation of physical / material factors."

I have seen (more than once) the allure that a prim and proper woman in niqab can produce with heavily made up eyes as she casts a single, darting glance with seductively flirting eyes. Conversely, a cold glance can put a man in his rightful place with the same eyes of a woman in casual Western attire.

An anonymous woman offered an extreme view that the practice of unveiling is harmful to Bahraini society. "Women are taught from early childhood that their worth is proportional to their attractiveness. We feel compelled to pursue abstract notions of beauty; half realising that such a pursuit is futile. Mothers who compel their daughters to take off the hijab, saying that they won't find husbands wearing it, are not educating their daughters to obey Allah and his messenger. If a woman will not obey Allah and his messenger, how can she be expected to obey her husband? The honour of a father is his daughter. The honour of a brother is his sister. The honour of a husband is his wife, and the honour of a son is his mother. Remember that when you leave the hijab and show the shape of your body (wearing jeans and t-shirts or even a tight fitting abaya) or, worse still, your hair and skin, then you are in fact dishonouring and insulting your fathers, brothers, sons, and husbands."

Lee Ann Fleetwood took issue with this opinion, countering, "honour should not be a burden on another person."

Annie Coyle, an Irish woman teaching Bahraini Arab adults conversational English, noted that in the past few years she has seen more women wearing hijab at the universities than previously. She wonders if it is from society's cultural pressure rather than religious belief. "I don't think anybody would ask anyone to change his or her culture. I think maybe the point is whether we have the right to judge another's culture. You have the choice to wear whatever you want, and respect what other people are wearing, without thinking that your way is the only right way. You should respect the culture that you live in."

"In Bahrain most women involved in public life and who have been well educated dress as they wish," contended Saara, who does not wear hijab. "Some wear abayas, some wear long and loose Western clothing, some wear tighter Western clothing, some cover their hair, and some don't. And yet, all dress within an acceptable range of 'modesty.' No one seems particularly concerned about dress, and I'm sure it is a non-issue for many.

"It seems that when a woman has achieved something worthwhile, it is almost an unspoken rule not to discuss her appearance. This does not mean that one's dress is entirely unimportant. It is just that it should never be the absolute emphasis of one's identity as a person. The inside is just as important as the outside."

"People in this country want you to wear hijab not for God, but for society and for them," contended Lee Ann Fleetwood. "I told my daughters that I didn't believe in it and I don't wear it, but I will not make the choice for them. My oldest daughter removed her headscarf for a month or so awhile back and got a lot of grief for that. She actually lost a friend over it, which really angered me. This friend told my daughter that 'if you were my friend, you would wear your hijab.' She should have said if you are a Muslim and you believe in God, you would wear it, not that if you want to be my friend you'll wear it.

"God says over and over in the Quran that He is the Most Fair, the Most Merciful, the Most Loving – every good word you can think about God – and He also says He does not distinguish between the genders; He makes them equal. He says that we are accountable for our own behaviour, and that each of us should behave ourselves, lower our gaze, don't look at forbidden things, and don't partake in forbidden acts. We should all behave modestly at all times. So given that He spent the whole entire book telling us how to behave ourselves, why then would He say, 'but because men are weak and always want sex and can't control themselves, in this case women should cover up their entire bodies and not let men see them?'

"Well, men shouldn't be looking at women's bodies. God already explained that. They should be behaving themselves, and God said that, too. If women's hair is sexy to men, then men's hair is sexy to women. So why don't men have to cover up from us? And also, don't forget that God is going to hold each individual accountable. You are not accountable for every man in this room if he looks at you. It is their sin if they look at you, not yours. As long as you dress modestly and behave modestly, it is not your sin if a man looks at you and thinks immodestly."

"This is what you see," countered Maryam al Sheroogi. "We see something else. In the old days of our culture, if a man saw a woman dressed provocatively, he would give her a poem about her body and her beauty. That poem brought shame to the girl's family because everybody knew the poem was about her. The Arabic poem is very bad."

BOKHARA OR BUST

by

Maeve Kelynack Skinner

In Bahrain's early expat days of the 1970s, seniority in a company was taken very seriously. The General Manager lived in a big house with paid-for servants, furniture and fittings, and wall-to-wall carpets. Whereas lowly junior employees were supplied with carpets that stopped one foot away from the wall. *I am superior to you, so I have a fitted carpet whereas you lowly person can only have one that sits in the middle of the room!*

All furniture was courtesy of the 'Company' and each newcomer inherited whatever had been left by the previous occupants. Furniture shops were rare; choice were limited to bog standard basics at extravagant prices, or the alternative which was made by labourers-cum-carpenters who banged together planks of wood with unshaven bits of bark and large nails protruding out of the sides to make a bed, or else flimsy chipboard cupboards held together by glue that listed to starboard, which meant the death knell for precious china or crystal glasses. A far cry from the exquisite handmade items handcrafted by artisans in Kashmir and Pakistan! Dark brown or mustard was the only colour choice of fabric, and carpets which were trundled out of the depths of the company warehouse.

The bungalow my husband was first allocated was pleasant enough with three bedrooms, two bathrooms and a cloakroom, open plan sitting room/dining, decent kitchen and a large garden with mature trees, shrubs and a gardener to plant whatever flowers he chose. But as this was one of Bahrain's earliest built expatriate houses, the interior was drab and dated, with a hideous brown and white speckled tiled floor, brown velour sofa-set with a gangrenous green tint and drab brown curtains that lolled against the windows like flailing sheets, hooked at irregular intervals to a wooden rail, their hems inches above the floor. Despair turned to relief when he was informed that the carpet men would be around soon. Anything would be better than this.

Shortly afterwards came a knock on the door and he was greeted by two smiling Eastern gentlemen who gestured to a Toyota pick-up parked at the gate, its open back stacked high with rolled up carpets, their myriad hues of brightly coloured silk, glistening in the sunlight.

"Great, so you're here with the carpets?" said my husband. "Bring them in." He couldn't believe his eyes as the pair proceeded to carry in countless rugs which they unrolled and placed one on top of the other. He'd never seen such a display of carpets in his life.

"These are beautiful," he gasped, wide-eyed as he ran his fingers over the soft richness of the carpets that would adorn his home for the next few years. He hadn't expected such excellent service from the Company who had already been generous in helping him to settle into a new life overseas. For the next couple of hours the two men displayed carpet after carpet for my husband to choose from. Those he liked went onto one pile, those he discarded were rolled up to be removed. He was in seventh heaven; the carpets were magnificent and would make such a difference to the drab and plain décor.

Finally he had made his choice and directed the men to place the carpets in the bedrooms, hall, corridor and main rooms until the house was filled with magnificent Bokhara, Qum, Kashan, Shiraz, Qashqai, Afghan, Turkoman, Kashmir – you name it. He had taken his time and had chosen with care. Smiling and rubbing his hands with glee he shook hands with the men, who also smiled and rubbed their hands with glee as he thanked them for their trouble and ushered them towards the door.

"No No. Now. Pay," the older one said handing him a piece of paper with an astronomical figure written on it.

"It's okay," explained my husband with an expansive smile, waving aside the note. "The carpets are from the company, they are supplied to me. FREE. I don't have to pay. Just give me a form to sign."

The two men looked at him blankly.

"This too much money. You must pay now," insisted the older man.

My husband was becoming a little annoyed. It had been an exhausting task choosing exactly which carpet was suitable for each room, and he knew that the carpets were supplied free and here were these guys trying to make a quick buck off him!

"No pay," he said firmly. "These carpets from the Company for my house. Carpets F-R-E-E," he spelt it out. I'm not putting up with any nonsense from this pair, he decided ushering them out of the house.

The two men muttered between themselves then the younger one slid past my husband and rapidly began to roll up the carpets; the beautiful blue and white silk Qum in the bedroom, the Qashqai runner in the hall, the magnificent Kashan in the dining room and then, he had the audacity to carry them out to the pick-up.

"Whoa. Stop," cried my husband. "What on earth are you doing? Why are you taking them away after all the trouble I went to in selecting which one went where. Put them down. Now!" My husband's voice rose in anger as he tried to get through to these thick-heads that the company had arranged for them to be delivered.

Watching his reaction, the older man suddenly burst out laughing. 'Now I understand. You are thinking these carpets from your company for house, Yes?"

"Well of course. I was told they'd be delivered this afternoon and here you are with the carpets."

"My friend," said the man gently placing his hand on my husband's arm, speaking slowly as if to a dimwitted child. "I am private carpet seller. These carpets not from your company. They are from my shop in Adliya. Every day I am coming to English man's house to sell my carpets. Very popular. Everyone want my good quality carpets. I give you special good price. Which one you want?"

My shattered and disillusioned husband shook his head, too disappointed to speak. His visions of living in an Aladdin's cave, stretched out on a magnificent Persian rug whilst listening to his music, vanished in a puff of smoke. Ruefully he watched as the parade of carpets disappeared into the back of the truck, until he began to see the funny side. "Maybe another day I buy your carpets," he called as the last rug was rolled up and deposited, far from his reach. He stood at the gate and watched the men drive off as they went on their way to make a small fortune, selling priceless, hand-spun carpets made by travelling caravanserai women as they drifted back and forth across the high Zagros and Elburz Mountains in the summer before journeying to the warmer plains in the winter. All the while spinning, weaving and mixing dyes sourced from the vegetables and flowers that they harvested as they travelled across Persia, Baluchistan, Afghanistan and into lands without borders on their timeless journeys....

LOVE'S GIFT

by
Madhavi Tiwary

Introduction to "Love's Gift"

This is a very, very special poem. I wrote it in my first few years in Bahrain. It was a time when my heart was healthy with a lot of love and romance. In those days I happened to pass through a village here called 'Malkia'. Although on that afternoon of peak summer, the village was not expected to exude much cooling charm, somehow it did succeed in tickling my heart with its pregnant silence on that scorching afternoon. Till now, I am not sure whether it was the love in my own heart, or the heated quietude of that village that ruffled my emotions enough to result in this poem.

I gift you this little village -
Which now has the sheen of both the worlds
For two mortals in immortal love
Happened to pass through it.

Dull lanes glisten with glory
Scorched trees have moist eyes
Cacti turned Veronica
Rusty roads stand a singing
Desertous fields dance -
To the heartbeats of newborn buildings.

LOVE'S GIFT

{ MADHAVI TIWARY }

The devilish orange of the sky
Only rains pink softness
Aimless urchins exude hope
The old look forward
Dreams replacing nostalgia
The young are lusty again.

A sweet breeze has blown off -
The veils of womanish misery
Smiles escape covered faces
Fingers twitch with eagerness
Feet have started walking
Heads at the right place
Hearts are exchanging abodes.

Fertility has wedded the sand
The village has an orchard of life
The mummied humanity
Now drinks from the vineyard of love.

This little hamlet, a freshly alighted piece of heaven
My love, I gift to you.

MY PEARL

by

Lillian Mills

Is it possible to have a love/hate relationship with a hunk of stone? Well, over the course of several years visiting the baby country of Bahrain, I seem to have accomplished just that.

He was the first thing I noticed (yes, foolish as it sounds, I have assigned my hunk of stone a gender) upon driving from the Bahrain International Airport on that fateful day in November 2008, to my tourist hotel for a vacation, other than the palm trees, minarets and road signs in Arabic that I had already come to love about this part of the world.

He was an announcement that I had arrived, welcoming me to a place I never thought I would be lucky enough years later, to call home.

During my vacation stay for the next two weeks, he was the first sight of my mornings, over-seeing the daily hustle and bustle of the central market when I opened my drapes to the new day. And he had moods as well; at times displaying a jubilation of fountains from within his spokes, in the evening he would light up in neon colours. Returning from my daily tours, the moment I saw him looming in the roundabout I knew I was approaching my hotel, he was my romantic landmark in an as yet unknown country.

He was also the last sight I remembered on the sad departure back to the airport for my dreaded return flight to New York.

Considering myself well-travelled by now, I could not explain my attraction for this simple form of a pearl reaching for the sky; surely less magnificent than the temples at Luxor, Michaelangelo's David or the Taj Mahal, but for me it held a special significance of the romance of Arabia, my land of dreams.

During the several months that followed, I came to hate this monument, for its mere existence, for the fact that I knew it was sitting here twelve thousand miles away where it would no longer greet my mornings and wish me a neon goodnight, living in a place I so longed for, but could not have.

Until I could arrange the next vacation from my tedious office job and tedious life in New York, anticipating the sight of him again like an old friend who has been waiting for your return. And he did not disappoint, bringing tears to my eyes at the first sight of him still standing in his assigned spot as I again arrived from the airport. So much did I begin to love this piece of stone that I insisted of the hotel management I must have a room from where I could see him.

Of course the affection worsened with time, making it almost unbearable to leave again when the days of my brief vacations ticked to an end. By now I had photographed this icon from every angle at every time of day, from the sunrise peeking through his spokes to gleaming bright white in the midday light, to standing at a perfect angle through which to see the sunset sinking leisurely into the Arabian Gulf behind him. Every photo brought tears to my eyes as I captured it since I was already dreading the next departure and the long months of cold greyness which would return to my sight in New York and replace this magnificence.

Of course I purchased all the standard tourist baubles in his image: key-chains, fridge magnets, miniature replicas, reams of post-cards. Which I found only worsened my longing to return every time I looked at them when I was back in New York, for what had now become just another stint in hell before I could get back to Bahrain again and my pearl.

And so it went, for the next two years, as often as I could return. Both the tears of joy upon arrival and the tears of despair upon leaving grew at increasing speed, like some horrible roller-coaster ride you subject yourself to for the exhilarating thrills until you feel the downward sickness overtaking them.

My existence in New York got progressively worse, first being diagnosed with gastrointestinal bleeding ulcers caused by stress and requiring hospitalisation for surgery, although not given a good prognosis from my doctor as to how long this stop-gap procedure would last, if at all, since it was at that point only experimental and not enough follow-up statistics had been gathered from surviving patients.

This wonderful news was immediately followed by the loss of my job due to the downward spiralling US economy, and so the ensuing days were largely spent hiding under the blankets of despair, worsened every time I looked through my Bahrain photo albums and saw this monument that haunted me. I reached a point in my depression where I wished I had never seen it or Bahrain, since it was now surely out of my grasp forever, given that I had been told by the doctors that it was not medically advisable to undertake such a long flight in my post-surgery condition.

Life in New York became a depressing monotony; I didn't even bother looking for another job largely because there were none to be had at my age, and so I subsisted on the meagre unemployment insurance payments from the government, which soon resulted in foreclosure notices being received from the bank, since this amount was not enough to pay the mortgage on my condo. The mailbox also began to contain salutations from other bill collectors.

At this point I no longer cared however, since my health was continuing to deteriorate, I was just waiting to die. And actually wanting to die if I could not return to my pearl and the country I felt I belonged in. I wanted him to be the last thing I saw in this life but knew I could not make the flight even to fulfil this wish.

Then one day I came across a quote, which I felt was a sign from Allah; it read:

'Happy Are Those Who Dream Dreams
And Are Willing To Pay The Price To Make Them Come True'

That decided it. I cashed in whatever savings I had, placed the condo for rental with a broker, packed the few things I wanted to take and had them loaded on an ocean freighter bound for the Middle East, and I purchased a one-way ticket to Bahrain, doctors be dammed. If I died during the flight, at least I would die trying to get back to my pearl for one last time.

Of course all my friends in New York said I was crazy, but I already knew this. I felt I had no choice. There was no way they could have understood.

And I made it, the bump of the aeroplane wheels on the runway at Bahrain International Airport being the most reassuring feeling I had ever experienced, knowing that in a very short time I would again see my pearl.

And there he was, as the taxi approached Manama, like a sentinel of security in my damaged world.

This time I decided to stay in the souq however, to make my little money last as long as possible, but I knew he was still out there down the road to insure a peaceful night's sleep, something I was never able to attain in New York.

Amazingly, upon a visit to my doctor here a few weeks after my arrival, my blood test results all showed a vast improvement, as did my low blood pressure which was now within the normal range, and I have had no further episodes of gastrointestinal bleeding since living in Bahrain. My doctor, who had hitherto placed me on a check-up schedule for every three months, told me that if my health continues to improve, he would then instead place me on a schedule of only every six months.

I am of course not claiming a miracle cure could be brought about by a sculpture, but I definitely feel it was instrumental in removing my stress, which was causing the ulcers, which in turn were causing the bleeding... like a vicious cycle.

Thanks to my improving health, I subsequently began searching for a flat and found one in Naim, coincidentally right down the road from my pearl, the first thing I see when exiting my apartment building each morning. And when giving directions to any visitor needing to find my building of residence, I happily announce: "I live right down the road from the pearl roundabout."

And every night when I go to sleep, I know he will be out there, my sentinel of security possessing the magic power to keep all the bad things of the world from reaching me. And I've never been happier in my entire life. Now I am secure in the knowledge that I will never have to leave him again.

I'm so glad I took the risk and listened to my heart instead of reason....

Note: Lillian's beloved Pearl monument was demolished on 18th March, 2011, by government forces as part of a crackdown against the Bahraini uprising.

HOORA

by

Hameed Al Qaed

Sleeping in the centre of my soul
oh … my Hoora
the pearl of all towns
the water nymph who has lost her sea
inside you birth of the dream
inside you the dream that will never end
you are living jasmine inside me
as the heart sustaining my body

Companions have deserted you
revolutionists fallen from their horses
the carts of time run over them
your best lovers have gone
dreamers ceased to dream
all those dear faces
all those eyes
which were swollen of dreaming
all disappeared in the breastwork of time
or extinguished in graves

you are yet alive, in the dim of my memory
'Hameed' is still playing
in your desecrated lanes
a child without a bicycle
dreaming on your sea-shore
which lies buried in coffins of sands

oh.. Hoora
the queen of all cities
the beautiful lady
whose jewels were stolen
I still find you dancing my blood
much like those good old days
though the years may have changed you
and me in their way

HOORA

{ HAMEED AL QAED }

oh… Hoora
memory of loneliness
our early innocence
in your soil we hide our slogans
our books
our pens
witness to a premature dream

oh… Hoora
you… grave of dreams and talismans
to whom will you tell your secrets
the lovers have gone
even your sea has gone
who will entertain you now
other than your busy memory

Hoora is a small town where the poet was born and lived part of his life.

THE VILLAGE CLOCK, A'ALI

by

Lorraine Charlesworth

The hands of the clock in the village square are stilled.
They hold time, frozen.
They are oblivious to the glory of the sunrise,
The shifting heart of the sun.
They are immune
To the blinding rays of the silver moon.
The winds of change will not touch them,
Memory of things past
Will not linger in their grasp.
The birds build their nests,
Spatter the face of time with dirt.
And still time does not pass.
No memory assails them as they wait, silent.
No heartbeat moves them onward.
The mechanics of their movements are mute.
The bells of continuance do not measure
Time as a treasure.

THE VILLAGE CLOCK, A'ALI

{ LORRAINE CHARLESWORTH }

They do not glory in the march of progress.
They do not wipe away the tears from the face
As the mind sees the lines of age.
They do not question and rage,
As the seconds turn into hours, the hours into days.
The endless days into week and months and years
That record the senselessness of life.
They do not mark the calendar with meaningless memories.
The hands of the clock in the village square are stilled.
They do not brush off time,
for time no longer exists.
It has no meaning.

THE MYSTERY OF BAHRAIN

by
Bron Vanzino

Bahrain was a mystery to me when I arrived two years ago. It was a very different place than Australia where I had been living. Solving the mystery gave me a sense of achievement but required effort. For me the effort was physical, emotional and mental, as I journeyed through Bahrain's unknown culture, religion, history and social practices. Getting to know Bahrain was complex but now Bahrain will always have a special place in my heart. I would like to tell you why...

BAHRAIN, A MYSTERY IN TIME

MYSTERY IN THE PAST

When I first came to Bahrain I was astounded to know how many old artefacts and historical remains were on the island. They seemed terribly precious to me because they were so ancient; our oldest house in Australia is just over two hundred years old. In Australia, we have indigenous Rock Art and stone tools but not the structures and details of past civilisations. There have been many 'visitors' to Bahrain, warring for a stake of the island, including the Assyrians, Persians, Arabs, Portuguese and British. The tension between nations around the island still continues, evidenced by the presence of the American Fifth Fleet.

'Bahrain' - the word - means 'two seas'. This refers to the presence of fresh water springs under the sea in certain places which flow into the surrounding salt water. The mystery deepens about these springs because legend says that Bahrain sits in a part of the original area of the Garden of Eden. Eden and two of its rivers are said to be covered now by the Arabian Gulf.

THE MYSTERY OF BAHRAIN

{ **BRON VANZINO** }

The enigmatic Tree of Life in the middle of the island which I have visited, is reported to be over four hundred years old and survives in a desert area, where there is no water supply. Its name is linked to the legend of the original Garden of Eden story and its survival connects the island to the original human habitation. Some say there are unknown springs of fresh water beneath the ground that feed the tree. The magic of Bahrain lived for me the day I went out to the tree and saw an archaeologist and his team uncovering a whole village, one thousand years old. There were pots on the stoves, he said, and I saw whole pottery artefacts intact being lifted out of the kitchen area of one of the remains. The dry hot sand had preserved the things over time, beautifully.

Many scholars identify the island of Bahrain with the land of Dilmun which the Sumerians believed was the original centre of culture and where agriculture and irrigation began. It was reported to be a lush place but, more importantly, held the very secret of immortality. In their sacred texts, the ancient hero, Gilgamesh, set out to find the flower of life in the land of Dilmun. It was described as the place where waters flowed together. He failed to bring the flower home but did reach Dilmun, the land of peace and purity. Dilmun was also the place where the survivor of The Flood had been directed to live and so all of these stories point to ancient Bahrain being a kind of starting point in human history. By being in Bahrain and learning about its past, I felt close to the early humans on earth.

All these legends around the dawn of human history were further enhanced when I later travelled the short distance to Salaleh in Oman and saw Ayoub's (Job's) tomb. The fact that he was fourteen foot tall and had left his actual foot imprints was just amazing. I had always admired him from my reading of his ordeals and faith but he became more real to me after visiting his land and his place of rest. After returning to Bahrain from Oman, I discovered Sinbad the Sailor lived in Oman and he was supposed to have built a ship in Bahrain. All these matters have made Bahrain a rich experience for me.

MYSTERY IN THE PRESENT

Bahrain is deeply shaped by its location. Above all as recorded in history, Bahrain was a port of call for traders. It connected Sumer with ships carrying copper from Oman. It traded with those going west to Arabia on the Silk Road, or even beyond to Egypt, and those coming from the Indus Valley to the east with cotton goods. Bahrain mixed many cultures through its trade and developed tolerance and respect for all people, after all that is good business.

The confluence of cultures has meant the identification of the face of Bahrain is a mystery because Bahrain has so many faces: Arab, Indian, Persian and European even Asian. Bahrain has a mixed lineage in its people. To come to Bahrain is to see many different types of Bahrainis.

Since coming to Bahrain I have discovered it is not far from anywhere. It has been easy for me to travel to other parts of the Gulf, to Asia, to North Africa while many of my friends have been to Europe and the Mediterranean. Similarly, many people who work in Bahrain travel, or have travelled, a great deal simply because they easily can, from here.

So Bahrain is exotic at many levels: its past and its present, its native people and its new workers. The island of Bahrain forces people to respect their differences because they are all in one small place, flowing together like the two seas.

MYSTERY IN THE FUTURE

People have different ideas about what they want for the future of Bahrain; these ideas sometimes conflict. History teaches that there are waves of change but none last. Bahrain gives the beauty of its timeless history to those who take time to discover its rich past.

BAHRAIN, THE MYSTERY IN ITS GEOGRAPHY

THE GEOGRAPHY OF ITS FIRST INHABITANTS

The earliest historical substance we have in Bahrain is the huge number of ancient burial mounds (over one hundred and seventy thousand) which are between four and five thousand years old. These are evidence that the Sumerians thought the island a kind of holy place suitable to deposit their loved ones. These graves give credence to the legend of Bahrain being an original site of human culture. The mystery remains of what exactly these ancient people were identifying with, in the land of 'Dilmun', as they called it. It seems it was the closest place to heaven they could find on earth to put their loved ones. Nowadays Muslims are buried facing Mecca and the Kabbah, the holiest place on earth for Islam, so their loved ones are pointed towards their hope of resurrection. There is no doubt that the Sumerians had specific beliefs, as the bodies are buried in a uniform way; infants are to the south of the burial chamber and orientation of the mounds laid out according to astronomical charts.

THE GEOGRAPHY OF ITS POPULATION

There is no doubt that the whole human family is represented in Bahrain today, there is someone from every country: the Middle East, Asia, the subcontinent of India, and the United States. You can meet Europe without leaving Manama. This has been a privilege for me to meet so many different cultures of people; in a sense, I didn't need to travel.

Trade is still the foundation of Bahrain. This is the reason why Bahrain is unique; its geographical position. Trade brings wealth but means getting markets, getting markets means being open to all prospective custom. Hence trade is the driver for much of the openness in Bahrain. Enhancing trade by a tax free zone has accentuated the attraction to the island.

Nowadays there has been such a large influx of people from outside countries because of the availability of jobs in the service and construction industries, that tension has developed about the limit of Bahrain resources to accommodate so many people. Some feel that huge numbers like this are endangering Bahrain and there should be restrictions on numbers coming in.

THE FACE OF BAHRAIN

As well as a huge 'guest' population, Bahrain has a number of people who have chosen to stay permanently after coming here for work. Native Bahrainis have roots in many countries but mainly Arabia, Iran, parts of Pakistan, India and Kuwait. Many of them maintain links with these original families and forebears.

With so many races represented, it is not surprising, food from every country can be obtained. Food is a main industry in Bahrain, from high end culinary design to exotic roadside sandwiches. There are also traditional Bahraini dishes but they are not staple diet of most Bahrainis instead Bahrainis enjoy a wide choice of food cultures.

Bahrain shares its hospitality with food and a wide smile, but helpfulness is also a big part of Bahrain. Respectful behaviour is mandatory in social life: 'everyone' must be greeted formally, and honour is especially given to elders, women and those in need of charity. It is a dignified society and to the credit of the nation, the younger generation in Bahrain have traditional values of respect. A high price is paid for crimes which break the social standards of honesty, safety and consideration of others at all times.

The beauty of Bahrain is that it does not 'belong' to any 'one' place or people. Some people would say it 'belongs' to the Arab world or it 'belongs' to the Arabian Gulf. The historical facts above show that such claims are too narrow to define the breadth of Bahrain. Bahrain is a truly international place. This is not to say it is neutral, no, there is a strong Arabic flavour, but it is blended with many, many nuances.

THE MYSTERY OF BAHRAIN'S RELIGION

A FORGOTTEN HOLY LAND

Sacred sites are sprinkled all over the world. Some are still relevant to existing inhabitants; some are forgotten. Bahrain's link to the sacred land of Dilmun is misted by time. Without written documents it is difficult to know the significance of what was identified in the Bronze Age in Bahrain. As I trekked to the desert to see the Tree of Life, the blank desert scene around with its nearby sea could easily be filled (in my imagination) with ships of people bringing their loved ones and hoping to achieve immortality for them by burying them in the land of Dilmun. The National Museum is filled with ancient treasures like ivory seals and ancient jewellery, thousands of years old, a preserved but silent testament to a lost world that Bahrain reminds us about.

A STRONGHOLD OF ISLAM

The Christian church in Bahrain was on the edge of the Roman Empire and at a distance enjoyed a measure of independence. Islam arrived in the seventh century, fourteen hundred odd years ago, recent by Bahrain's ancient history standards. Islam overtook Christian Bahrain and was a launch pad for the spread of Islam in the region. Now there are Christian, and other places of worship on the island to cater for the diverse working population. Muslims in Bahrain are tolerant of other faiths and have remained fairly impervious to extreme ideas of Islamic religion. Calls for prayer echo over the island as Bahraini people remember their vows to Allah. Because of the working week, Friday is the Sabbath for Christians and the only day off for many. Bahrain's society is a testament to the reality of completely different faiths living together peace, something that some other countries are not yet able to achieve. Bahrain gives dignity to all Godly faiths.

THE MYSTERY OF BAHRAINI CULTURE

A LAND OF UNIQUE PEOPLE

One day I met a stranger in a sleek modern designer café in Bahrain and we fell into conversation. She had lived in Bahrain many years before when her family was young and had come back to visit her old friends. After talking about various places she had lived and travelled, I asked her what she thought was special about Bahrain. She did not say the history or the geography as I expected. Instead she said:

> *"The thing that is special about Bahrain is the people themselves. They are special."*
>
> A woman from Seychelles

The people in traditional Bahrain grew up in houses without roads between them. The children all played in the narrow pedestrian walkways between houses. These were their backyards for games. Generations of families lived together. Men worked together singing, whether fishing, pearling, weaving or praying. There were drums and music and lots of songs. There were stories and legends. Traditional meals were had together in houses. Families ate together and celebrated together. Daughters worked with the older women of the house. People were hospitable to their neighbours, strangers and travellers. It was a communal way of life. Somehow modern Bahrainis have preserved the strong sense of human bonding and community that many other modern societies have lost. That is what makes Bahrainis unique and beautiful. The mystery is they are living according to their religious instructions.

Dilmun means 'dignity' and that is what Bahrainis give to modern life. This ancient land has kept its link with the centuries old ways, the 'old days' when travellers depended on hospitality, when sailors worked together as a team for their survival, when there was time for family and for God. The family was the social welfare system. This is the true heritage of Bahrain: it link with traditional human culture.

A vestige of this social principle can be seen in Kurar House where tourists can discover the traditional craft of gold thread being embroidered on the decorative border of traditional clothes. Women spin the gold threads and then as a team plait and sew the delicate threads onto the fine cloth. The work must be done together; it takes many hands and synchronisation as well as a great deal of love.

THE FINAL WORD

A powerful symbol of Bahrain is the pearl, a thing of great beauty. Bahrain pearls were famous for their unique colour which derived from the fresh sweet water springs which streamed into the shallow saline oyster beds. Even Bahrain's pearls are unique. It is a land specially favoured and I am glad that I discovered it: its history, its human geographical diversity and the kindness of its people.

THE ARAB HORSE

by

Lorraine Charlesworth

Fly with the wind, my Arab steed, across the desert sands.
Dance in the swirling storms of dust, and swim the restless seas.
Oh, that my heart could beat with yours, in the first light of day,
When the mist drifts beneath the palms and the world begins to play.
When the seas are mirrored silver, and silence stills the air,
If only we could gallop into the future without care.
Run with the wind as it breathes o'er the land,
Answer to the touch of my guiding hand,
With your lengthening stride, speed away from those who do not understand.
Your spirit bold and rare.
Oh, dance, my Arab steed, through the star flecked night,
When the crescent moon is gravid with sorrow,
And you flee the darkness of tomorrow,
With your neck stretched you race the shadows drawing near.
And your breath is heavy with fear.
The darkness of the present rides with crop and spur.
Fly from the future when the tracks of time are marked by rubber wheels.

When the water of life is dense with oil,
And pollution is on the wind.
Our souls touch through eternity,
Your beauty and grace are the realities of fantasy,
Your tossing mane and flowing tail,
The deep chest that is filled with heart,
The soft eyes and the flaring nostrils as you breathe deeply of life.
The horse that has danced through the dreams of man,
The Arab horse.
You are valued for the grace and beauty of your breed.
Oh let us ride together with pride, my Arab steed.

MY BAHRAIN MY HOME

by

Hasina Patel

It's 6am. The golden sun slowly rises over the azure waters of the Arabian Sea, casting a reflection that looks like liquid gold. A gentle breeze rustles in the air and the water crashes against the wave breakers. Fishermen are slowly trudging around getting ready for a day of work. Early morning joggers beat the paths on their road to fitness. A plane lands in the distance and the roads are bustling. I am filled with a sense of calm and joy. It's been five years since we moved here from South Africa, and I can't imagine living anywhere else, Bahrain is my home.

I remember when my husband told me we were moving to Bahrain. I was both excited and afraid; excited because I had always wanted to live in a foreign country and afraid because I had never even heard of this place before I went online to research Bahrain, and could barely see it on the map; it was a tiny dot. I was thrilled though to find out that it is an archipelago made up of the mainland and many smaller islands. Our move was so impulsive there was little time to think about the implications, we just packed up and moved. It was an adventure of a lifetime; we were both young, with no responsibilities and the world at our feet. And if it didn't work out we would just go back home and start over.

I had been waiting for this adventure my entire life.

Bahrain is pronounced 'Bahh' 'rain,' and not 'Ba' 'rain' as many non-Arabs refer to it. It is a tiny desert island in the Arabian Peninsula about an hour's flight from Dubai. In some ways it is very much like Dubai, but also completely different. Bahrain is a forward thinking and modern Arab nation; there are skyscrapers and big shopping malls with more than enough shops to accommodate any taste. But the best part is that Bahrain has maintained its Arabian culture; family is the cornerstone of Bahraini society with the mother being the most important member, and it is not unusual for Arabs to sacrifice their own desires and goals to make their parents happy.

In the Arab world smoking is a part of the culture and in the evenings you will find Arab men gathered together in the outdoor cafés smoking shisha, while the women sit on their doorsteps chatting away. Shisha is the traditional eastern way of smoking using a water pipe in which the water cools the smoke, (this is something you have to try in your time in the Middle East, and I highly recommend the double apple flavour).

Bahrain has always been famous for its pearls and this was the main source of income until the discovery of oil in 1932. It was the first country in the Arabian Gulf to have oil wells sunk. The discovery of oil in Bahrain brought prosperity and modernity to the country. The Bahrain National Museum houses many ancient archaeological artifacts and shows the growth of the country from its ancient roots to the modern country of today. Visiting the museum was the first time that I discovered that Bahrain has both a rich and interesting history. It also gave me a very nice introduction to the Arab lifestyle and is a must-do for anyone visiting or new to Bahrain. The exhibits I enjoyed the most were the ancient burial mounds. There is an actual mound which dates back to 2800BC, taken from the desert and reconstructed in the museum showing the structure and the content of these graves. These burial mounds used to be scattered all over Bahrain, but today there are very few left. Driving past them, they are very easily mistaken for mounds of dirt but hidden underneath are stories of an ancient people.

Other very interesting exhibits in the National Museum are the ones that display the culture and lifestyle of Bahrainis. They show scenes in the life of a typical Bahraini, from birth to death, with life-size models and using music and sounds to set the scene. One of the exhibits also displays a Bahraini wedding, which is such a colourful and joyous event. I once had the opportunity of attending a Bahraini wedding, and there were many similarities to Western weddings, like the beautiful white wedding gown and the beautifully dressed women, but the Arab culture was also very conspicuous. All guests were sprayed with perfume as we walked in the door as a welcome gesture. The ladies were dressed so beautifully in revealing designer clothing, all made up with lovely hair-dos, and there wasn't a man in sight! The music was blasting and all the ladies got up onto the stage to dance. Then suddenly there was a hush and within seconds every woman covered themselves from head to toe; the groom, with his father and father-in-law had come to see the bride. I think it's just so wonderful how they manage to include their religion into their culture so perfectly. The thobe and abaya are more Arab culture than Islamic attire as is commonly misunderstood. They were actually invented to serve as protection against the weather and elements faced by Bedouin on a daily basis in the desert years back. In fact non-Muslim Arabs wear also abayas as part of their culture.

Bahrain embraced Islam in 629AD and was one of the first places in Arabia to become an Islamic state. In Bahrain people are allowed to practice their faiths freely and you will find many places of worship here besides mosques. Growing up in a Western country, as a Muslim we have always had to make more of an effort when it came to religion. Here our religion is built into our daily lives. The Bahraini flag has five points which reflect the five pillars of Islam; belief in God, Prayer, Fasting, Charity and going on Pilgrimage. Malls have prayer facilities and everyone breaks for prayers during events or meetings.

Ramadan is a joyful month where everybody fasts collectively, and then we all celebrate Eid together. We don't have to use valuable vacation days for Eid or other important religious days, since in Bahrain they are already public holidays. For Muslims, all the food here is halaal so we are not limited to the non-alcoholic, vegan options on the menu! Halaal means permitted or lawful in Arabic, it describes the food that is allowed to be consumed according to Islamic guidelines. Prohibited food includes pork or pork by-products, animals that were dead prior to slaughtering, animals not slaughtered properly or not slaughtered in the name of Allah, blood and blood by-products, alcohol and carnivorous animals. The only downside to being able to eat anything is gaining a lot of weight, buy hey... you only live once, right?

My first thought on arriving in Bahrain was that it was so clean. The roads were perfectly lined with palm trees and lovely white and red flowers which I later discovered were the colours of Bahrain. Cars actually drive within the lanes, which was not what I experienced in other Asian countries where the road markings are ignored and driving requires some serious skill. Don't be surprised if you see a turquoise BMW, cerise pink Lamborghini or even a metallic gold Land Cruiser on the roads, as people like to make a statement with their cars. Residents are always complaining about the traffic which I find so amusing since Bahrain does have traffic, but it's by no means as bad as the traffic in most major cities around the world. That said, I have used traffic as an excuse many times for being late and it is easily accepted! I used to get so lost when we first moved here because no one knows the street names. They give directions using landmarks, most of which I didn't know. Now I'm one of 'them' and have gotten completely used to giving directions using landmarks, in fact if someone mentions a road name I get confused because I don't pay attention to that any more.

In Bahrain you are surrounded by water and driving almost anywhere you will be able to appreciate the beautiful sea views. The land reclamation here amazes me, one day you are in an apartment that has a sea view, and the next day there's a huge building in front of you. The lovely pink Gudaibiya palace used to be on the sea-front but now there is a whole new area in front of it. Bahrain is developing at a very rapid pace. I don't recall buildings back home coming up so quickly.

I remember finding the newspapers here so amusing. Where was the real news? Someone lost their wallet... and it was returned! Some kids robbed a cold store, and got caught the very next day! Someone broke into a house and fell asleep in the bathroom! This was hilarious compared to the murders, hijacks and rapes that are common in my, (and many other) countries around the world. I thought burglar bars were actually part of the windows until I moved here; you won't see them anywhere in Bahrain. Sure you may ask about all the problems that are happening in Bahrain with the protests recently, but we expats have a joke that as bad as it is here at the moment, it is nothing compared to our daily lives in dangerous cities around the world, where muggings are commonplace and you have to get a new cell phone every few months, not because you want but because someone else has helped themselves to yours and where friends are hijacked, people are murdered in their homes, children are kidnapped every single day. Things like that don't happen here and I know for sure that I feel very safe in Bahrain. My husband, like a lot of other people here, has to travel out of the country for work and he leaves me and my daughter alone without having to worry about our safety, whereas this would not be an option at all in most other countries.

Bahrain markets itself as 'Business Friendly', and the Investor's Centre at the Seef mall is a true testament to that. It is a one-stop-shop for everything you need to set up a new business. We came here to open a business and spent our first two weeks in the Investor's Centre finding out how to do this and gathering all the things that we needed and by the end of it we knew almost every person's name and the entire process of opening a company, from start to finish. It was the most amazing feeling walking out of there with a Company Registration and Bahrain Residence permits in our passports. We had arrived! Many people that we met had originally told us we would need a wastah to get anything done in Bahrain. A wastah is like a 'connection', someone with influence that is prepared to do you a favour; like the saying, 'It's not what you know, it's who you know.' It's a good thing that we didn't listen, because our Company Registration was very smooth since we followed the correct process. I do feel we would have never opened the company as quickly if we had tried to find a wastah and building a connection with him or her. I believe most Middle East governments, and especially Bahrain, have taken steps to eradicate this practice anyway. I am sure finding a wastah occurs all over the world, it's just that here there is a name for it!

Unfortunately for us our business didn't work out and a year later we sold it, however we decided to stay here and see if Bahrain had anything else to offers us. I am so glad we did, otherwise we would have always associated Bahrain with our failure and never gotten to know the true nature of this country. We had realised that in our first year of being here we had hardly experienced Bahrain at all, because every waking moment was spent getting the company going. As difficult as our time was, we somehow found ourselves drawn to stay. I don't know if it was the relaxed lifestyle, or the safety aspect.

Getting a job once you are in Bahrain is not easy, so if you are thinking of doing that, I would advise you to think again. After we sold our business, it took my husband and me a long time to find jobs and get settled. As a local hire, you don't get many of the benefits that expat staff get. However I was fortunate to eventually get a job in a Ministry and I feel it was a perfect way to get to know the locals, since most of the employees are Bahraini. They are such courteous, friendly and generous people and it was such a pleasant surprise to discover how respectful the men were, as opposed to the awful comments I had heard about Arab men. People have the misconception that working in a Ministry is one big party but don't be fooled, during my time there I feel like I grew the most in my career and had a dynamic boss who stayed in touch with the trends and was always prepared to try out something new.

From personal experience, and those of friends, it seems that the workplace in Bahrain is more relaxed than many countries, and people here manage to have a very good work and home balance. It can be frustrating when you first arrive, but if you stay here long enough you actually start to slow down and become more relaxed. I feel this actually makes you more productive in the end. Of course another big appeal to working in Bahrain is that it is tax free. I still remember the days when a huge bulk of my salary used to go in taxes which just makes me appreciate Bahrain even more!

I grew up in a very small town in South Africa which didn't even have a movie theatre (actually there still isn't one today). Going to the city for studying and university was a huge adjustment for me, and I never really got used to it. It took me a whole year to build up the courage to drive on the busy highways, and even after years of practice I was still so stressed. Moving to Bahrain has been like going back home to that small town atmosphere with an upgrade! Here, everyone knows everyone but with benefits like big malls and - most importantly - movie theatres. I feel that Bahrain has that small town atmosphere again with a city-like lifestyle. You get the best of both worlds. The way of life is very relaxed and that is one of the major reasons that people find it so hard to leave. Where else in the world can you just toot outside a restaurant and get someone to come take your order, or if you don't feel like going out then your favourite restaurant probably offers home delivery service. Having a maid and driver is a norm and not a luxury. There are laundries all over, not the kind where you go to do your laundry yourself, but the kind where you drop off your clothes and pick them up cleaned and ironed the next day all for small change. If you feel the need, many laundries also offer a pick-up and delivery service, in fact you can get almost anything delivered to your home. It's very easy to get used to all this convenience and luxury.

We live in an apartment that is fully-furnished; our rent includes water and electricity, internet, satellite and twice a week housekeeping. All we had to bring was our clothes! Or not, because Bahrain is a shopper's paradise and the shops stay open till late at night. There is actually more traffic at night than during the day, with all the families out and about. I love the sale season because the sales here are different; the entire store goes on sale and not just a few items that no one wants and that probably won't fit anyway. In Bahrain you are so much closer to wearing designer clothes with many sales going up to seventy percent or more off! I was once almost the proud owner of a nearly affordable pair of Christian Louboutins, if it wasn't for my silly legs that can't handle super high heels. Now I can't help but wonder if I should have just bought them anyway.

You must buy gold jewellery while in Bahrain, the gold is of a very high standard and Bahraini gold is stamped. Pearls are also a very popular souvenir of Bahrain due to the high quality available. You can rest assured that your purchase is the real deal, since cultured pearls are not allowed in the kingdom.

The weather in Bahrain is hot most of the year. The hottest months are June, July and August, with August being the hottest and most humid. Nothing can prepare you for the onslaught of heat as you walk out of an air-conditioned building, but don't worry; most places are air-conditioned and you manage to adjust your life around the heat. People always ask me how we survive the heat of the summer and I don't even feel it any more because we go from an air-conditioned home to an air-conditioned car to an air-conditioned mall. In fact the malls are sometimes so cold that I keep a shawl with me even in the middle of summer. Bahrain gets very quiet in the summer because everyone wants to escape the heat, which it makes it my favourite time here because we have the place all to ourselves.

The best months here are from October to April because the weather is cooler so we can spend more time outdoors taking walks or barbecuing. In December and January it does occasionally get cooler and you will need jerseys but it is by no means freezing.

My husband and I are passionate about travelling, and travelling from Bahrain is very easy too, due to its central location. Fuel here is dirt cheap and it makes road trips very economical, however Bahrain is so tiny you can get from one end to the other in less than an hour and driving through Saudi to get anywhere makes the journey very long and is through the desert. We chose to experience this once and drove from Bahrain to Qatar through Saudi. Getting out of Bahrain over the Saudi causeway is beautiful and you enter Saudi within thirty minutes. The sight of the golden desert with the camels was wonderful and the little patches of black gold brought lots of excitement for the first hour. But then the next five hours were a dreary repetition of everything we had seen, it was like we hadn't moved at all. And most notable for me was that the bathroom facilities on our journey were not very friendly, which is the main reason that we will not undertake a road trip again. However the proposed bridge to Qatar might open doors to future road trips.

During our time here we have travelled to Kuwait, Qatar and UAE in the Middle East, Turkey, Germany, Belgium, Netherlands, India, China, Thailand, Malaysia, Singapore and Indonesia. With our lust for travel this is not halfway enough and we have an even longer list of places we would still like to visit.

Bahrain will always hold a special place in my heart because my darling daughter was born here. After years of focusing on my career I have now chosen to stay at home with my daughter and where better than Bahrain? There are so many activities and groups for kids that we are spoilt for choice. Most places around the island are kid-friendly which is such a blessing. I have been shopping around for schools and there are so many good options, how will I choose just one? It is so comforting to know that my child is safe here. I don't need to worry about her being kidnapped or us being car-jacked. We go around to our activities without a care in the world.

Bahrain is a hodgepodge of different cultures and lifestyles and the Bahraini people are very warm and welcoming. The greeting marhaba is a true testament to this as it means 'welcome'. Locals have managed to preserve their culture and incorporate it into the modern world just as my ancestors did. My heritage is Indian, my roots are South African and Bahrain is my home.

MANAMA SUQ - A CULTURAL FEAST FOR THE SENSES

by

Mary Coons

Cultural immersion distinguishes a tourist from a traveller. And what better way to experience the Arab culture than exploring the historic Manama Suq in Manama, Bahrain.

Located in the Arabian Gulf near Saudi Arabia, this small desert island nation is readily recognised as the leading financial hub of the Middle East. With its rich pearling history prior to the discovery of oil in 1932, the Kingdom of Bahrain has made it a priority to develop and showcase its heritage to visitors under the direction of the Ministry of Culture & Information.

Manama's liberal cosmopolitan city, a popular stopping off point for cruise ships, embraces visitors with its warm Arab friendliness and hospitality. If you find yourself in the kingdom, an evening exploring the historic Manama Suq is an experience not to be missed.

To know a place well, one must walk the ground, talk to the locals, and soak up the history. Let's begin at Bab al Bahrain.

HISTORIC LANDMARK

Built in 1945 and refurbished in 1986 to incorporate Islamic architectural features, Bab al Bahrain – which means 'Gateway of Bahrain' – marks the main entrance to the Manama Suq.

When constructed, this arched building was very near the water. Due to extensive land reclamation over the years, it's now a hearty five to ten minute walk over to the new Bahrain Financial Harbour buildings in order to even glimpse any water… and then the area is punctured with ever-constant construction and further reclamation.

Bab al Bahrain's ground floor houses the Tourist Information office and shop brimming with guidebooks, handicrafts and natural pearls for sale. This might be a good first stop for tourists. Taxis are readily available here for transport back to your hotel or ship.

The Suq's bustling marketplace with its traditional and contemporary shops recently completed two phases of renovation. The prime goal of the project, initiated under the directives of His Royal Highness Prime Minister Shaikh Khalifa bin Salman Al Khalifa, was to re-brand the Manama suq into a significant and self-sufficient urban centre, according to officials, by returning the suq "back to its prominence within the daily fabric of life in Bahrain."

As pedestrians pass under the low arch, they are immediately greeted by a covered roof canopy high overhead, connecting buildings on both sides that are now sporting new facelifts. There is also an exterior walkway on the second level. Known as Bab al Bahrain Avenue, the shaded pedestrian mall – a former one-lane street – features traditional wooden doors and Islamic architectural detail of Middle Eastern suqs, along with and an eclectic mixture of beckoning shops and shopkeepers. The deeper into the suq you venture, the more original and historic details you will see.

VIBRANT MARKETPLACE

As the hot desert sun begins its evening descent across the horizon, the suq begins readying itself from a day-time of deserted alleyways and shuttered store-fronts to a flurry of hustle and bustle of life at dusk. With shops opening between 4pm and 5pm, visitors should plan their outings accordingly. During the week the suq closes at 9pm, but many shops remain open longer on the weekends. In Bahrain, the weekend begins on Thursday evening and ends Saturday night.

The smells and sights abound. Don't miss out on the spice suq. Shopkeepers welcome the opportunity to tell visitors about the history of spices and beam when you comment in awe on the multicoloured spice pyramids they painstakingly create. Suq air is thick with the smells of spices – cumin and saffron – while only a few alleyways over, strong oil-based Arabic perfume fills the air.

Wandering into a corner perfumery shop is a pleasant deviation. The shopkeepers are more than willing to explain the origins of their scents. You'll quickly run out of untested wrist and neck space from sampling the exotic oils. And the Arab men – appreciative of Arabic perfume's seductive scents – will take notice when you pass.

Hawkers and traders are not shy as they vie for your attention and summon you over. Whether you are interested in Arabic perfume, knock-off designer watches, 24carat gold jewellery, coveted antiques and regional handicraft, or modern appliances, unusual trinkets, traditional clothing or bright coloured Indian fabric, bargaining – and sometimes intense negotiating – is welcomed and expected. Don't worry about language barriers; English is widely spoken and understood. Although most dealers are Indian, the massive weekend crowds comprise all ethnicities and walks of life.

Most foreigners know about the flowing black robe (abaya) many Muslim women wear, but few are aware of its array of style and embellishment options. In the suq there are literally dozens of shops selling black abayas, yet their embellishments are of every colour possible with highly detailed embroidery and beadwork, and adorned with matching headscarves. Don't believe anyone who tells you that Arab women are not interested in fashion or wearing the most popular clothing and shoes. I can't count the number of women's ornate stilettos I saw peaking out beneath elegantly flowing abayas. And the way they carry themselves as they walk is strikingly dignified yet always respectfully.

Visiting the suq is not just about shopping however. This is an enriching cultural and social experience. Be adventurous. Plan to take your time wandering the narrow streets and passageways of rows upon rows of open stalls, and don't be surprised if you find yourself temporarily turned around. It happens to everyone. After all, that's part of the intrigue of discovering new sights and meeting people of a foreign land; offering an ideal opportunity to converse with locals while asking for directions.

First-time visitors can wander for hours ducking in and out of small alleyways finding themselves originally in the fruit and vegetable area suq only to have spilled out into a paved lane leading into the textile suq with its sensory overload of multi-coloured fabrics. Navigating these narrow, often chaotic, lanes is part of the thrill along with a chattering mix of nationalities and the rise and fall of unknown accents.

MIDDLE EAST CUISINE

Small local ethnic restaurants and coffee shops are everywhere. Cuisine ranges from Thai and Indian to Filipino and Persian. Prices are remarkably reasonable, the food fantastically tasty, and the people-watching immensely interesting. Most restaurants have a family section and Men Only areas. These do not apply to foreigners however.

The Arab locals and Indian expats swarm into the suq during the cool evenings after sunset to sit beneath the cloudless sky playing dominoes, enjoying a flavoured smoke of sheesha and discussing politics. Although spilling over onto the narrow sidewalks, their friendly smiles reassure you that you may indeed weave your way in and around their chairs and tables as you continue on your way. They welcome Westerners and cherish the opportunity to talk if approaches. Although very friendly and interactive, local Arab men will respect your privacy and not draw you into conversation unless you seek it. And if you do, chairs will be instantly offered, a cup of hot tea or Arabic coffee will magically appear, and you can plan on some very interesting conversations with everyday Arab men.

If jewellery catches your fancy, you are in for a rare treat. The suq has two gold suqs. Gold City, located between Al Khalifa and Government avenues, is characterised as a suq within a suq, offering a dazzling array of Middle Eastern and Indian jewellery along with a number of local perfumeries and watch stands. And yes, bargaining is expected here also.

The Gold suq, tucked away in a two-story building off of Bab al Bahrain Avenue, similar to Gold City's jewellery is all 18carat and 24carat gold items. In the Middle East, 10carat and 14carat gold items are not considered or accepted as 'gold' jewellery.

If pearls are more to your liking, Bahraini natural pearls are one of a kind and available for purchase. There are no cultured pearls in this country; only natural – actually, the only natural pearls in the world today – and sold by the gram. It is illegal to bring cultured pearls into Bahrain to sell. Take note that if you do spot an item of interest, it is best to haggle and purchase then and there. Chances are very good that you'll be unsuccessful in retracing your steps to return later.

SPIRALLING MINARETS

Unassuming mosques are interspersed between old and not-quite-so-old buildings throughout the suq where their call to prayer offers a welcoming repose to the constant chattering of foreign dialects. Visitors and those living within the suq neighbourhood quietly slip away to prayer as evidenced by the neat rows of shoes lined up outside mosque entrances. Since the doors are left ajar, passers-by can freely glimpse men in various stages of prayer. Some seven to ten minutes later, they are back within the throngs of shoppers or perched again inside a dark alleyway immersed in hearty conversation.

There's so much to absorb and experience in this traditional Arabic marketplace that given the opportunity of a repeat visit, spending another evening in the Manama Suq would never be a decision regretted.

THE RARE BIRD OF BAHRAIN

by

Maeve Kelynack Skinner

It's not everyday you discover that a tree outside your front gate is a roost for one of the world's rarest species of bird. 'Our' tree was a large acacia growing on wild palm scrub and acacia land in a rural area of Saar.

The first inkling we had of this phenomenon was shortly after we moved into the house when we awoke on a November morning to find four men crouched in the long grass opposite, wielding cameras, tripods and telescopic lenses. Relieved to discover that their lenses weren't trained on us but on the tree, we wandered out to find out what was happening.

"Shhhh – don't disturb the birds," whispered one twitcher (as bird watchers are commonly known). "We're watching the Grey Hypocolius take off on their dawn flight." He indicated the tree which we realised was completely covered in birds, when suddenly a number of them perched on top branches, shot up into the air and in seconds had vanished from view.

For the next ten minutes we were spellbound watching this spectacular avian performance which followed the same pattern over and over again. A new flock of between fifty to one hundred birds would appear from deep within the acacia and assemble on the topmost branches, fluttering and chattering in a distinctive high pitched 'mewing' sound which seemed to summon fellow birds from the surrounding palms. At a given signal undetected by us humans, they rose in a cluster, flying high into the wind and disappeared. Their flight was so fast and so high, that it was impossible to follow their route.

The Grey Hypocolius is apparently the only bird of its particular species in the world. It is small, only about eight inches long; the male is dove grey with white and black tipped wings which when spread, reveal a soft pinky/peach underbelly and it has long tail feathers. Its most distinctive feature is a sleek black mask around the eyes rather like the khol blacked eye of a beautiful eastern woman. The female is merely brown/grey with none of the male's markings.

Its breeding habitats are believed to be in Turkmenistan, Afghanistan and western Baluchistan. It migrates during the winter season between November and April before continuing south into Iran, Saudi Arabia and across the Red Sea to Egypt and sometimes as far afield as Palestine and Oman. Although flocks of Hypocolius have been sighted in these places, for some reason the greatest numbers appear to gather in Bahrain and in particular, around the large acacia tree directly opposite our house in Saar.

The Grey Hypocolius is a very shy bird and rarely spotted due to its mainly inaccessible habitats, so once we realised how privileged we were to be able to monitor the activities of this rare bird from our bedroom window, we became avid twitchers. At dawn, we would pull back the curtains and watch the extraordinary spectacle of the tree come to life from the comfort of our bed, while sipping freshly squeezed orange juice and enjoying a cup of tea.

We don't know why this large acacia was chosen as the pivotal hub of the Hypocolius, but it became clear that the birds treated this particular scrubland area as a winter roost – and had apparently done so for years. In fact a bird-lover came to visit friends of ours in Bahrain and told them that he was desperate to see the Grey Hypocolius which, according to bird spotting experts, could only be seen in Bahrain as it was impossible to gain access to their roosts in Iran, Saudi or elsewhere. His reference was an internationally published book of birds that specifically identified the birds' roost in Bahrain as the very location where our tree stood. Our friends brought the bird-lover to our house and he was was in seventh heaven when he realised his luck in being able to see, close up, the activities of the incredibly rare Grey Hypocolius. We learned that the location of this large acacia tree was in fact the site of the highest ever recorded colony of Grey Hypocolius to roost at one time, numbering one thousand, five hundred.

Over the next few months we grew to learn more about the birds. Unlike other species that fly in a straight direction from one perch to another and usually at a leisurely pace, the hypocolius flies directly upwards at speed into the wind, flying high into the sky where it catches the air stream to propel it towards its feeding grounds. The birds usually arrived in Bahrain in late October and remained for almost six months before they departed in April.

Their daily routine never varied. At night, one large group would spend the night deep inside the sweeping branches of the large acacia, while others slept in nearby palm scrubs and smaller acacias. Perhaps the large acacia dwellers were the 'senior' or 'leader' tribe and the rest came from different migration areas. At sunrise, the site came alive as hundreds of birds darted out of the surrounding thickets and swooped to the large acacia, decorating its branches in a mantle of grey. It was transformed into an avian 'Heathrow'. Their soft 'mewing' became louder and they would chirp and chatter excitedly as they discussed their plans for the day. Fluttering, darting back and forth, swapping places, jostling for position on different branches, they prepared for take off.

Monitoring the precision of their flights was like being a plane-spotter; first, at a pre-arranged signal, one flock would flutter to the topmost branches and perch, facing into the wind, and then suddenly, more than a thousand birds ceased chirping and remained in absolute silence until the 'take-off" signal was given. Then, the first group shot straight up into the air like a NASA space launch to catch the wind, and within seconds had climbed so high that they were barely visible.

Then another flock took their place and settled on the top branches, each passenger jostling for the best seat until there was a full planeload. Again they all fell silent before take off, then rose as one, into the air to catch the wind-stream before veering off in a different direction to the first flock. Just like at Heathrow airport, this pattern continued in regular intervals, taking off a minute or so apart and continued for about twenty minutes until the tree was empty. The birds were well behaved; no queue jumping was tolerated as any miscreant was hustled off the branch. At times up to one hundred birds took flight simultaneously and reached heights of a hundred metres before they found the right flightpath.

On misty mornings, the birds would make a few false starts if they hadn't reached their desired height and would flutter back to the treetop until they gained their equilibrium. Then they would try again to catch the current which propelled them high into the sky.

One very foggy morning the flight plans were badly delayed. When the fog lifted slightly, the first group took off hesitantly, followed too closely by another flock. They all became disoriented in the mist and collided, then swooped back down into the lower branches and postponed their flights, allowing smaller groups to take off before them. This lot cleverly flew low, beneath the mist. It was fun to watch the local bulbuls trying to imitate the Hypos but lacking the streamlined thrust and skills of their feathered colleagues, they kept colliding and falling back onto the tree. Cheeky sparrows who were normally no match for the Formula One speeds of the Hypos thought their luck was in and tried to sneak onto the 'take off' branches - but they were chased off.

At sunset, tiny specks appeared high in the in the opal twilight sky as the birds returned from all directions, flying at full speed towards the acacia where they circled briefly to get their bearings, before plummeting down on closed wings, their long tails stabilising their descent like jets. The chirping and warbling again reached a crescendo as over one thousand birds jostled for space, chatting, sharing news and at sunset, similar to the sunrise take off routine, at each landing, the noise ceased for a second before starting up again.

The precision and timing of the birds' flight routines were spot on. At dawn, they had all assembled by 6.15am just as it grew light and by 6.30am, they were gone. At sunset they appeared en masse at 3.15pm and had all landed within fifteen minutes. The Grey Hypocolius is really an incredible bird.

The Hypocolius alight briefly to drink water from lawn sprinklers or irrigation channels in quiet, private compounds but are rarely seen eating from the ground, preferring to feed on unharvested dates, fruit morsels and insects hidden deep within the foliage of palm trees and thickets. Occasionally aerial feeding on insects has been observed.

Sometimes in the mornings when our red pepper tree was in bloom, the birds would hang around eating the berries and perching on our telephone wires, but they didn't stay long enough to make it a regular feeding stop.

Word about the birds' Bahrain habitat reached the outside world and to our amazement, tour buses of twitchers began to arrive at our gate from the US, Sweden, Holland, France and neighbouring Gulf countries. At one stage there were at least two bus loads a week filled with eager birdwatchers who couldn't believe their luck when they were able to view at first hand, the rare Grey Hypocolius. Cameras clicked, videos rolled as the visitors crept quietly around the tree so as not to disturb their prey. My sons were contemplating setting up a booth to sell water and juices and even hats with 'We've seen the Grey Hypocolius in Bahrain' emblazoned on them!

"This is my seven thousand, six hundred and ninetieth bird sighting," said one elderly American grinning broadly as he climbed back onto the bus. "I've travelled all over the world to see as many species of birds as possible and this is the first time I have seen the Grey Hypocolius. I never thought I'd get the opportunity. Now I can rest easy."

In 1999 we returned from leave to find that all the trees in front of our house had been bulldozed. The lofty, majestic acacia with its large welcoming branches was gone, not even its stump remained. That October, the Grey Hypocolius flew in their thousands from their lofty mountain retreats in the high Karakorams to their favourite roost here in Saar. But when they arrived at the site, they whimpered and mewed in consternation, fluttering around nervously, no doubt wondering where their tree had gone. They tried to find shelter in the scrappy palm scrub on an adjacent empty piece of land and to carry on their traditional lifestyle, flying off each morning to hunt for food but their flight pattern was disorganised; they had lost their citadel.

The Grey Hypocolius left early that year and over the next few years their numbers dwindled, although some valiant souls continued their journey to Bahrain, searching for possible roosts. Before the birds left forever, I was walking my dog one evening trying to spy the occasional small flock when I stumbled upon a group of twitchers from the Bahrain Royal Irish College of Surgeons, who had sadly missed the glory days of the Grey Hypocolius but were then capturing and 'ringing' the birds to identify and count their numbers which at that time, they reckoned were about four hundred.

Shortly after the loss of 'our' acacia, a friend recalled noticing that a large tree in her compound had attracted an unusual type of bird to roost in its branches. One day it was cut down and she watched in dismay as these birds fluttered and circled all night, making crying sounds when they found their home had disappeared. The next day they were gone; she never saw them again.

The country lane outside our gate is today a main highway linking two major arterial road systems and the land of the Grey Hypocolius is now filled with housing estates. In common with much of the world, urbanisation of Bahrain's original farmlands and wilderness finally drove the birds elsewhere. Few people are aware that an acacia tree in Saar once held the still unbeaten world record of hosting the highest recorded number of Grey Hypocolius ever spotted at one roost.

SAILORS COME, SAILORS GO

by

Phari Poitier

Sailors come
Sailors go
Whether they tell the truth or it's a game only them and the good Lord knows

Fantasy Island this is where they will be
Where all your wishes, dreams, and desires can be lived out and no one outside of Bahrain will see

A huge multicultural population where people come from near and far
Having exotic beauties at your disposal 2, 3, 4, or more

Café's, coffee shops, lounges, souq's and shopping malls
Bahrain is the place where you come to play and pay to have it all

No matter what day of the week there is ALWAYS a ladies night somewhere
For what you will pay to fill up a tank of gas in the U.S you can have a spa day, movie date and a five star dinner with a little cash to spare

Salacious rumours, inconspicuous activities, what scandal will be released this week?
Everything can be a tell all book and nothing less than juicy

SAILORS COME, SAILORS GO

{ **PHARI POITIER** }

Men loving all the ladies, ladies loving all the attention
Better be careful 'cause you'll never know whose switch hitting

Mud ducks and chicken heads Bahrain will not exclude
Heck, you can come here and create your own 2 Lame Crew

Tongues telling lavish tales of having whatever you like
But it's really a false statement that always ends in PSYCH!

Marriage proposals, shacking up, 'local spouses' running rampant
Not knowing that there are loved ones else where while they are here doing damage

Misleading, misguiding of what intentions people are truly hiding
For those on a virtuous path BEWARE the temptation of backsliding

Sailors come
Sailors go
If you've never been here then you will never know

This is life, this is Bahrain
Is it Beautiful? Let certain men tell it and they'll gladly exclaim;
"This is my beautiful Bahrain"

HOW THE PEARL GOT ITS LUSTRE

by

Nawf Al Bassam

"Gardens of Eternity will they enter: therein will they be adorned with bracelets of gold and pearls; and their garments there will be of silk. The handsome young boys in paradise are similarly depicted"

(35:33)

Beneath all the layering and the romanticism of history and words, Bahrain can be translated into one word for those crossing the bridge from Saudi Arabia: relief. It is the difference between wearing a completely buttoned shirt and wearing a shirt with the collar unbuttoned. And, like the destination to Eden, there is a bridge…

There are exactly six sections that separate you from restraint, to a sense of normalcy. Three belong on the Saudi border and three on the Bahraini. And, frankly, I cannot begin to count the number of times I have pleaded to God that nothing goes wrong on the Saudi section of the bridge. I always double check: passport - check, permission to travel (from my father) - check, copies of permission - check, twenty riyals to pay for the causeway tax - check. I always had this check-list when going to 'the island,' and never leaving it. Never would it be a problem if I were ever left behind on 'the island'.

In the hours, and sometimes minutes, I travel through the causeway (as if a right of passage), my heart skips a beat and I start to smile when I see that my cellular network has changed from "STC" to "VIVA." My fingers begin to drum to the rhythm of freedom. Bahrain definitely has a beat to it, or at least it did for that particular October weekend…

***

As I walked to the taxi stand outside the shopping complex, I gripped the fingers of little LuIu. Her walk was more like a skip as we left the complex, as her weekly pampering (suited for a six year old her age) came to an end. These four hours of six year-old heaven are a back to back series of gifts, gifts, and more gifts. The slight caveat being that my niece be on her 'best behaviour' … and if lady luck had it, I would take her to buy Hello Kitty, and that is what we did.

Lulu, has the features of her mother and soft yet piercing eyes. There was no way one could get away with a lie around her. Her smile was always that of an expecting curiosity. Over the years I have learned to tolerate the nags, tantrums and the Bambi- looking eyes reeling me in. I learned how to say 'no' to a six year-old, similarly I have just recently learned how to say 'no' to the six year-old within me too, when I saunter into a jewellery shop.

In the midst of cars, a straight row of white-orange taxis aligned themselves and that is how Lulu and I first met Zain; a taxi driver from October to June and a pearl diver from June to October.

I silently sat in the cab, taking note of the Quranic verses on a red velvet fabric with gold tassels hanging from the mirror of the car, and the low volume of the Quran recitation playing in the background. On the dashboard, he had his ghutra, a white cloth that he would wear when he read the Quran. I had hoped that Lulu would not fidget, as there was no telling how long the ride would take in the sea of traffic that lay between us and our destination. Consumed with her Hello Kitty, she paid little attention to the fact that we would be caught in traffic for a while.

"Please take me to the Seef Residence", I requested.

He took his eyes off the road, "No problem, let me just start the meter. Where are you from Shaikha? Are you and your daughter enjoying your time in Bahrain?"

Lulu's silence was broken. She jumped at the taxi driver and said, "Aunty Khulood is not my mommy."

Yes, my dear niece, I am not your mother. I am the poor Aunt who just got her wallet maimed by this darling six year old.

Smiling as my niece set the record straight, I reply "very much so, in fact, I studied high school in Bahrain."

★★★

With the cracking of his knuckles, Zain adjusts the posture of his back as he sits on an old teak wood chair. He grips the side of the table and looks into the map. He then begins…

"I am a diver and thus I will start this story with the ebbs and flow of the sea. The level of the sea was much higher then. I am told that it was four to five meters higher than the tide today. The limestone at the centre of Bahrain is from the sea. The sea made it so that this land was not for ordinary people. You do know that we're going back to 3000BC? That is how deep the layering of this pearl is."

I lay down the tea cup, rummaging through my bag, hoping to find a pen and paper inside the volcanic clutter of belongings; I silently wished I had cleared out my bag today. I was rummaging in a way that I did not lose eye contact with Zain. I wanted him to know that he had my full attention.

Lulu had gone to the edge of the water-front, as if the voice of Zain, along with the ebbs of the waves, took her into as contemplative a state as a six year-old could be in.

I had finally found a pen and started to spell out the date and place of this encounter. '*I want to remember, I want to remember and I want to remember. I want the future to remember, I want the future to remember and I want to remember*'.

As I silently committed to the documentation of this moment, Zain dismissively says, "Khulood. this is not a lesson. You do not need to write anything down".

"But I want to remember, to use it for when I write."

"What will you be writing about?"

"Well, I was thinking of discussing the layering of the pearl, and how the more layers it has, the more of a lustre, and how that really is Bahrain; a composition of layers but all give out one beautiful lustre. I don't know, what do you think?"

"I think you should just listen to me and not write. You can write when it is time for you to write. If information is what you are after, then go to the museum or talk to the historians. I am just giving you a story. Are you ready to listen?"

"Yes, sir".

The history of a story is not simple. It is not written and maybe that is why a part of our history is never pure but rather tainted with the storyteller's perspective. My grandmother told me stories. I never wrote them down.

"The story of Dilmun is the story of ideals - a wish-list if you would like to call it that. I am sure you know that before Islam, the people residing in this land had a different set of beliefs, beliefs that included many gods. I am sure you've heard of this. Well, it is said that the gods looked favourably at this land, so favourably that the god of water supplied us with fresh water for the pearls. At least, that is what is said to have been in scripted on the tablet rock found by the English when they came around. Anyway, these gods were in charge, and thus decided not to save man from a flood. Ziusudra, the last of the Sumerian kings, built an ark and weathered out the flood for seven days and seven nights. Sound similar to the story of Noah's Ark? Anyway, Ziusudra sacrificed sheep and oxen as he submitted to the God of warmth who came out in the middle of the storm, the breaking of the sea and the howling of the winds, to warm Ziusudra. As a reward to Ziusudra, he was sent to Bahrain - Dilmun at the time; 'the place where the sun rises,' known for its peacefulness."

***

The moment I had mentioned that I studied in Bahrain, I knew I had accomplished one of three things in Zain's mind: first being that I positioned myself in the complexities of the fabric of Bahraini society; second, that I understood what Bahrain is in some way; and most importantly third; that this island has given me an education. As I looked outside the window, the reflection of the sun setting in the background of the buildings, mosques and sea-shores never looked so beautiful. Any moment, we would hear the melodic call to prayer. I thought about Monet, and how he could catch the reflection of light onto the water in his paintings. I am sure he could have not captured this sunset.

The calling to prayer is not an interruption but rather a reminder of all that one encapsulates. It is a moment of silence in time. I was told as a young girl that if I were to ask anything of God, it would be granted as I kneeled on all fours during the Maghreb prayers. I was told that one recites verses from the Quran to protect themselves from the Evil during Maghreb Prayer. It is in these moments, I am reminded that the past, present and future were not about me, but something far greater.

"You studied here? So you are our daughter! How did you like it?" interrupted Zain, noticing my wandering thoughts that led to my past. It is so easy for the present to entangle itself with the past and to romanticise. I welcomed his nudge to being present.

"Yes, I graduated in 2003. I loved it."

I remember how the entire school was divided into four houses. Each of the houses would be in competition with one another: Dilmun, Tylos, Argos and Awal. I was in Awal. Once on PE day, the entire school had gone in a shuttle bus to the National Stadium. The stadium was filled with a palette of blue, red, yellow and green against a grassy green backdrop; each colour representing a house.

My performance in the shot-put competition had put in motion a conspiracy to move the Dilmun team. I redeemed myself in the javelin tournament. I never understood the names - and most importantly, the why.

"It seems that Bahrain was good to you," he gently said. He had noticed my grin. Yet, again, I was gently nudged into the present. I looked to the left of my shoulder and saw Lulu with her seatbelt on, kneeling against the window, slowly but surely moving Hello Kitty along the edge of the closed window. She had commenced on a fictitious journey of 'playing house,' as I did when I was her age. Only this time, Hello Kitty was the daughter and Lulu was the mom.

Taking note, I reply to Zain with a reminiscing smile, "Yes, it is. We definitely have a charming relationship."

"Insh'Allah even better times are to come my daughter".

"Listen, could you tell me more about you?" I asked.

★★★

"Look at this pearl, I can taste its layers in my mouth," Zain tells me while holding between his index finger and thumb a tear-drop shaped pearl with a twinkling glow. The lighting in the room gave it a more of a mysterious feel. It was like I was looking at the earring in Vermeer's Girl with a Pearl Earring. It brought out the pool blue colour of the maid's eye in the painting, only to add more to her mystery. When looking at the painting there was no doubt of the beauty of the floating model, or the tear-drop pearl, but there was also a distance and I couldn't understand it, but I definitely appreciated it. Similarly, I could not understand the layers of the pearl Zain held in awe.

In Zain's tiny shack, overlooking the coast and the view of a dhow nearby, which I assume was his, I noticed a closed pearl mussel resting in the weaving of a cotton net on a worn out wooden table, the intensity of Bahrain's summer humidity an apparent cause for the cracks in the wood. The net would be placed around the pearl diver's neck, along with a rock inside of it. A tea-stained map was used as place mat on the table. It was very interesting to see the circling around the different bodies of water. Mounted against the wall was a faded and aged photo of a man posing in front of a dhow. The man's face was dark and eyes were deep if only to point out that this person lived a life in the sun. I could only assume that this man was Zain's father, and that it was no coincidence that Zain was a pearl diver.

Zain offers me some red tea while directing me to take a seat facing the sea. I sit in a manner that would not interrupt the culture of the room.

The sun had set, and the moon reflects itself onto the waves. The stage was set for a story.

"Can you tell me the story of pearls, Mr. Zain? I ask.

"Pearls are not simple. It is a story of layers, but it is beautiful". He says as he takes a sip of his glass of red tea, I can see the tea droplets condense against the glass as he slowly drinks. He then begins…

"The story of the making a pearl is very different than the pearl itself. For example, the red tea that you now drink is very different than the three leaf stem it came from. The making of a pearl, is a story of accepting the other. The pearl itself is a story of layering, and how the beauty of pearl comes from the layering and complexity."

GIBRAN KHALIL GIBRAN, THE PEARL:

"Said one oyster to a neighbouring oyster, 'I have a very great pain within me. It is heavy and round and I am in distress.'

And the other oyster replied with haughty complacence, 'praise be to the heavens and to the sea, I have no pain within me. I am well and whole both within and without.'

At that moment a crab was passing by and heard the two oysters, and he said to the other who was well and whole both within and without pain, 'Yes, you are well and whole; but the pain that your neighbour bears is a pearl of exceeding beauty'."

"It is said that the story of a pearl is a story of Aphrodite's tear when she emerged from the water. Young Greek brides used to wear a single strand pearl necklace, so that they may not shed a single tear throughout their marriage because they carry the tear of Aphrodite around their necks. It would be nice to think of pearls that way. The truth is pearls are nothing more than an oyster's reaction to a foreign object intruding into their inner space. So, why does this become a story of acceptance? Well, it is very simple. The oyster did not fight off the object, but rather took it in; it did not assimilate, but rather accepted the presence of something other than itself. I am trying to teach you something here. I hope you understand why wisdom is of pearls and pearls are full of wisdom."

"The layering of the pearls are even more interesting. It is what gives the pearl its lustre. The more depth it has, the more meaning it holds. The first layer is acceptance and through that a joint history develops, as in the case of Dilmun, through the history, consecutive layers develop. It is very hard to separate one's identity from its history. Once the oyster accepts the foreign object, it develops not only a beautiful object, but a story with it; a story that may become an ornament of a man's love for his wife to place around her neck on their twentieth anniversary. This is how the pearl gets its lustre. Bahrain pearls have the most lustre. So, do you see this pearl? Do you understand it?"

★★★

As I sat in the cab, the mirage of colour and lights, got the best of me, and I got to thinking about Zain as he invited me along with my Bahraini baby niece to his dhow. I left Lulu to her mischief, there was no telling of what the future will be like for Lulu, my pearl. All what mattered was the present. Her story will come. And I hoped that one day I will be able to give her slight anecdotes of mine and she will accept it and build on it...

I was in a completely different realm, the realm of authorship, and thus I speak to you my reader: *"I, the author, have externalised these passages with black ink- hoping that the spirit will somewhat be translated into your realm of consciousness. This country is beautiful, for many reasons- but it is mainly beautiful, in my eyes, because it is a country that embraces. The historical and cultural metamorphosis of this island is reflected in the aggregate of identities, accents and mini-cultures. Like the pearl, Bahrain has many layers and that only further adds to its lustre. The past attests to its present and the future is silent in waiting for its becoming. The beauty in Zain's name, the eternal in my own and the lustre in little Lulu's- she is our future; the eternal beautiful pearl."*

Author's note: The diver's name is Zain- which means beautiful and good. My name is Khulood- which means eternal, and my niece's name Lulu which means pearl. In some way this influenced the narration of this story. Bahrain may be many things, to many different people, past, present and future. Nonetheless, it is a pearl with eternal beauty.

GROWING UP IN BAHRAIN

by

Dilraz Kunnummal

I was born right here on the island of pearls, the Kingdom of Bahrain, or simply Bahrain. My name is Dilraz Kunnummal and I have almost a quarter century of calling Bahrain home, and I doubt if that will ever change.

Every country grows up and my Bahrain too has changed so much that many who lived here long ago would hardly even recognise it today. Even the political set-up has changed and the people are now a lot more international and a lot more open to ideas and cultures, but the warmth and hospitality, that's one aspect that will definitely last forever.

My father is a businessman and he has been here for over thirty-five years. Bahrain, in my opinion, is the most perfect place in the Middle East to live with your family. It's neither the too fast and modern blink-and-you'll-miss-it pace of Dubai, nor the all burka wearing, no entertainment conservative attitude of Saudi Arabia. It is liberal, comfortable and relaxed. There is something about Bahrain that everyone who comes here falls in love with.

I first opened my tiny eyes twenty-five years ago at the Bahrain Defence Force (BDF) Hospital, and I still get a smile on my face every time I drive by there. The first house I lived in is still intact, in one of the by-lanes of East Riffa. The second and third houses, where I spent most of my childhood, have both been demolished to give way to Lulu hypermarket, and I still feel a jab of pain when I drive by where the hypermarket now stands. There used to be a residential compound; thirty-two villas, a nice pathway, swimming pool... the works. My dad's store stood there too, once upon a time. And our flat, prior to moving to our villa, with the shawarma shop, the video store, the garage and the dry cleaners on the ground floor. Now just a big shiny mall! Do note that I have nothing against Lulu, but I just miss the place I grew up in, and when I walk inside the supermarket I silently wonder if that was the place I first fell on my bicycle or if this is the spot where we used to dive into the pool. None of it is there any more, but what's really nostalgic is the fact that if you take two steps back and look around, everything else is still there; the mosque where my dad used to go for his prayers, the football club where my brother first enjoyed the game, the fruit and vegetable store across the road, everything remains except the place where we spent our childhood. Those are now just sublime memories.

Growing up, I didn't live in a Bahrain full of malls and cafés and water parks. The Bahrain I grew up in had none of these. For us, the biggest fun outing was a trip to Al Areen Wildlife Park; feeding the camels, seeing all the animals, gushing over how amazing it all was. Mind you, these treats were only for special days like birthdays or Eid.

And must in everybody's to-do list, was a stay over at Zallaq; take a shack, stay, enjoy the BBQ. I should confess though, I have never actually done it and I have been supremely jealous of everyone who has! It used to - and still does - sound like so much fun, and I vow to do it someday soon. But yes, we did have our trips to Zallaq to enjoy the sun, sand and sea. It was such a pleasure to dip your toe into the waters and to write your name in the sand.

The National Museum was usually the chosen spot for all our school picnics. It was the museum, Zallaq or Adhari Park. But I was one of the few who were always excited about a trip to the museum. It had no beach-front hangout back then, but to me it was still fascinating: the traditional section, with all the women in colourful clothes, weaving, the pearl diving section and the creepy, scary burial mounds section which still gives me the jitters. There was one time when the museum organised a special section on dinosaurs and pre-historic creatures, which came fully equipped with moving dinosaurs and scary noises, it was awesome.

Adhari Park was our favourite too. All the rides were so much fun. I used to love the mini Ferris wheel, the zigzag slide - as I called it - and the bumper cars! They even had a boating ride, if I remember rightly. Although a popular place for many families, for some reason the Hadika Almaeeya water garden in Gufool was not too popular with us; Adhari was where we went as a family and the water garden we went to hang out with our friends.

Every weekend, the family used to head to Marina beach; pack up our dinners and go eat out in the open. Running around with my brother, dad and mum, playing with the beach ball till we got exhausted, and then enjoying a good meal and heading back home for the night.

And everyone who grew up in my generation will tell you how anxiously they waited for the National Day, Dec 16th. Every year on this day the skies of Bahrain would light up with a fantastic show of fireworks. We all would bundle up in our best winter wear and head to the ground in Riffa, or to the National Stadium to watch it, and the area would be thronged by hordes of people; children holding onto their mummy's hand or standing on top of their vehicles or sitting on the shoulders of their fathers. People from all backgrounds and nationalities and ethnicities would be present to witness that spectacular show, year after year. I still wait for 16th December each year, hoping for the replay.

The movies were another very rare treat for us, 'till we became teens and started going off with our friends. My father may have possibly watched only two movies at the cinema in Bahrain, one was Independence Day which I think we watched at Awal cinema and the other Titanic, at Delmon Cinema. Oh wait, I think he also saw Devdas as well. Awal cinema was considered the best when we were growing up, and then Delmon started, and these places were exclusive too. Only the latest English movies, and the tickets were valuable treasures!

My elder brother and I grew up without the luxury of cable television. We had only Channel 55 and some of the other Arabic channels. How we anxiously waited for the 5pm bell. It started with a reading of the Holy Quran, followed by cartoons! Every single day at 5pm, we'd be glued to the telly, if we were home. And the Bollywood movie on Wednesdays, that's one thing we never ever missed. And if I did miss it, I used to be gloomy as hell the next day.

I remember buying our first VHS from the video store: It was Aladdin and it cost a whopping BD3,500fils. We then collected a lot of other great animations like *Snow White* and the other parts of *Aladdin* and *Lion King*, right up 'till *Toy Story*.

One of the most awaited times of the year was the rainy season. We used to run out into it, with our umbrellas and rain coats and boots just for those few drops of rain. It was such an exciting time, we'd wait looking at the darkened skies, just hoping, praying even that it would pour like there was no tomorrow.

I remember the time Seef Mall opened. It was like a totally different world, so thrilling and fabulous. It had so many shops and even a Multiplex. It was so cool to hang out there but now every weekend we go to Bahrain City Centre mall, however, as exciting as it is to shop, I do sometimes miss the old-world charm.

Every time anyone visited Bahrain, our itinerary would more or less be the same: it would include the museum, Al Areen Park and Zallaq, or one of the beaches. A trip to the souq also was must. I still love the look and feel of our souq, it's so earthy and traditional, and so charming.

More than being a religious festival, Eid is a time for national celebrations here in Bahrain. Every Eid, growing up, we used to get up or rather not sleep at all in the process of getting ready. Painting our hands with henna, new clothes and what-not, we'd all be ready in the wee hours of the morning and bundled up in dad's car to go to the Grand Mosque.

It was always one huge happy family gathering. We'd meet so many people we knew, and so many people we had never met before, all smiling at each other and wishing '*Eid Mubarak*' with the three kisses on the cheek. Jalabiyas, thobes, kurtas, long dresses, abayas, we'd see people dressed in clothes from all across the world. That atmosphere is truly representative of life here; it is indeed one of joy, of a blessed life, of multiculturalism and of celebrating moments together.

I am Indian and one of the best aspects of being Indian in Bahrain is that you can revel in it. Honestly, you get to enjoy the best of both worlds. I have never had to compromise on my Indian identity while living here, but that doesn't make me any less of a Bahraini, even if my official citizenship states otherwise.

I have realised I have celebrated more Indian festivals that my cousins and friends who actually live in India, and I have been exposed to more Indian culture, arts and crafts than I would have living in India. It only goes on to show how welcoming the Bahraini community is. Possibly because living in any place in India you are only exposed to that one culture, whereas here you have people from all across India and other parts of the world. We have communities and places to practice, not just religion but our own native cultural aspects and have a large number of organizations in Bahrain catering to the different backgrounds of Indians; there is the Indian Club and the Indian Ladies Association which are open to all. Then we have associations like the Bahrain Keraleeya Samajam, the Young Goan's Club, Maharashtra Mitra Mandal and so on and so forth. We are exposed to a multitude of cultures and are able to learn and imbibe the best from them.

I am a Keralite and I have practically grown up and spent years of my childhood at the Bahrain Keraleeya Samajam, which is an association for all people hailing from Kerala. I remember when it used to be a small building in Gudaibiya where the South Park restaurant is currently situated. Now it is a sprawling campus in the heart of Segaiyya with three halls and parking for over three hundred cars, and that in itself is a testament to the faith and strong relation between the Bahraini and Indian community.

Growing up, I have learnt Bharatnatyam, Mohiniyattam and Kuchipudi, which are all classical dance forms of India. And there are many like me who have also learnt these dance forms. It was only possible because of how easily available this has been in Bahrain. There are teachers all across the country teaching these classical dance forms and, more importantly, there is more than one platform where you get to showcase these talents. We are now even able to buy the costumes and jewellery for these dances here, we no longer need for them to be specifically brought in from India.

Right up 'till I returned to India for my higher education, for more than eight years, without fail I had celebrated Eid, Diwali, Onam and Dussera. Every year I also enjoyed the Onasadya and the Dandiya during Dussera. But during the five years that I spent studying in India, there wasn't a single year where I got to do this.

By the way, I really do think that every Keralite who comes to Bahrain will feel perfectly at home because of the large number of Malayalam speaking crowd here. I doubt if there is any cold store or high-end office where a Keralite is not present. I have also even come across a few Bahrainis who speak Malayalam fluently.

Bahrain also has some absolutely great Indian restaurants, where we can enjoy the cuisines from different parts of India. We even have a chaat place and even a puttu-kada, which specialises in the rice cake delicacy of Kerala. Fine dining, or a full meal for just 1BD, there is a complete range of choice here.

And I have been pleasantly surprised time and again by the sheer love Bahrainis have for Bollywood. Even though the Wednesday movie no longer comes on Channel 55, the latest movies are always released in the theatres here. Hey, not just Bollywood, even regional Indian movies are released here on time!

I remember when Indian superstar Rajnikant's film *Shivaji* was released in Bahrain, the entire Gudaibiya area where Al Hamra Cinema was located was flooded with people. They were crowding onto the roads and it looked like a sea of people. For a moment, it felt like I was back in Chennai.

Just recently, as editor for a magazine, I interviewed a young Bahraini photographer whose dream was to do a photo-shoot with Bollywood star Aishwarya Rai Bachchan. His knowledge on her life and her movies was quite in-depth, I don't think even I knew much of it.

During my days as a reporter, I have covered numerous activities of the Indian Embassy and was thoroughly impressed by their efficiency and by the support that the Embassy has had from the Bahraini authorities.

There are also plenty enough stores here selling Indian fruits and vegetables, and other Indian foodstuffs, and even Indian clothes; Sarees, salwars, lehengas all of them are easily available, and not at a price that will kill you. As a matter of fact, believe it or not, I actually purchased my engagement lehenga from right here in Bahrain.

Even in terms of education, we have the option of choosing the Indian Central Board of Secondary Education (CBSE) and, as far as I know, Bahrain is one of the few countries in the region where both locals and Indians are allowed to study the Indian syllabus.

I am an alumnus of the Indian School and I am proud to say that I was part of it during its glory years. At school, we all grew up with a large number of Bahraini friends, and it was always a pleasure to teach them about India and its culture.

I remember when one of my Bahraini friends came home for dinner and we had to teach him how to eat and enjoy our meals. He was so confused and didn't know what to eat with what, and it was also so funny to watch him eat with his hand. Not that he couldn't enjoy the food with cutlery, but all of us, him included, had more fun making him eat with his hand.

At school, we were taught both the Indian and Bahrain national anthems and most of us sang both with equal pride and fervour. We also hold up the Bahraini flag with as much respect and love as we do for the Indian flag. I have always loved watching dances to Khaleeji music and I must say that it has caught on so well that now more and more non-Bahraini students participate more in the Arabic dance competitions at school.

Over the years, one of my only regrets has been that I haven't learnt Arabic. I do hope that it becomes compulsory for all students in Bahrain to at least learn the basics of the Arabic language. Not that I require it professionally, or even socially, but I am truly embarrassed that I don't know the language of my 'home'.

I believe Bahrain is so popular with the expat' community because of the lifestyle that Bahrain has to offer and we are never made to feel like we don't belong. I can say with a hundred percent conviction, that this indeed is an island where there is no racism, at least not from the Bahraini folk. I have never been made to feel inferior to anyone, in any sphere. I have always been treated like an equal, and I have always been respected and treated right, which is more than you can say about many other Arab states. Many who have lived and worked in Bahrain find it unacceptable to move to another Arab country because of the culture difference. In Bahrain, it has always been an all-inclusive society, always a smile for a stranger, always an open heart and warm welcome.

I remember when we were in school waiting to graduate, so that we could leave Bahrain and go off to see the world. Everyone always said; "we won't come back to Bahrain, it's too boring. Nothing exciting ever happens in Bahrain," but ultimately quite a large number of people who grew up here do eventually return, and start families here. There is something about the life here that brings us all back. Sure, it may not be the most exciting oh–my-god-I-have-no-time-to-breathe kind of life, and yes it may seem even slow at times, but there is a certain charm, a unique warmth, and a special sense of belonging here.

My passport may not be of the red colour that Bahrainis hold and yes I am an Indian, but Bahrain is my home. I was born here, had my childhood here, went to school and grew up here, evolved into the person I am today and now that I am married, I am definitely looking forward to giving my family and my kids - when they arrive - the sweet and beautiful life that Bahrain provides. Maybe the one reason that I love it here is that sense of belonging, And when I do travel, I always look forward to that wonderful the feeling I get when my flight lands at the Bahrain International Airport. You know... the feeling of finally coming home.

It is indeed *My Beautiful Bahrain*.

STRANGE PLACE

by

Osama Arshad

At fifteen, daddy came to this strange place,
knowing no one, knowing nothing.
Daddy came to help out with work.
Little did he know, this place would become his everything.

Sea and desert it was and that was all,
development came, he saw it with his own eyes.
Life continued, a beautiful wedding,
a baby boy, his little prize.

That baby boy grew up soon,
was an introvert and a pessimist.
He dreamed big and brave but
never was really content.

Time went by, and he remained the same,
until two wonderful men he met
native to this strange place.
These two men showed him different.

Change came to him easy with them.
Mingling was not a problem any more.
Before he knew it, he was becoming
part of this strange place, this culture.

Soon he was no longer the lonely son
of the fifteen year old who,
who had come from far away to this strange place
with deserts golden and skies blue.

In this strange place, no longer strange,
he found opportunity and friendship,
like he couldn't have found far away.
Life even brought him courtship.

This was it, life falling into place;
his happy ending,
in this strange place.
It was only the beginning.

SAAR SURRENDERS ITS SECRETS

by

Maeve Kelynack Skinner in conversation with Dr. Robert Killic

The Land of Dilmun has fascinated many archaeologists and historians, not least Dr. Robert Killick and his wife Dr Jane Moon who arrived in Bahrain in 1989 to discover the secrets of an ancient settlement lying in the shadow of the burial mounds. Under the patronage of the late Amir HH Shaikh Isa bin Salman Al Khalifa, the two archaeologists formed the London-Bahrain Archaeological Expedition, and began to dig.

"Uncovering the ancient city was like lifting the lid of a toy box," said Dr. Killick of the settlement in Saar, near the north-west coast of Bahrain. "It was a perfectly laid out 'Lego Land' city, with walls, streets and a temple which had remained intact for four centuries. Lying undisturbed on the temple's sandy floor were numerous seals, platings and sealings (small irregular shaped seals) indicating that food and drink offerings used for ceremonial rites had been stored there." Seals were imprinted with cuneiform and used as jewellery and marks of identification. They are button-shaped with two holes pierced at the back for a string to hang around the neck, or as a signature or mark of ownership.

"The Saar settlement is a perfect example of a Bronze Age site. It is unique because it's the largest horizontal exposure of its type and period in the Middle East and has never been built upon, thus has no after layers so is relatively easy to excavate. Whereas other sites, such as the Bahrain Fort which dates from the same period, was built upon in later centuries so archaeologists had to uncover layers of civilisations to reach the earliest period."

Over a ten year period, the London-Bahrain team uncovered a complete settlement including a temple, ninety-two dwellings, a well, limekiln, copper storehouse and storage units. They pieced together the social structure and economy of a four thousand year old society of six or seven hundred people who occupied different areas at different periods. The south of the settlement was occupied in 2000BC but dwellings in the northern area had been abandoned perhaps because they may not have been worth restoring, so people built new houses. As in modern life, there are gradual contractions of populations in one area and growth in others, Dr. Killick pointed out.

Uncovering the temple was the first project as it was the pivotal point of the city. There are two central altars, each bearing a crescent moon, one of the oldest religious symbols in the region. The crescent could also be a stylised representation of bulls' horns, another symbol of divinity in the ancient Middle East.

The settlement consisted of narrow streets lined by blocks of two or three-roomed houses with an L-shaped courtyard-kitchen around an inner room. A definite pattern showed that each house had a distinct doorway to differentiate it from its semi-detached neighbour. The houses were not much larger than traditional village dwellings in the Middle East today and shared characteristic features such as a central hearth and a cooking area with supports for pots or jars. From the skeletons unearthed in nearby tombs, the average height of the people was about 5'4" (1.52 metres).

A deep circular well once fed by sweet water from an aquifer was uncovered, the fresh water inlet clearly visible at the lower end of the well. Stone hand and foot holds were set into the sides. The team also found a limekiln which revealed how the settlers built their houses and made pottery and other items. The circular structure resembled a well, but a gap in the stonework signified a doorway which led to the discovery of the kiln, further evidenced by hard baked walls and burnt plaster on the floor which differed to that found elsewhere on the site. The rock at the top of the kiln was fired from below to turn it into lime plaster used to build the houses. The walls of the structure gradually narrowed which indicated a domed roof - similar to the structural formation of the pottery ovens used in nearby A'Ali village today, and the firing technique is also similar.

"We assumed that a ruling class or administrative tier did exist in the Dilmun era because of the large tombs found in A'Ali and Janabiya and the superior quantity and quality of the artefacts found beside the skeletons inside," said Killick. "These denoted a king's burial place. But the defined street patterns, stone tools, pots and artefacts found in smaller burial mounds above the Saar settlement, pointed to ordinary households. Apart from the temple, there was no evidence of an administrative or public building, although they did discover an unusual eleven-roomed house in which a large amount of copper was found in one room, so the house may have belonged to a wealthy copper merchant."

Saar was occupied for about three hundred years but then abandoned. The reason why, is uncertain. The archaeologists believe that the fisherfolk accessed the sea via a tidal inlet from Tubli Bay which widened into a lake, a kilometre away from the settlement. Apparently a drop in sea levels around 1800BC caused the inlet to dry up and the coastline to disappear, so the settler's livelihood would have been lost. During that period, Bahrain had also lost control of the copper trade, so Dilmun ceased to be of major significance.

Archaeological treasures on display in the Manama Museum discovered at the Saar settlement include ninety exquisite cuneiform seals, four hundred seal impressions, pearls, carnelian, turquoise and amber beads, obsidian arrow heads, stone tools, fish bones, date stones and pottery sherds.

So much evidence of Bahrain's history, which includes the Sumerian Epic of Gilgamesh, shows what amazing stories are still waiting to be found in the Land of Dilmun.

BREATHING LESSONS

by

B.M.Engel

"You are expecting too much from me," Sami declared quietly and gave the pre-school reading book a firm push.

Startled by the earnest tone of his voice, she glanced at her little boy.

Hunched over the cool marble table, his head buried in his folded forearms, she could only see a bobble of dark, sweaty hair. This fluffy crown made his head appear much larger than the rest of his body. Bony shoulders poked through his red and white cotton shirt. 'Not fully hatched yet,' she observed one wiry upper arm sticking out its sleeve. But, hiding under rosy tinted, soft skin, she noticed a display of fine sinews, twitching nervously. She smiled and with aching wistfulness absorbed the full site of his sweet existence down to its ten restless, dirty, boyish toes.

"Come over, darling," she murmured, gently touching his rounded shoulders.

Reluctantly his head turned towards her. With a firm grip she lifted his flopping shoulders and pulled his tired body gently onto her lap; a pair of lifeless, dangling legs with the famous set of bare feet reaching her last. She smiled.

"You see, Sami, sometimes," she continued, "sometimes we have to be brave, take a deep breath and embrace what we don't know."

"But, mummy, you are expecting too much from me!" he answered back promptly, straightening his back and glancing at her reproachfully.

"Perhaps, darling," she answered, looking down at him, again surprised at his sincerity. Slowly she combed through his sweaty hair with one hand, the other holding him in place before continuing: "But we must be curious about life and pick up a challenge in order to grow, don't we? Come, let's rest for a while and try again later!"

She felt his body relax, huddling closer to hers, eyes shut. Satisfied with herself she leaned back holding her son tightly. With each inhale she savoured the moment and the light, sweet-sour sweaty odour emanating from his exhausted body. Slowly breathing in and out they surrendered to a peaceful lilt.

In their slumber they didn't give heed to the taxi chaotically speeding down the quiet road, coming to a screeching halt in front of their house. Neither did they notice the heavy thumps of closing car doors, nor kerfuffle and clanking and the scraping of paraphernalia sliding over garden tiles and the distinct rustle of numerous plastic bags. Completely oblivious they were, to the light clatter of the wood-framed fly net, protecting the main door which caused a first fluttered din. It didn't reach the sanctuary above yet. The solid tone of the double-winged teakwood door behind, though, forcefully being pushed open and then rhythmically plodding back with some delay, tolled up to the first floor.

Sami raised his head.

"*Alhamdullillah Rabilallahmin*! *Uch, wa alleiyeh, wa alleiyeh! Ana ehnee! Habeeba! Weiynech inti? Weiynkum intau*?!" (Thank God, the Merciful! Uh, poor me, poor me! I am here! Habeeba! Where are you? Where is everybody?).

The imperative force of an older woman's voice condescended onto their house, plummeting and swelling with each intonation. It absolved everyone merciless from their midday break at once.

"Fareeda Ameen!" Sami shouted in exhilarated expectation.

"Fareeda Ameen!" echoed his baby sister Yasmeen, half aroused from her afternoon nap, still holding on to her patou.

The young mother sighed because she knew there was no holding back now. Down the staircase her children galloped, shrieks and laughter accompanying their descend. Overpowered she leaned back and stretched her arms, arching wide over her shoulders, shaking her head, "Fareeda. Always this Fareeda Ameen!"

Slowly she rose from her chair and walked towards her kitchen, desperately in need of a strong cup of tea.

The completion of her kitchen was the last project of a continuous string of extensions that had lasted the entire year.

It had been their joint decision to stay with his widowed mother after they got married and therefore room was allocated to the young couple on the first floor. Grandmother occupied the ground floor of the villa. Both architectural engineers, they thrived on the challenge of adding much needed room to suit their growing family.

Pleased, she looked around into the airy and bright, well organised modern flat. Custom made book shelves filled the study and glowing watercolour paintings adorned the white walls of their family room. A comfortable, oversized Italian sofa, dressed in aquamarine blue linen, two white, swivelling leather armchairs and the round marble table with five chairs accentuated the loftiness of their place. With combined efforts, she and her husband had created a true sanctuary.

This delightful space was of great importance to her, the young, foreign wife. Despite being well received and integrated into her husband's family, she needed room of her own. It was a necessity for her to re-energise away from his extended, energetic family. Guarding her privacy was also important in view to raising their children. Equally amused and concerned she had noticed, that their offspring had learned quickly to bypass her rules. Quietly they would sneak downstairs, preferring grandmother's relaxed style instead. If things got tense from now on, she would simply lock the upper entrance door until order was established and peace prevailed.

"Exactly," she nodded encouragingly at her image reflected by the hall mirror, as she passed by. Then stopped and blew a breath of air on its surface. She pulled the hemmed sleeve of her fine cashmere cardigan up over her knuckles and polished the tiny blind spot with empathy.

"That should do!"

She noticed a few rays of sunlight squeezing through the half-closed shutters adorning the windows of the main rooms, living, dining and study. Big, almost frameless, they bordered on the adjoined, generously sized terrace facing the sunny south side of Bahrain.

It was her favourite spot. The view was spectacular with its apparently infinite view over their neighbours' lush, green gardens, almost an adequate replacement for the abundant woods and fields, mountains, rivers and lakes of her own country that she had left behind.

Quickly she stepped outside to open the wooden partitions to ward off the intense midday heat. Now, soothing afternoon sun streamed in, bathing the interior in its mild light.

Their bedrooms and bathrooms, on the cool north side, faced another green belt; their own garden with swaying palm trees, indigenous, colourful vegetation and a collection of animals of all sorts. A paradise for their children and little cousins next door.

Just looking at the thoughtfully orchestrated flow of inter-connected space inside and its soothing tranquillity, gave her tremendous pleasure and peace. But sudden shrieks coming from downstairs made her shiver and urgently reminded her of preparing her cup of tea.

"Oh no," she sighed, "no more left!" With disappointment she stared into the little container, almost void of precious tea leafs. This special blend had been sent to her by her mother from Europe.

"Enough for one last cup", she moaned and started to prepare water, sugar and cream with utmost reverence. Who could foretell the arrival of another parcel?

Carefully she placed her favourite porcelain cup on its saucer, added a tea spoon together with a shiny nugget of candies to the right. Then she heated the cream, checked the water temperature, poured the bubbling water over the hand rolled leaves and set the minute timer to obtain the perfect strength.

Fascinated, she watched the dried dark leaves unfold, slowly releasing a translucent, copper red- tinted swirl of tea.

"One, two, three," she counted and with each count, a single drop of cream gently plunged into the cup, until its contents magically changed into a gold coloured fluid.

"Mhhhhh," with relish she drew in the distinct aroma, malty and pungent.

Images of green Indian highlands, heavenly dark blue skies and moist monsoon showers jostled for her attention. Instead, she resolutely placed the spoon in the sink, lifted her cup of tea carefully with one hand, opened the door to the staircase with the other and slowly descended downstairs, leaving her Nirvana behind.

Walking through her mother-in-law's kitchen, she noticed that preparation for the afternoon tea was in full swing. A plate heaped with scrumptious samboosas, another holding a delicately flavoured, sesame-covered agaile had been placed on a trolley. Anika, the maid, was holding the dainty, hand-blown estecaans filled with steaming hot tea, ready to serve the happy crowd inside grandmother's majles.

Still balancing her own precious cup, followed by Anika carrying her tray, she stepped out of the kitchen and advanced through a dim, narrow corridor. Under the arched entrance of the majles she came to an abrupt halt and stared disapprovingly at the ungainly sight.

"Typical."

Her mother-in-law's tastefully decorated majles, had undergone a transformation beyond recognition. Big boxes, unprofessionally held together with tethered washing lines or gigantic brown duck tape, adorned the supposedly meticulously clean place. Some parcels were being ripped open while others lay still closed undisturbed. Soft brown wrapping paper lay carelessly strewn all over the place. Cheap plastic bags in various colours dotted the mess here and there. Two were empty and sailed aimlessly through the air. One white, one blue.

In disbelief her eyes wandered across the room until they met her mother-in-law's.

'Let gool shei (don't say anything), Marie,' they were signalling back to her, and another amused twinkle spelled: 'Let it be, this is my valued guest!'

"*Ya Allah, ya Allah!* (Oh God, oh God) *Weinah, weinah* (where is it)?" A voice wailed, immediately seizing everybody's attention. And there, in the midst of the room, surrounded by her precious paraphernalia, squatted Fareeda Ameena!

She was facing her host Habiba, who sat gracefully, slightly elevated on a sofa. Her five grandchildren, two from one son, three from the other, nestled around her. Spellbound, they were watching a promising show unwind, delighted by its impressive leading character.

Marie gazed back at Fareeda. Legs spread apart, she was sitting right in the middle of the Persian carpet, covering its entire beautiful centre medallion with her enormously huge bottom. A well worn, cotton-printed, striped jalabeeya barely covered her heavy figure. With impertinent curiosity, Marie's eyes moved slowly over voluptuous body parts, until they got stuck at the sight of a grand, half exposed, moist cleavage! The young woman took a deep breath.

"Good gracious! What a display!"

She jolted but couldn't help but complete her observations from head to toe. Now she noticed a rivulet of water trickling down Fareeda's loosely pleaded and greasy, greying braid, making its way along the back of the jalabeeya down to a pair of unkempt feet.

Mama aud's (Grandmother's) bathroom must be in a state again! Marie resigned. She was accustomed with the habit of taking wothoo. *But using the hand wash basin to wash your feet?! Why don't they use the shower tray instead? It would be much more comfortable for the old ladies, wouldn't it. And less messy!*

In contrast, her mother-in-law's petite feet, a size three and a half, were clean and beautifully soft and manicured. She was dressed in a sky blue, satin jalabeeya. Its neckline, hand embroidered, showed off a garland of tiny daisies, which echoed the colour of her head cover; a white chiffon scarf. Looking closer, one could detect a small pair of golden, pearl studded earrings. With each of Habeeba's moves, they would flash up and quickly disappear again under her neatly trimmed French bob.

Indeed, Fareeda embodied the exact opposite to her mother in law!

"How can they be best friends?" she had asked her husband once.

"We respect and value her because her mother was my father's wet nurse," was the answer.

Marie shook her head. His argument didn't convince then and so that strange alliance remained an unsolved conundrum still.

"*Weinah, weinah*?" Fareeda's cry wanted to be heard again.

Agitated she turned paper by paper, box by box in search for the missing object.

"Did he cheat me or did I lose it?" she continued in a stream of never ending complaint.

"*Haade, haade* (calm down, calm down) !" Habeeba bent down towards her friend, comforting her with an appeasing smile.

"What are you saying? What are you looking for, habeebety (my darling)?" Her kind eyes twinkled at her friend.

"Uh, I bought the cuuuuutest little dalla in the souq, today! I must find it!" A distressed Fareeda continued loudly rummaging between her luggage.

"Tell me, how is life at home? How is your family?" Habeeba asked, trying to distract Fareeda.

"Uuuh, don't remind me of that deserted country! I wish, I would still live in Bahrain!" Habeeba scoffed back.

Marie looked at her mother-in-law. She was the one telling her, that Habeeba was born and raised in Bahrain, but being moved to another Gulf country after her marriage, leaving friends and family behind. Her children and grandchildren, now grown ups, had left her and settled abroad, except for one. Old and divorced, Fareeda was living alone.

"Rich or poor, young or old, they are always welcome in my house," Habeeba once declared on a busy day, when the stream of women friends visiting her didn't seem to stop. Her house was indeed a refuge for everybody.

"Uhhhhh, there it is! Look at this beauuuuutiful, cute little thing," Fareeda cried, "and so cheeeeap!"

Relieved she raised a tiny, polished dalla overhead. A beautiful smile transformed her face as she turned to Habeeba. Still sitting, she bowled over and with a sweeping, generous gesture she presented the dalla to her dear friend.

Now Marie's two children and their three little cousins got restless. Overwhelmed by their curiosity they climbed down the sofa and gathered around their grandmother's unconventional guest.

"Ya ainy (the apple of my eye), ya habeeby (my darling), ya haleeleh (my sweetie)," Fareeda greeted them heartily. With each intonation, she pinched their little cheeks until they showed painful red marks. Then, pulling them over one by one onto her huge lap, she smothered them with wet kisses.

Suddenly she paused, clapped her hands and cried in feigned disbelieve: "Oh, my God, I must have left your presents at home!" There was no holding back now. They cajoled and giggled until all of them wrestled a present off their guest, which suddenly had appeared out of nowhere.

Marie, still standing under the arch, solemnly rested her eyes on the boisterous crowd.

*Paradise is at the feet of mothers**, it suddenly echoed in her mind. She looked at Fareeda's feet.....

"Careful," she shouted the next second, giving way to her youngest, little Yasmeen, who, followed by Fareeda, was chasing her present, a gigantic balloon. Trying to save her cup of tea, Marie stretched her arm and made a half turn ....

"*Shukran* (thank you), ya habeebety (my dearest)," Fareeda shouted and relieved Marie from her precious load. She downed the delicate brew with one single gulp and wiped her lips with the back of her hand. Looking with fondness at her benefactress she continued: "And I always thought, you don't like me!"

Marie stood stock still.

Without leaving the young woman out of sight, Fareeda put cup and saucer down, stepped closer to Marie, opened her arms wide and seized her with one generous embrace.

And slowly Marie closed her eyes. She felt the warmth of Fareeda's huge chest and took in a deep, long breath.

*Narration from the life of Prophet Mohamed - A man once consulted the Prophet Mohamed about taking part in a military campaign. The Prophet asked the man if his mother was still living. When told that she was alive, the Prophet said: "(Then) stay with her, for Paradise is at her feet." (Al-Tirmidhi)

BAHRAIN

by

Kathleen Dodd

There is the August heat to face,
when stepping out resembles
stepping in a slow roast,
sizzling searing
sand dust lies bone dry,
on parched land
and black robed,
faceless women
drift through
heavy heat,
to market stalls
of spice and silk,
magenta, turquoise, gold,
There are the palm trees,
languishing on stark white sand,
the green sea
and a poignant past
of pearls and simple life.

And then there are
the high rise works of art
and worldly malls,
cool for ardent expats
searching for a taste of home.
There is ambivalence;
a deep and complex blend
of bounty and the beauty
of the Call to Prayer.
the ancient and the new,
and seeking for the true
Bahrain.

A NEWBIE!

by

Pooja Rajpal Kasala

I am a newbie here! A toddler in Bahrain and love it already!

At the time of writing this, my husband and I are just over three months in this country and the vibe, energy and exuberance of this island is infectious! Am taking baby steps and every day here seems like a new adventure!

There is something in the air of Bahrain, is it that it's a small island so the people are all inter-connected, close knit and merrily going about their daily life? Or is it that the country has consciously attracted easy going, sanguine, positive folk? I can't fathom, but the vibe for sure is addictive!

At first I was terrified at the thought of moving to a new country. A new country means we start life afresh, make new friends - which seems to become decidedly tougher as years go by. Looking for new work opportunities and keep busy while the husband establishes himself. Basically uproot oneself and begin life anew!

Anyhow, we got here! I behaved like an imbecile most of my first month, constantly complaining about being dislodged from a life familiar to me, having to leave my 'lucrative career' and no more the thrill of meeting deadlines or working round the clock for a presentation. A wise man once said, '*We must be willing to let go of the life we planned so as to have the life that is waiting for us,*' and now I am learning how to implement this statement on a day to day basis.

The first task at hand was to quickly get ourselves a house. I began my search with some trepidation, thinking how I would find a good house with my multiple needs, within a budget. I began my search, I looked at houses, oh yes I saw some! Over a hundred of them in fact! And not because I wasn't finding one, but because I found so many! Each one better than the other. I was spoilt for choice; should I pick up a villa with beautiful pink and while bougainvillea blooming in the garden and a small pool for the kids, or do I take a swanky penthouse overlooking the Arabian sea? Then there were regular flats replete with amenities, studio apartments or deluxe houses with classical or contemporary furniture. Toughie isn't it? I had mind boggling options, do I pick up a house with open kitchen or closed, do I choose between twice a week housekeeping or a laundromat next door, and a few apartments also had breakfast on the house. How much better can this get? And most houses or apartments came with roof-top or indoor swimming pools, and fully furnished gymnasiums. I finally settled on a flat, about two minutes walking distance from four 24/7 supermarkets and a food street comprising top of the line food chains across the world. The foodie in me won hands down!

Bahrain spoils you, spoils you rotten.

By the time I finalised the house I was already familiar with the island, I had met some very helpful agents who shared a lot of interesting trivia and helpful information on the country and now I'm sure I could become an estate agent myself. Not bad for someone who has hardly been here, and a pretty lucrative career option I must say, specially in this country.

The thing I like about Bahrain is that it's definitely not Wall Street; working professional can unplug and enjoy their well-deserved evenings, at the same time there is enough to challenge the jet-setters. I like the fact that my husband comes home at a reasonable hour, I know it's never too early for us girls but if I had to be fair, life in Bahrain is a lot more balanced than many other countries.

I get super excited on weekends, as that's when we take off in our car and drive around the coast. One of my most favourite places is the Al Dar islands, about a half an hour drive from the city. This may just be the cutest place to visit, a tiny island with a restaurant and pristine blue sea surrounding it. I love chilling there with a cool cocktail, smelling the salty sea air and gazing at the minuscule sun soaked beach and then finally heading for a spin on the boats, what freedom, what exhilaration! Easy on the pocket and what a delightful way to spend the day!

A day out with new found friends at the Bahrain Sailing Club at Zallaq beach is guaranteed fun and a fabulous way to spend the weekend. Warm, shimmering waters, mellow surf and crowd lazing in their beach-wear, while people with a passion for sailing and kids keep themselves busy with their chosen water sport. I could go there again and again... and again!

When in a mood for some adrenaline, I head to the Juffair food street, I have concluded that this street never sleeps. Flanked by restaurants on either side, we would invariably see people ripping by on their Harleys, Ducatis or Honda's, high-fiving their buddies on the way. I like to sit in one of the many open-air restaurants and enjoy a casual conversation with a kindred soul, or just watch the crowd buzzing by.

I love exploring the malls on the weekends, am pretty sure all of us girls do! The shopping is to die for; brand after brand. Oh I am so greedy, I want it all. I have been inspired to shed off a few kilos just looking at the gorgeous dresses hanging on the mannequins.

As winter approaches there is a nip in the air, it also rains once in a while and this is the time I like going to my nearest Starbucks and grabbing a hot cup of coffee. Everything seems tastier and cosier. While walking the streets I am frequently greeted with a customary yet cheerful 'hello' and hand-waves by people driving by, the chatter that I hear is all about Christmas cakes and baking!

Winter is also the time to take long walks by the beach or just stroll in the by-lanes of Bahrain looking at majestic villas, stunning landscaped greenery and colourful flowers blooming outside many a house. I immensely enjoy the sights of little children riding their mini-bicycles, while their moms animatedly chat with the neighbours. The seasonal rains seem to have spruced up the flowers and trees, and they look greener and more colourful as if all set to welcome the Christmas.

A first for me was the visit to Bahrain's biggest mosque, the Ahmed Al Fateh Islamic Centre (Grand Mosque). What a magnificent place with highly informative guides who shared insights into the religious aspects and highlighted the architectural facets of the mosque. I truly experienced the Arab culture and hospitably that day.

I have met some incredible ladies on this island, many of these women, just like me, have left their familiar world to join their husbands but have managed to create a niche for themselves. Some blog, some are regular columnists, others teach or volunteer counselling sessions, some bake and sell their yummy goodies. It's inspiring to meet these women who don't get deterred in a new place but establish themselves on their own merit. Taking a cue from them, here I am, penning a few thoughts of my journey thus far in this chirpy little country.

A great experience for me has also been joining local cultural associations or groups or local coffee meet ups. I have managed to meet some very interesting folk at these organizations. There is this extremely ingenious and a now a good buddy, who organises dolphin watching as his hobby. There is another gentleman who conducts poetry writing workshops!

I don't complain about not working, in fact I know I will soon land a job for myself but in the meantime I am enjoying the deliciousness which comes with the newness of a country, I am happily soaking up the culture, sights and traditions of Bahrain!

This is the first time in my life I am taking a break from my career, and might I say I am pleasantly surprised at how busy I can still be. I made friends with my neighbour who in turn introduced me to a big bunch of people who welcomed me and who I visit occasionally for a game of cards or sometimes just to meet up to chit chat.

Deciding to gift my husband an art class on our wedding anniversary, I walked into a quaint art gallery in the jig-sawed lanes of Adliya, and so feel in love with the artist's work that I have decided to get out my never used paint brushes and try and paint my own little rainbow.

Life is interesting, it leads one to never visited junctures.

I, for one, find it hilarious when I lose my way, which happens all the time while trying to reach a new destination, much to the annoyance of my husband. But that's the fun; we get lost so we drive more and we see a lot more of Bahrain in the process!

Bahrain is indeed a gorgeous country and something or other will always catch your fancy. There is so much to do, I love this place! I know I just need to go out there and there will always be something 'newer' to do! Life is good. In the words of Joseph Campbell;

"The big question is whether you are going to be able to say a hearty yes to your adventure!"

And I am saying YES!

MY PRINCE, MY PRINCESS

by

Natasha Khan

She held it between two fingers and gazed at it reflectively. The small cluster of tiny pearls seemed to reflect her own thoughts back at her. They gave her nothing of their own. No – they were hard, opaque - like small, shiny stones. Their soft brilliance began to oppress her.

She put the ring down, and took her hand away from it. It was a small gold ring, with tiny Bahraini pearls. Her engagement ring.

Her mother had warned her against it when she first saw it.

***

"Hmmm… Pearls." Her mother frowned at the ring she showed her. Emily looked at her mother nervously, the first bloom of her happiness beginning to wither underneath her mother's dry, satirical gaze.

"D... don't you like it, mother?"

Her mother turned back towards the stove, answering her daughter in a practical sort of manner. "Well, Em… You know what they say. Pearls are unlucky at weddings. They symbolise tears."

No, Emily did not know what they said. She looked from her mother to the beautiful gold ring, set with tiny pearls from the Middle East – from a country called Bahrain. When he had slipped it on her finger, in that wonderful, beautiful moment she had said yes… When he slipped it on her finger, and she gazed at it for the first time ever, she had been swept away in an exotic dream. A dream full of colours and fragrances, and the scent of rich spices. A dream that seemed to lead her to the door of a new opulence, which her old mid-western self could never even have imagined. She was no longer Em, short for Emily, daughter of poor dairy farmers in Wisconsin. She was the fantastic, wonderful, beautiful Emily, standing on the threshold of a world where she would be a well cared for, well-loved princess. A world where she would be a Scheherazade.

Emily steeled herself against her mother's lack of enthusiasm.

***

And here she was. The colour was gone now. So was the fragrance, and the scent of rich spices – if you chose not to count the meaty smell coming from the shawarma stand, just below.

Emily looked around her. Here she was, in a stark, 'semi-furnished' apartment in Bahrain. When she had first expressed her surprise at the interior, her husband had quipped: "Oh yeah… This is the Arab interior designers' attempt at 'modern.' Guess they still don't really get it."

Of course, this had been when he had first brought her in. The time when he still found moments, found little words, to speak to her – to reassure her that she was there with him. But that seemed so long ago now.

Emily stood up, shivering suddenly. The air conditioner must have been set too low. She crossed her apartment to reach the temperature controls – crossed the hairy nylon carpet, the gargantuan purple sofa, the faux wood and glass coffee table. Emily pressed the buttons on the controls to raise the temperature – raise it significantly. It still felt cold though. "I guess it'll take some time to warm up." She turned towards the rest of the flat once more, and it looked coldly back at her. The furniture, the walls, even the blind flat- screen TV… They all looked at her indifferently. Not shunning, not disapproving – no, that would still have been something. Just indifferent. Cold.

"But it's been some time now…" She thought to herself. "It's been some time now since… Since… Hasn't it? Hasn't some time passed? Shouldn't it be warmer now?"

She could not tell. The endless moments all seemed the same, all stretched out to eternity before her.

She moved forward, and looked towards the clock. Its steady tick-tock did nothing to reassure her, and both the needles on its dial moved on with a surgical precision that she found unnerving. Nothing paused, nothing stopped. Nothing had paused or stopped since the beginning of time. Bodies, trees, mountains, countries, continents; the whole world would crush and crumble under the great burden of time as it rolled along… Time would be indifferent. It would not stop to look.

Emily sat down heavily, perched on the edge of the purple sofa. It offered no comfort, and no reproach. Where was her husband? When would he come home? Emily decided to wait. Clasp her hands on her knees, perched as she was on the edge of the sofa, and wait...

★★★

"Em! Are you engaged?"

Emily looked happily towards Denise, and nodded; a shy smile curled her lips, which could not hide the immense joy that flowed from within. Denise jumped forward to hug her colleague. The retiring Emily was not new to the workplace, but the warmth between both women was new. It had taken a long time for Emily, reclusive as she was, to open up to the more confident Denise.

"But what an unusual ring, darling!"

A little confused by Denise's southern effusiveness, yet still too happy to retire, Emily spoke.

"Yes – yes. It's from Bahrain. That's where I – my hus... husband and I will live."

"Bahrain! And what is that place, my dear? Where is it?"

"Well, it's…" Emily struggled to remember all that he had told her. Of course, at that time, she had hung on his every word about Bahrain; he had told her of the sea, and the quaint fishermen, and the divers who had brought the very pearls she wore on her finger from the depths of the ocean. He had told her of the souk, the market place, full of spices and rich cloths. He had even told her of Bahrain's gold souk. But since then, she had added so much of her own colour to the picture he had painted, that it had become difficult to separate… What were the facts that he had told her, and what were her own imaginings?

"W – well… It's an island. A small island… In the Middle East."

"In the Middle East! Oh Em, you're going to the Middle East?" Denise rose and turned around, announcing to the forest of cubicles that surrounded her: "hey everybody, listen! Emily is going to be married and move to the Middle East!"

Emily blushed profusely as scores of colleagues, many of whom she had barely spoken to before, crowded around her bidding her congratulations and shaking her hand. Yes… This was the start. The start of what she had dreamed of… From plain old Em, to Arab princess. This was the start.

***

She did not know how much time had passed by. The clock went on. She sat there with her hands clasped before her, resting on her knees. She stared ahead, her blood-shot eyes unwavering in their service to her.

Was it the same moment? The same hour? The same day? Or perhaps a few days had passed. The phone had rung several times, and each time, she had risen and crossed over to answer it. Not to answer it, but rather to listen for the voice she sought at the other end. But each time she brought the receiver to her ear, it was some other concerned, anxious voice. Some other curious voice. Some other hard, official voice. It was never the voice she wanted to hear.

Suddenly, she began to feel tired. So very, very tired. The phone would ring, ring, ring… But she had no will to reach it any more. She no longer strained to hear that voice. That voice… Maybe it had left her long ago. Left her stranded here, in what was not Bahrain.

When was the last time she had heard that voice? Did she remember?

Her thoughts walked down a road… Was this what they called 'Memory Lane?' Walked down a road, and ambled on into the distance. It went without her. She was left watching, watching…

Watching.

***

She sat on the sofa, watching him listlessly as he worked on the tiny dining table. Hunched over as he was, he barely lifted his face – and thus never looked at her. And she sat there watching him.

Finally, she spoke. Her voice was quite even. "When do you think we'll go?"

He ignored her. Perhaps he had not heard.

She spoke once more, just a shade – a touch louder. "When – when will we go?"

There was a pause. He snorted. Then turning a few pages, his voice finally spoke. "Go where?"

"To Bahrain."

He frowned. Though he glanced in her general direction, he did not really look at her. Perhaps he thought she was joking. He did not answer. So she tried again, this time with a pleading urgency in her voice. "When will we go to Bahrain?"

He shook his head in some irritation and sighed. Then, perhaps because he thought an annoyed, sarcastic response would not be worth his time, he spoke: "We are in Bahrain."

She hadn't heard his voice after that. She sat staring at him, staring at him from the purple sofa.

***

The doorbell rang.

She did not have the will to go.

It rang again. And again. It was incessant.

Someone called from outside. She could not make out the voices. She tried to shut them out. There was a dull thud. A thud as if some body – or bodies – had hurled themselves at the door. Then more voices. More shouting. Then a moment of silence. The sound of keys clinking together came through the door. She shut her eyes tight.

***

He kissed the hand he had just put the ring on, and then looked up at her – a broad grin on his face. "Can you believe it, Em? Can you believe it? We're going! I'm going, and you're coming with me… To the Middle East! To Bahrain!"

She laughed a heady laugh – the laugh of the intoxicated. Yes, they were going to Bahrain.

"Oh, Em… You don't know what it's going to be like. We'll live like royalty! You don't know how much those Arabs have got, how many opportunities there are… Em, I'll be like a Prince by Wisconsin standards! And you'll be my Princess. My Arab Princess."

He laughed in his excitement, and she laughed with him. Bahrain, the land of riches, where he would be Prince, and she would be Princess. Together, they would live in a world of love and unbelievable luxury. If she had a doubt, all she had to do was glance at the glitter of the gold ring on her finger, and it's cluster of glowing pearls.

Bahrain. Bahrain! Where she would be Princess, and he would be her Prince.

***

"Madam? Madam! Please get up."

The voices surrounded her. The whispered to one another in Arabic, in Hindi, in Urdu, in Bengali. "Madam, are you all right?"

She finally looked up, but her eyes were vacant. Some one stepped forward and helped her up. She could probably stand.

It was in the same moment. Or no, the same hour. Or perhaps, the same day… Or some other day. She did not know. A man sat before her, dressed in a clean blue suit. Sunlight streamed in from the picture window to her left.

She did not look up. Her gaze never left her hands.

"Ahem. Miss...Miss Emily? May I call you that?"

She looked up. Her eyes were still vacant, and she made no response. But she had been like this since they found her, and the doctors could find nothing wrong. Perhaps she was just a shade dull. He chose to continue.

"Miss Emily… The task we have before us is a somewhat painful one, but we trust you to cooperate. Ahem… Your husband. You haven't heard from him for a while, yes?"

Her vacant gaze was beginning to unnerve him.

"Well, we know that you haven't heard from him in a while. And we're looking for him. But all evidence shows that he's fled the country in… In less than honourable circumstances. Of course, that affects your stay here as well. Uh… Do you understand, Miss Emily?"

She made no response. He became irritated, and now spoke brusquely. "Miss Emily, your visa here was attached to your husband's work visa. Now that his work visa has been terminated, you must be asked to leave Bahrain."

For the first time, some recognition entered her eyes.

"Leave – Bahrain?"

A smiled cracked her lips. A gurgle issued forth. The gurgle became a giggle, and the giggle became a laugh. The laugh became a hysterical peal of laughter.

The Officer rose in some alarm. "Miss Emily...?"

The laughter continued, only growing in hysteria.

No one ever could tell between Em's laughs and Em's screams. They were all the same...

PEARL EPIPHANIES

by
Bron Vanzino

Pearl Epiphanies in my life: a personal narrative and introduction...

Pearls first entered my life when I was four years old: a little necklace of seed pearls. They were pretty, harmless, and of no significant financial value, merely evidence of being a flower girl at a wedding; part of a happy childhood.

As a young single adult, my mother gave me a single pearl ring. I became conscious of real pearls at that time. This pearl had a 'depth' that I trained my eye to see fake pearls did not have. Fake pearls are like a surface reflection of the Moon Mother. My mother's natural pearl had a setting that was old fashioned and I did not like it, at that time. I wore it only for a short while and later gave it away, only to realise the beauty of its balanced perfection after it was gone.

Later, for my engagement ring I chose a single pearl ring with a beautiful delicate floral wrap of gold on either side. That ring made me feel I belonged to the elite club of 'chosen ones', engaged young women whose betrothal can be identified by the wearing of a decorative ring. As fortune would have it, that pearl itself was lost many years later as I did the housework. It felt a huge personal loss but not as great as when it was replaced by a much smaller pearl. This pearl could not fill the setting space adequately and seemed shamed compared to its older sister pearl. Like an omen, it foretold the empty shell that the marriage would become.

Yet I still continued to love pearls despite the reminder of pain and failure they brought. I accumulated quite a lot of pearl jewellery, most of it given to me. I loved it all because of the love associated with the giver. So in my later life, I had a wide collection of pearl jewellery because of the wider values I chose than those I had as a young person. Ultimately I was given the most magnificent and unexpected pearl ring by an undreamed-of new lover, discovered late in life. My conclusion is that pearls have slowly illuminated my life. As I have meditated on them, I have sensed a growth in understanding of them and life.

THE EPIPHANIES: WHAT THEY ARE?

The grain - the revelation of initiation

The grain of sand irritates the soft oyster which lives vulnerable, without protection, inside the oyster shell. That grain of sand is the interface of a new life, the life of a pearl: a world within a world. Just so I began as a tiny grain inside the womb of my host. At times I irritated my mother's body and made her sick. Every day waves of nausea washed over her, whispering of my invasion. I held my ground against the convulsions of stomach, steadily putting on covers of delicate flesh knitted in seamless perfection. I was her unseen pearl, her darling seed.

The little girl wove her dream of future beauty as she gazed on the tiny seed pearls. One day she would allow seed to grow in her and bring forth living souls to be admired by men and angels, souls whose faces shone with reflected divine glory. These pearly stones each contained a sacred name yet un-deciphered by the Hand of Fate. Her eye saw wonder in each tiny shape that portended an individual yet matched design.

Pearls need time and patience to grow: a revelation of reciprocity.

Many dangers face the growing pearl: without enough time it will be without size or significance; its life aborted before a chance to breathe is given. The oyster, early on, can be freed of its guest and feel the continuing comfort of undisturbed existence, a soul unchallenged by proximity or sharing until its inevitable day of reckoning comes with un- trumpeted harvesting of oyster meat. However, the enslaved oyster who could not rid itself of the foreign body will eventually feel accommodated around its demanding guest only to be suddenly shed of all its patient fruit.

Never 'seeing' the treasure, the traditional gold setting held, the girl now a young adult, disposes of the ring undervaluing not only the gift but the giver. She had not yet appreciated the love of her own mother but the girl's judgement of beauty was based on the harsh light of current fashions and the sterile style of minimalist geometry. To her young mind the old ring was full of the sentimentality of poetry about the moon and the Moon Goddess, old myths of femininity and the impoverished status of satellite submission. With time she learned more life lessons about true values, the wholeness of truth and things not being what they seem. Perhaps, the metaphor of 'things not being what they seem' is never truer than with Nature's metaphor of the oyster growing a pearl.

Pearls are a result of the active union of the oyster and the growing grain: the revelation of effort.

The pearl is not just the result of time, but the work of the oyster is also vital. The truth of this statement is in the variety of shapes that can be produced, not only shape but colour variety. The cultured pearl has commercialised an artificial method of pearl growing. It has also minimalised the variety of pearls that are produced while multiplying the profit and lessening the work.

The oyster works blindly, just reacting to its annoying visitor, without a blue print of the final work of art and yet that is what the oyster is capable of, the finest artwork. This craftsmanship challenges human efforts. God has glorified the oyster as a tool of creation, a master craftsman though it has not even the fundamental levels of higher creatures.

The mature woman on her developmental journey, discovers an initial crown of love in her marriage where she is held in great esteem by her husband. He buys her a single pearl which fits snugly into the floral tendrils of gold on either side. The pearl like the marriage seems immovable, but it is lost through carelessness of its priceless value. Just as the love in the marriage is taken for granted and replaced with a token kind of human routine. The woman is shocked not only by the sudden loss of the ring, which is never again discovered but also by the replacement pearl which to her accustomed eye falls short of the tendrils that are fixed in the setting of the original ring. She begins to despise the meanness of the new ring and the emptiness of the marriage. The joy of the ring and the marriage are gone. Love known and love lost are bitter to her so that the meaning of pearls is changed just as others have told her they are suspicious of pearls because there is an association of grief in their making.

The sacrifice principle of love is seen in the oyster and the pearl: the revelation of death.

If the oyster just grew the pearl, accumulating it as a manifestation of its pain and irritation would be negative and meaningless. So it is if we just accumulate wealth. No, we are meant to be givers and the oyster is included in that. The oyster is a reluctant giver, the epitome of a stubborn man. It never gives in, just keeps working at making that pearl. The oyster also has to be forced to give up the pearl, it does not do so willingly.

Older but as a single woman again, I was able to appreciate pearls. Again they simply became things of beauty. I could not wear the small pearl any more but stored it away in a small box, not knowing what to do with it but thinking it could be redesigned later. A new relationship brought a large new pearl. The death of the old marriage prepared the way for the possibility of a new marriage, just as the sale of the man's entire wealth in the parable enabled him to buy the pearl of great price. No longer could the man, in the parable Jesus told, love or hold on to any of his wealth. To do so would mean he was not able to purchase the beautiful new pearl, so too we are taught not to hold onto our possessions or material things but to embrace spiritual values. Metaphorically letting go is a kind of death. So the final revelation of the pearl comes through death: the oyster must die to release the treasure he has unwittingly created; so too we must let go our riches and even our poverty and problems so we will not be held back from embracing the new future, the greater treasure, the final truth.

THE PEARL OF GREAT PRICE: THE CENTRAL MESSAGE, BEING AT THE HIGHEST LEVEL.

The Teacher

So the pearl is the great teacher in nature about initiation, reciprocity, effort and death. Therefore, the pearl is a metaphor of the cycle of life and death. If we meditate on it, we can understand life with our hearts and not just our eyes, but unfortunately we could be like the oyster and stay inside our dark shell resisting, resisting anything that is not 'of us', resisting anything that is not harmonious with our own doctrine. The consequence of the choice of exclusion of every grain of new truth, every breath of change will be to give away our treasure and to miss out. Just like the oyster accumulates pearls that others eventually enjoy. To lock out the world as the oyster does, thinking he is protecting himself, is to lose.

The Treasure

Not only is the pearl our teacher but it is our treasure. The man in the parable recognised the value of the pearl that enabled him to sell all his wealth and purchase it. This is a situation of making no compromise: the price of the pearl is so great that it costs all our accumulated riches. The decision has to be made between the pearl and wealth. If we do not purchase the pearl of great price by selling up/ giving up our present pile of understanding, money or any gifts we have, we will miss out and someone else will own it. The oyster can never have or enjoy the pearl, it does not even know what a pearl is, all it knows is irritation and discomfort, negative emotions. He wants to lock out the world, the oyster is the perfect picture of selfishness. The selfish cannot buy wisdom. The selfish do not recognise one greater than themselves.

The Moon

Once a connection of truth is made with Nature, there are many connections that can be made. The full moon is the image, the original image, of the pearl. The greater Nature connections must be meditated on to be seized through a heart understanding. At this higher level, the connection of the pearl to the moon can be seen directly. It can be seen through the oyster. First, the open oyster with the pearl inside is the picture of the human eye, its structure: eyeball within a lid and socket casing. The pearl then is like an eye, the moon is like an eye. Thus the whole of nature becomes poetry. Pearls are pure poetry in the sense that they carry the truth in pictures. To further explain this thinking, the pearl becomes the seed, the eye, or the initiation of further revelation. The moon and its nature will help us to understand the world we live in. The pearl epiphanies become a cycle. The moon causes the tides, it also controls the sea which is the habitat of the oyster. The oyster depends on the moon. The oyster produces the best work of art about the moon and therefore reciprocates the gift of supplies provided by the moon. The effort of the moon providing the tides is matched by the oyster's effort. Each month the moon dies and is reborn just as the oyster must complete its cycle of life, but in a sense its life is reborn in the creation of the pearl. Thus the cycle of epiphanies is at this higher level as well.

The Engagement

Pearls are the embodiment of wisdom because they teach us the inspired truth. The final step in the life of the oyster is the pearl itself. When the pearl is removed from the oyster, when it is recognised for its great beauty and is no longer a secret, that is when the pearl finds fulfilment. For a young man, to find someone to share his life, to give himself, once he is mature and perfect, makes the struggles of coming to maturity worthwhile. The undiscovered pearl is worthless. The pearl to the oyster is worthless, even lower because it is a nuisance. The oyster misses out just as the selfish miss out on the joy of giving. The young man looking for a pledge of his sincerity can take the pearl ring and give it to his beloved. Thus finally it becomes a symbol of his word, a pledge of his worth, of the worth of his life. To accept the ring the young girl (whatever her age) becomes captive to the man, she also becomes rich and finally she becomes enfolded with love, set in beauty like the pearl wrapped in the delicate fronds of gold of the original engagement ring. Ultimately at the higher level, this relationship is played out between the earth and the moon: the earth binds the moon to itself but the moon lovingly serves the earth and its creatures, faithfully loyal to them as predictably as the changing of the tides and the cycle of the moon phases.

For the earth to lose the moon would be sure death.

MEMORIES OF MY LIFE IN BAHRAIN

by

'Krazy' Kevin

Unbelievably, it is already twelve months since I moved from my beloved Bahrain to Australia. I lived in, worked, played, and loved the island for over a decade, having arrived in 1999 to work as a DJ in the new JJ Murphy's Restaurant and Bar, after touring much of the world since winning the title of UK DJ of the year. Originally I thought my stay in Bahrain would probably be around twelve months, and that I'd then continue on somewhere else; globe-trotting and working my way around the world. But how wrong was I?

Bahrain was life changing for me in so many ways; I met my beautiful wife Wendy (who is Australian) and we had our gorgeous daughter Hannah, who was born in Bahrain and still thinks of herself as half Bahraini.

On arriving in Bahrain I was struck by the lovely laid-back attitude of the Bahrainis. I first encountered the word '*Inshallah*' whilst having my car fixed at a garage; it needed a service, so I asked the mechanic Ali when would it be ready, and he said; "tomorrow *Inshallah*". OK, so the next day I arrived at his garage only to be told "it's not ready, please come back tomorrow and it will be ready, *Inshallah*" So again, the next day I arrived to be told "it's not ready." Now, I'm generally a very laid back person, so I said to him "Please don't say, it will be ready 'tomorrow *Inshallah*', if it takes a week I don't care, as long as I know when it will be ready." Ali gave me a mischievous smile and said, "OK three days" I said "fine", and as I walked out, he quietly added, "*Inshallah*"…Ha!

Another great thing about Bahrain is that it's a melting pot for so many different nationalities. I would never had believed you if you had told me before I arrived that I would be compèring events such as the Indian May Queen Contest, the Sri Lankan Festival, the Poppy Ball Celebrations and many others! The diversity was endless and I never knew what I was going to do next, and it made my life fun and exciting.

Let me tell you about how I started on Radio Bahrain. As I said, I was working in JJ's when a lovely lady with lots of hair came up to me and started talking. She asked whether I'd ever thought about doing radio and I said 'yes', but 'had never had the time'. Well, the lady in question was Marie-Claire, and she set up a meeting for me with Salah Khalid, the head of Bahrain radio. I went to the Ministry of Information in Isa Town to see him and what a lovely man he was. His only vice (which is a big one) is smoking. I came out of his office smelling like an overflowing ashtray. Salah said that I could do the Friday morning Breakfast Show (from 6am till 9am). I thought fantastic! BUT I was also working every night DJ'ing until 3am, so, my first morning on the radio I slept for two hours on the sofa and trundled off to the radio station with all my CD's in a bag.

Now there's a big the difference between DJing to a live audience and DJing to a microphone in a little room all by yourself! The response you get from the 'live' crowd is instantaneous, whereas in the radio studio on my first morning I felt so alone!! The newsreader that day was Nadia Swan, and luckily, we hit it off immediately. We had a chat after the news, live on air, which wasn't really 'done' at that time on Radio Bahrain. I did the Friday morning show for about four weeks before I was asked to also fill in for a DJ who was having a three week holiday. The time slot was great; 3pm till 6pm. I absolutely loved it, but then came a bit of a bombshell; I was asked to take over the weekday daily Breakfast Show. Having no sleep one day a week hadn't been too much of a problem, but how was I going to combine working at JJ's till 3pm and then going to the radio five days a week? Actually it was easy - I decided to just sleep all day!

Lots of funny things happened on the Breakfast Show, some (err) I can't tell you about, but others I definitely CAN reveal…

During one of my first morning shows, the music was playing when Nadia came in with a welcome cup of coffee. Then, just as my lips touched the edge of the cup, the CD unexpectedly stopped! I quickly turned my microphone on and said 'Ooh, thanks for the luvely cuppa Nadia' and had a quick on-air slurp whilst changing to another CD and then just carried on with the show. Well, the DJ coming on after me (who had worked there a long time and, I think, still is) berated me; saying that I had been very 'unprofessional.' Being the new boy, I took this rather to heart and the next day I apologised to the listeners, but I had so many calls saying that it was good and natural (as well as few saying they didn't like it because they were driving to work and wanted a coffee too after hearing me talk about it). Ha, when I present a show it's just me, Kevin, that you get, nothing contrived and nothing put on!

If I could help it, life at Radio Bahrain was never dull. When we had a new Minister take over, one of his directives was a new dress code stipulating that shorts could not be worn on the premises, only long trousers. So me and my 'Krazy' dress sense, headed off to the souk to see Mohammed; my amazing tailor, to give him some rather loud fabric and to ask him to please make me some suitably long trousers for the radio. Talk about multicoloured and BRIGHT!

While we are on the subject of trousers, another funny 'trouser' story was when we had the Australian V8 Races at the Bahrain International Circuit. I had been interviewing drivers in the studio, and on that particular morning I got a call at 7am from Martin Whittaker, the CEO of the BIC, saying that he's at the gate with Jamie Whincup (the reigning V8 Champion) and security won't let them in 'cos Jamie's wearing shorts. So, I said "Martin you come in", he came into the studio, I took my trousers off and gave them to him and he arrived back fifteen minutes later with Jamie wearing my nice bright trousers, and I did the interview with him, whilst sitting in only my underwear. It was so funny, but of course we couldn't say anything about it on air.

On the morning show I also loved working with the kids and, when I have put them live on air, some of them have put me in some rather funny, but awkward situations. Like the time a little girl called Amy rang and asked if she could tell me a joke. I asked her how old she was, she replied "six", so I put her on air. She then said: "How do you make a pool table laugh?" I said "How"? She came back and said; "tickle it under it's balls!" Oops…quick put a song on… out of mouths of kids 'eh?

One really positive thing about becoming well known in Bahrain is that it opened a lot of doors for me, giving me opportunities that I'd have never thought possible. Some of the opportunities were perks that benefited only me and my family, but sometimes being able to open doors meant I was able to help others too...

One morning on the radio, I received a telephone call that really hit home. It was from a Sri Lankan friend who told me he'd just found out that he'd lost a close relative in the Boxing Day tsunami. Immediately I felt that I wanted to do 'something' and started telephoning around. From a few people working together to raise money to help victims and their families, it culminated in a twelve hour music fund-raising event at the Diplomat Hotel called 'Hands across the Water.' My goodness, the coming together of people for this event was inspiring. On the day we had raffles every hour, DJ's, bands, and at the end of the night we had so much stuff left over we auctioned things off. Then I got a shout from the back of the crowd; "Krazy Kev, I'll give you five hundred dinars if you shave ya head." So in a shopping mall two weeks later just as Steve the hairdresser was going to shave my whole head, I said "shave half of it off"! For three weeks I walked around Bahrain looking like a loon, but raising even more money, then the last of my golden curls were shaved off too. My hair has never really been the same since, but it was so worth it. We raised nearly fifty thousand dinars which I presented to the Bahrain Red Crescent Society.

Another big moment for me was when I proposed to Wendy live on the radio on Valentine's Day. I invited her into the studio on the pretext of helping me out with all the dedications and requests. Everything was going well, I'd ordered a bunch of flowers to arrive at the studio, and had asked one of the newsreaders to come in and say; "would you like a coffee" to let me know that they'd arrived. Anyway the time flew by as we enjoyed doing a great show together, until I looked at the clock and thought "oops, there's only twenty minutes left of the show, where's the flowers?" Suddenly, in came the newsreader and I thought, hey here we go! Of course, I didn't know the size of Wendy's ring finger, so I'd bought a (temporary) plastic ring with a smiley face from a vending machine. I stopped the song, got down on one bended knee and asked her to marry me, and what was her reply? "What with this plastic thing..!!" Oops, I gulped, but then she said, "Yes!"

So, Bahrain has really played a very important part in my life; meeting Wendy, and having our daughter Hannah, a name we chose because it means joy / happiness in Arabic. We added Ruby as her second name, so she could have the initials HRH; our little Princess.

With all these fond memories wafting through my head, I really can't believe that it has already been twelve months since I was last in Bahrain. In my final week I was privileged to have a going away party at the British Embassy. I'd received a telephone call from Jamie Bowden, the British Ambassador (at first I thought that it was a wind up) but, when it dawned on me that it wasn't, I thought me, 'Krazy' Kevin having a farewell party at the British Embassy… Wow! You just couldn't ask for a better send off!

When Jamie spoke about things that I had done over the years with charity work, I became very emotional and just about managed to string a few words together (I know you don't believe that) to say thank you. But Bahrain has done so much for me.

Thank you Bahrain!

THE EMBRACE

by
David Hollywood

What an astonishing embrace and sense of touch to receive from a complete stranger!

I initially thought this was all a consequence of the inspiration that occasionally and unexpectedly occurs at peculiar times in a life when certain people meet each other for the very first time, and from that gleaming they instinctively anticipate something special may be happening which will form a relationship that was unforeseen but shall spontaneously develop and formulate into something lasting and good.

Therefore, and naively, I firstly thought that I was an intrinsic ingredient which had contributed towards being part of a dynamic that was creating a sudden atmospheric charm which had become real as it manifested itself at that time. And that thereby I was a necessary constituent to the moment being experienced and witnessed, and which without me could not otherwise have happened.

Silly me!

My expressions of friendliness upon meeting this stranger were allied to my innocence in terms of what I was about to go through, and had combined for the first time in my life into an introduction of what it actually meant to be greeted by humanity.

I impulsively understood at that instant that this acknowledgement of my existence was exactly what it should always be upon any first meetings, but I was surprised and confused by the dawning in my head and my heart that while I recognised it; I had never seen it before.

My reflection now is that such privileged instances, as rarely experienced within a life, are so uncommon as to be momentous, and if after the magnificence of the revelations we don't latterly disregard, abandon or forget them, then I suggest these exceptional occurrences add to a small and such insightful catalogue of human behaviour, experience, understanding and feeling as to be witnessed by us as life at its most sublime.

What had actually occurred to me upon the occasion of my new vision was actually uncomplicated but, and from a practical perspective. was simply that I had been greeted shortly after my arrival in Bahrain by a Bahraini man who also happened to be enjoying the hospitalities and conviviality of the hotel in which my family and I were staying, and who amongst a welcoming group of people, had been introduced to me by another foreign visitor and acquaintance who had arrived earlier.

When I met this Bahraini associate of my friend, it were as if I had just come across an old companion, but whom conversely as it happened, I had never actually met before. However, this person was nevertheless happy and prepared to greet and accept me into the familiarity of my being part of a trusted friendship which had arisen and bonded us all together, and to which it were as if I was already acquainted and accustomed to the circumstance and background of our mutual reasons for being there together. This was startling because I had never witnessed the like of such a warm greeting and open friendliness before! By virtue of my presence, it were as if it was naturally and joyfully assumed that I must be a good and worthy person, and consequently all sense of trust and kindness was unconsciously being displayed towards me, and why should it ever be otherwise!

It seemed to evidence that while everything around me was apparently normal in a palpable and continuous manner, and demonstrated there was nothing in reality to otherwise reflect upon, that I was being odd within myself because I had been surprised by the considerations being shown to me as if they were undue. Yet this additionally proved, felt and demonstrated to me how anomalous, inadequate and unnatural were my reactions to such enthusiasm.

Now, over two years later I am writing and elaborating upon my first impression of what in the end I have come to realise is simply the natural and everyday affability of the citizens of Bahrain.

To reflect upon and compare this revelation to my previous conceptions of human behaviour, I need to look at the experience of being in Bahrain and qualify my credentials as having lived at various times in other parts of the world. Therefore my background, combined with the media intrusions of television broadcasts, newspapers and other formats, have given me to somewhat witness the illustrations of what it might be to live in and appreciate what happens in other societies, and this by extension has given me a generalised glimmer and limited knowledge and confidence about my comprehension and awareness of the world's standards of behaviour.

Possibly I am educated towards an appreciation that has followed and provided for through an internationalisation of my life and which has allowed me to have certain imperfect insights into the separate elegances of cultures that exist around the globe.

While prospectively being accused of being obvious, I acknowledge that these two influences of travel and media have, to a certain extent, braced me with enough knowledge to realise that not everyone I journey towards is going to be of the same style as the people I have just left, and consequently the appearances of a newly visited culture won't just throw up differences in languages, manners of dress, types of clothing, physical variances, ways of thinking and gosh knows what else, but also an ability to detect that the emotions of people are influenced by their own personal and separate surroundings, beliefs, traditions and history, and that consequently I need to be sensitive to what may otherwise be valued differently to and from my own and other peoples inheritance.

However, upon deciding to live in and thereby arrive in Bahrain, what I had not expected was that I would quickly and suddenly discover a population so completely at ease with its nature and civilisation as to be totally confident about its relationship with any of the rest of the world's population which happened to visit its shores.

I therefore subsequently came to realise that in Bahrain and, as compared to the behaviour of the majority of the rest of world's peoples and structures, that within this country to consider being, and behaving in anything less than a compassionate, generous, graceful and tactile manner would demonstrate rudeness, coarseness, puzzlement and a neglect for the dignity of the human condition.

The particular depth of this almost unique manner of consideration within Bahraini society has shown to me since I came to live here, that on an almost daily basis what might be regarded as extraordinary friendliness and invasiveness of feeling towards acquaintances within other locations around the world, is perfectly normal here.

This has stretched my imagination into wondering what privileged circumstance has stimulated what it must mean to be a Bahraini Arab, and how can they be so relaxed about the new contacts that are met and greeted, and that to be otherwise would be inordinate and unnatural.

With this addition to my experiences I sense, and hope, I may be gaining an insight into our everyday lives that I had not previously detected and which is motivated by a natural kindness which orbits around caring for others, and from that perspective I might learn more about what it means to share in ways that expect nothing back except the simple joy of companionship.

This forces self examination of how I may have previously measured, participated in or understood compassion, and why this necessarily leads to a re-consideration of my earlier views, which are now challenged as deficient because of what I have found to be humanity behaving at better levels of sensitivity and thoughtfulness within Bahrain.

It seems Bahrainis are brought up unconsciously knowing that mankind surrounds them, and this acceptance may seem evident to all others, but it is my observation and that it is the un-reflective practice of being in a family, community and having acquaintances which form the natural priorities for developing a decent and moral life in Bahrain and this is based upon the kindly insensible, involuntary and instinctive emotion of easily giving to and providing for others.

Consequently it is normal to wish to embrace the world upon first and subsequent meetings, and to therefore show and demonstrate friendliness and generosity whenever welcoming a guest or friend into one's environment, and that this becomes a standard for the guaranteed maintenance of happiness and respect for all the experiences between peoples.

When viewed from the perspective of an outsider, this amity must stem from a culture that is sufficiently confident about itself to accept without judgement all of the mannerisms, looks and dress of a foreigner without comment or involvement. It has to almost be understood that because we are different, this makes us distinctive rather than foreign and thereby does not make me or anyone else right or wrong as to who we are, but simply shows that we are citizens of a diverse world.

A supporting aspect of Bahrain's hospitality is the appreciation which emanates as a consequence of our making the physical effort to visit the country, and that this call upon Bahrain somehow entitles us to a grace and respect that flatters our reasons for being here.

It feels as if, or while, our reasons for being here are never in doubt or questioned, it is perceived that we particularly wished to work here, and that now we are here, we deliberately want to know about Bahrain and its economy, culture, society, geography and its everyday activities, and therefore what we see as being interesting and enjoyable about the country and its citizens is as if we admire it and wish to engage with it. If we also happen to prosper while we are here then this is to be expected and will be celebrated as being good and a positive reflection of Bahrain's ability to enhance our lives and expectations for decent standards of existence, and that this reward is desired for us in a way that we should always experience, understand and want. It is tenuously felt as a pleasure among Bahrainis and as a compliment to us that Bahrain brought us the success we looked for.

These exchanges have for me brought about a personal love of Bahrain which I hadn't expected, felt or sensed the full depth of in any other nation, and while I have known a number of other countries, all of this goodwill is represented and reflected by the embrace I initially received from a stranger in Bahrain, and which I subsequently received from the population as a whole throughout my daily movements within the country.

So often as we travel around the globe and visit places for what they are within the beauty of the landscape and the beneficence of the climate, and which are further supported by the history and culture and intelligence of the population that lives there, these considerations ought to be sufficient to determine whether a society is worthy or unworthy, and whether it is secular and accepting of the worlds citizenry.

However, in Bahrain you quickly come to acknowledge that the aesthetics of the countryside are challenged and limited by virtue of it being a desert island and therefore not of dynamic variance.

But that is only until you meet the people! Then the enigma begins to develop.

Within the Bahraini need for communication, there is a continual requirement to be polite and hospitable. This is so universal in its practice that the history of contact between this country and the world appears by now to have made it innate.

Because Bahrain is located almost half-way down the Gulf, it is geographically positioned to perfectly capture all passing trade between the continents of Asia, Africa, Europe and The Middle East, and traditionally Bahrain is also acknowledged as being the original location where the Garden of Eden is placed and mentioned in the Old Testament. As this is geographic advantage and reputation for abundance is reflected into the pages of history, it can be seen and read that Bahrain was an essential trading and staging point for the passage of goods between diverse cultures.

Necessarily this passing to and through the country of many separate types of peoples and their varied goods brought about a consequent integration and degrees of influence over thousands of years of commercial activity (this essay ignores the details of history and who the various invaders were and how long each may have stayed), as well as developed relationships with other regions and environments that must therefore have naturalised the population into having an inherently international talent and ability for the provision of warm, hospitable and friendly greeting, and capacity for the entertainment and hosting of intercontinental visitors. This historic advantage must have reflected itself down the years into a position and confidence which today shows that Bahraini's know for themselves who exactly they are in the world, and that this is enhanced by the sophistication of centuries of welcoming visitors to Bahrain.

It is further complimented through the easy grace and style of movement that is demonstrated through and by the wearing of refined and elegant traditional and practical Arab styles of clothing, and this is further expressed by the regular demonstration of modest gestures which deny elaboration and yet offer open arms of friendship (I have rarely met a Bahraini who folds his arms), and the warming smile in the eyes and face.

Within the simplicity of everyday relationships and greetings, my experiences have witnessed in Bahrain an honesty and nature of caring for the condition of fellow mankind which is done through a sympathetic and civilised expectation that we are all intrinsically good and worthy, and I continually marvel at the openness of friendship which carries no burdens or suspicions or untoward mannerisms, but rather expects, imagines, develops and envelops decent behaviour and a reciprocal alliance of friendship. Bahrain is an example to the world of what can be achieved through an embraced respect and a mutual regard for the person and dignity of us all.

LAST RANDOM THOUGHTS

by
DaVonda St.Clair

Moments in time…Thoughts in action…Sounds turned into visions…Visions turn in to art… Art turns into a beautiful Bahrain.

Waking thoughts of a peach sky as morning twilight approaches.

Birds playfully chirping outside my window.

The weather of the Middle East is different than any other as it is currently changing seasons.

Several months of summer, weeks of fall, a month or two of winter then beautiful awakening of spring.

Monotony can have you miss the beauty of this kingdom.

Morning walks to work, ceasing moments of splendour.

Hearing mysterious squawks from a bird unknown.

Crowing from neighbourhood cockerels.

Parakeets flying above the corner villa…. Parakeets?

A yellow crowned cockatiel lands in my path, so I take a picture, who would believe that they fly freely and that I see them daily.

The aroma of gardenias, adeniums (desert roses), perennials and flowers blooming from a tree over-growing from someone's property onto the street.

Glimpses of magnificent landscapes when a set of towering metal driveway doors part.

Side-walks stained of dates not yet picked.

Waving with a smile at the security guards patrolling the perimeter of a high white wall.

Occasionally accompanied by a stray dog or two, longing for playful interactions.

A gentle breeze…refreshing.

Proud Nation flags wave gloriously atop Embassy buildings.

Detailed ornamentation of minarets and mosaic domes.

If driving, all this will be missed but so much more will be discovered.

Traffic…ugh!

How long is this light? (Hear car horns blowing).

Yellow light…why are most people in a rush?

Who taught YOU how to drive?

Construction, accidents, diminutive inconveniences when on the road.

Roundabouts, one-way streets, people driving down one-lane alleyways.

Shopping cravings cured by A'Ali, Seef and City Centre malls.

Souqs filled with shimmers of gold and the glistening of silver.

Calls of "My friend, my friend, here I have a good deal for you!"

Tailors, seamstresses, fabric stores.

Fruits, vegetables, roasted nuts.

Smells of curry, a few puddles of soot.

Cafés, lounges, coffee shops.

Swarmas, lambchops, cheese naan, chicken tikka, freshly made juices.

Friday brunches, mmm………….. Friday brunches.

Hookah, shisha, hubbly bubbly.

Camel farms, camel races.

F1… speed!

Horseback riding, equestrian clubs.

Al Areen Wildlife Park, Rally town, WahOOO, Adhari Park, Lost Paradise, Beit Al Quran, Barbar Temple, Al Khamis Mosque, ancient burial mounds, Al Jasra House, Arad Fort, King Fahd Causeway, Al Faith Fort, First Oil Well, Dilum, the Tree of Life.

LAST RANDOM THOUGHTS

{ **DAVONDA ST.CLAIR** }

The remarkable architecture of the World Trade building, Financial Harbour, Almoayyed Tower (Dark Tower), Sommerset, Novotel, Sofitel, KFC, McDonald's.

Toothbrush / toothpaste, gum, water, ice, juice, dry cleaning, all delivery quickly to your door.

Amwaj, Saar, Seef, Hidd, Riffa, Al Areen, Juffair, Isa/Hamad Town, Manama, Sitra, Adliya, Durrant, Hawar Island.

Without the Pearl roundabout nothing will be the same.

All these words, sentences, phrases make up My Beautiful Bahrain.

BIOGRAPHIES OF CONTRIBUTORS

AARON MAREE

Aaron Maree started cooking at the age of thirteen and quickly found his forte as a pastry chef. By the age of seventeen he had won such notable competitions as 'Patisser 88' as well as numerous medals for his works. Leaving Australia to travel the world he worked around the UK with some of the best chefs of this generation before returning home at the age of twenty to an Executive Pastry chef position, and as one of the youngest Pastry Lecturers within his country. Consulting, demonstrations and publishing quickly ensued. Under the watchful eye of Australian Columnist Bob Hart, Aaron was taught how to write for magazines and newspapers whilst at the same time publishing cookbooks and continuing his cookery career. Between 1990 and 2001 Aaron Maree published fourteen books in Australia, Canada, New Zealand, North America and the United Kingdom under the Harper Collins, Angus and Robertson, Bay Books and Cassell UK imprints. In 2001 Aaron took a ten year break from writing to re-focus on his cookery career. In 2010, after travelling over eighty countries Aaron, is now living in Bahrain where he wrote *Arabian Dreams – new age desserts for the modern generation*. It went on to become named one of the top fifty-seven cookbooks in the world, and the 'Best Arabic Cookbook' in the World at the Gourmand cookbook awards in Paris. As well as achieving great rewards in his cookery writing Aaron has also achieved commercial success in his literary work via magazines and newspapers in several countries. Writing under a slew of pseudonyms Aaron uses his thirty years of culinary experience, his travels to more than a hundred countries and his life adventures to write for a variety of mediums, as a journalist, copy writer and syndicated columnist on lifestyle, travel, comedy and food. Aaron is currently penning his first novel after successfully publishing sixteen non-fiction cookbooks worldwide and is proud to have his fiction writing involved in *My Beautiful Bahrain*.

Books:

1990 - *Cakes, Tortes and Gateaux of the world - 100 Cakes and Tortes of the world.*
1991 - *Cookies, Biscuits and Slices of the World / Shortbreads, Cookies and Tollhouse of the World*
1992 - *Petit Fours / Chocolate Delights / Festive Treats / Sweet Treats*
1992 - *Patisserie; The Encyclopedia*
1993 - *Chocolate Cookery with Aaron Maree / Cadbury Chocolate Cookery with Aaron Maree*
1994 - *Sweet Health*

1995 - *A Passion for Chocolate* (Co-author)
1997 - *Classic Desserts*
2001 - *Dip Me In Chocolate*
2011 - *Arabian Dreams, New Age Ideas with Middle Eastern Desserts*
Aaron is currently writing freelance for numerous magazines under several pseudonyms within the Middle Eastern and Gulf Region, Australia and the UK, everything from humour/comedy to fiction and non-fiction articles.
E: arabiandreams2010@hotmail.com

ANA CORRADINI BORELAND

"As a journalist, I have worked for several newspapers and magazines in Brazil, writing mostly about science for *Folha de S. Paulo, Scientific American Brasil, Saúde!, Astronomy Brasil,* and *Superinteressante*, among many others. In 2003, I published my first book for children, *Almanaque de Harry Potter e outros Bruxos*. This magical ride has brought me to fourteen books published so far, most of them for kids and young adults, and two travel guides. Some books have been adopted as support material at several schools in Brazil for the 7th and 8th grades. In my last job back home, I worked as editor-translator for *Disney's Club Penguin*. In Bahrain I have been working as a freelance reporter for *Bahrain this Month* and *Woman this Month* magazines, and translating children's books for Brazilian publishing houses."
E: anacorradini@gmail.com
Blog: http://vemprobahrainvocetambem.wordpress.com/
Blog: http://olhosdagua.zip.net
Blog: http://dubliniana.wordpress.com

ANITA MENON AND NAMIT BHATIA

Anita Menon is a Supply Chain Consultant turned aspirant writer, who now divides her time chasing her hyperactive toddler and writing blogs. After five years of hectic career in consulting, she chose to take a break to raise her daughter and move with her husband to the Kingdom of Bahrain. She is extremely passionate about food and can spend endless hours browsing cookbooks and watching re-runs of food shows. She pours that love for food in her food blog, where she writes about her experiments with everyday baking and cooking. So it was only natural that she chose to write about the food and culture of Bahrain in the aptly titled: *Bahrain: The Culinary Oasis*. Not many people know that Anita is an obsessed food container collector and can speak five languages. An avid reader, she is a compulsive book buyer and loves to buy them randomly without reading the blurb. She feels she wants to give the author the opportunity to surprise her with

their story. The other thing that she absolutely loves doing is telling stories. Stories from her life, of the people she loves, of the wonderful characters in her head and above all stories about her daughter. She pens down her stories in her literary blog and is currently working on a fiction novel on this blog as series of posts, and is looking for a publisher who would help her see it in print. Anita was supported by Namit Bhatia, a closet photographer which may not necessarily mean he prefers photographing wardrobes. Being in Bahrain since his early years, Namit takes to Bahrain as his second home and this proved to be an advantage while sharing ideas with Anita on this story.
E: dazzler29@gmail.com
Blog: www.sliceofmylyfe.wordpress.com
Blog: www.dazzlersdiary.wordpress.com

B.M.ENGEL

Barbara was born in west Germany and lives, together with her Bahraini husband and their two children, in the Kingdom of Bahrain. Since arriving on the island almost thirty years ago, she appreciates Bahrain's multicultural, cosmopolitan and liberal environment, regarding its diversity both as a challenge and asset. An Architect by profession, she started writing short stories a few years ago. Her stories are based on the belief that one should concentrate on matters that people of different origins have in common, rather than their differences. Compassion and humour are the characteristic elements she employs to weave her tales together. The plots are fictional but characters, scenery and moods are inspired by her knowledge gained living abroad in a foreign, multicultural society. Barbara writes letters, short stories and prose in both German and English. Where writing in German is a rather natural process for her, writing in English proves to be an exciting and welcoming challenge. She thoroughly enjoys the venture of expressing herself no matter which language. In 2007 she joined a writers' course and rediscovered her love for the art of the short story. Consequently with friends and enthusiasts alike, she formed her own writing group in order to support each other to develop their skills further and attain a professional standard. Barbara founded the German Literary Circle Bahrain in early 2011, which welcomes all who have a love for the German language and literature written in or translated into German. *Breathing Lessons* is Barbara's first published short story. She is currently working on a series of short stories with view to getting them published in the near future, both as a book and in journals.
E: bekhonji@hotmail.com

BRON VANZINO

Bron Vanzino has taken her first baby steps as a professional writer recently in Bahrain. We at the Writers Circle are very proud of her small achievements inside and outside of the Circle. She has been involved in the publication as writer for the latest Alba (Aluminium Bahrain) publication about their forty year record of expansion in Bahrain. In addition, she has written for a travel magazine on her unusual stay in a Berber village in Morocco. Bron aims to use her writing to touch hearts – to bring them back to life and healing, or crack them if they are hard and closed. Currently she has begun writing a history of the last hundred years of her family called *Born for the Hard Times*. It tells of cruelty and destruction, courage and determination in the twists and turns of fate within the lives of past generations. She focuses on the five generations within her reach, conscious that these family forebears have a voice through their history for the inheritance they provided for the young Australians of today. In the future, Bron hopes to train 'toddler' writers to take their own independent steps of success by nurturing them within her own writing studio. As she departs from a career of teaching English to business students from all over the world, Bron plans to step into a role of research writer for a government institution while she realises her dream of starting up the studio. Bron plans to take this writing role to wherever her husband finds his next job which, she tells us, could be just about anywhere. Wherever she is living however, she can always be reached by other writers
E: bvanzino@hotmail.com

CATHERINE PURCHASE

Catherine Purchase is an avid reader and aspiring fiction writer. Her educational background includes a B.A. from the University of Toronto and an M.F.A. from the American Film Institute. *The Little Pearl Merchant* is her first short story to be published.
E: cp@townrent.com

DAVID HOLLYWOOD

"I shall start by declaring I am Irish and rejoice in my wife Ruth and four children. By virtue career circumstances' and necessities, I frequently have had to travel and live in different countries. However, we have been happily residing in Bahrain since August 2009 and look forward to being here for a number of years to follow. My background is as a Trade Consultant and Advisor to Government Departments interested in creating incentive programmes for commercial development, and also as a Marketing Mentor for industries looking to promote their portfolio internationally. I have twenty years personal Directorial experience of founding and establishing, managing and leading international trading companies. Currently, I am assisting the Bahrain Small & Medium Enterprises Society to identify and establish commercial structures and incentives necessary to create trade prospects for the future. In addition I help a small select number of restaurants with their wine lists and provide training for staff in their efforts to recommend wines as well as know how to pour and appreciate wine. I have an amateur's enthusiasm for classical history and certain sciences, particularly cosmology. Over the past number of years I have been involved in amateur dramatics and appeared on tours throughout Ireland in a selection of dramas and comedy performances. Since arriving in Bahrain I have become a member of the Bahrain Writers Society, as well as the Bahrain Writers' Circle, and additionally joined the creative arts group Elham, while also being involved in dramatic productions for the Manama Theatre Company. I have hopes to establish a community oriented drama society where we can develop themes which have an emphasis upon the traditions of the Gulf and consequently shall require high levels of Bahraini input and participation. Earlier this year I was privileged to become the Chairman of The Second Circle workshop on poetry appreciation and creation, and which operates under the auspices of The Bahrain Writers' Circle. With regard to my writings, they are inspired mostly by the extremes of finality, uncertainty, occasional unhappiness, emotional and physical pain and the joy that then comes from release. I think my poems have manifested themselves in terms which reflect an ongoing stimulation of sensations and passions, combined with abstract impressions of the real, imagined, sensed and available, and consequently they may expose the uncomfortable fears or lack of confidences we may sometimes have. Additionally, I have attempted to face the directness of love, death, loss, ruin, rejuvenation amongst a variety of themes and feelings which may drown or embarrass our relationship with the everyday world. I started writing when I was eighteen but was too sensitive to criticism at the time and therefore gave it up for many years and only started again in my late forties whilst living in America and at a time when circumstances were very difficult. These inspired me to find expression through poetry because, as a medium for communication, it allowed me to formulate feelings and ideas through entangled perceptions of frustration. If I were to ponder what it may be about my work which emerges as a consequence, it is that it is largely unembarrassed by the reality that we feel what we feel and see, and that no matter how much we may pretend to the contrary and thereby move and say and act in a manner which protects our veneer of personality, the truth is that we all occasionally, and sometimes unwittingly, allow ourselves to see, recognise, accept and run away from the truth of what is actually inside of us."

E: davidhollywood23@hotmail.com

DAVONDA ST.CLAIR

DaVonda St.Clair, hailing from Cincinnati, Ohio, has always been surrounded by the arts and the creative talents of her family, not only inspiring her by being positive role models but also by nurturing her imagination and her artistic abilities in creative writing, dance, visual arts and music. Her mother, Sharon, was extremely active in the arts by teaching body movement (contemporary dance) classes at Over-The-Rhine (OTR) community centre while others in her family showcased their diverse talents through song writing, singing, drawing, painting in addition to successfully producing entrepreneurial business ventures within the Greater Cincinnati Area. DaVonda's creative writing skills improved throughout her school years by journal/freelance writing, an array of speech/writing competitions, entertainment and arts classes, creative writing programs and poetry workshops. Winning impromptu speech and writing competitions fuelled DaVonda's desire to write along with meeting Nobel Prize and Pulitzer Prize winning American novelist Toni Morrison, award winning poet Nikki Giovanni and award winning magazine editor Susan L. Taylor. She credits her family especially her mother, great grandmother Rebecca (RIP), great aunt Nancy (RIP), her aunt Terri, counsellors, mentors and teachers to fostering her development and commitment to values such as leadership, integrity and scholastics. As a member of the Cincinnati Arts Association, DaVonda continues her commitment as well as her sense of social responsibility through global philanthropic initiatives to include donating and being involved with the Freestore Foodbank (Cincinnati), Artists for a New South Africa (ANSA), Feeding America and the Bahrain Society for the Prevention of Cruelty to Animals (BSPCA). Look for upcoming works of poems, non-fiction and fictional novels from DaVonda starting with two book series The Nasty 'Nati and A Single Woman's Travels. "Poetry is an outlet for my body, mind, and spirit. Life is my inspiration as it is filled with so many emotions, experiences, and expeditions that can not be held internally…it has to be released, this is what frees me, writing is my release."
E: davondastclair@yahoo.com

DILRAZ KUNNUMMAL

Born and brought up in Bahrain, Dilraz Kunnummal has always had a penchant for writing. Armed with a Bachelor's in Business Administration and a Masters in Broadcast Journalism, she has worked in Mumbai for a while before moving back to Bahrain. Over the last two years, she has worked with *Signature Bahrain*, the *Daily Tribune* and is currently the editor for *Sabaya Magazine.* She is an avid reader, a trained Indian classical dancer and choreographer, and is on the continuous journey to dabble in her passions; finding fun, knowledge and smiles along the way.
E: dilraz@gmail.com

EVA L BURNS

Eva's writing career began when her family passed her letters to each other. People questioned whether her exploits really happened. Her response was "Do you want the truth, or a good story?" Unable to stand the idea of being poor, she studied finance and found herself surrounded by millions. During her eighteen years in banking, she honed her technical writing and developed over a dozen classes about 'safe lending practices', which were obviously put on a shelf somewhere after she left. By day a banker, by night she was a theology student specializing in Feminist Spirituality. Inspired by nuns, she practised academic writing and began preparing herself for a Ph.D., But her female professors were no match for an Arabian Sheik. His call led her away from the seminary and into a desert nursery where her three children were held captive by her stories. After discovering the Bahraini government stamped 'Not Permitted to Take Up Any Employment' in her passport, she started listening to the voices from her past that whispered "Why don't you write?" So she began a novel and submitted a chapter to writing guru Sid Stebel for his review. His comment was "You can write but what story are you trying to tell?" To find her direction Eva took Deonna Kelli Sayed's writing course. When Deonna abandoned Bahrain to hunt ghosts in the US, Eva teamed up with three international writers. Together they wrote short stories and critiqued each other. After writing a dozen stories that had a beginning, a middle and an end, her confidence grew. But she still searched for a story that would fuel her passion. In 2009 a burping Korean healer inspired Eva with his tales of healing ghosts. She wrote a non-fiction narrative about her discovery that her grandparents' spirits still walked the earth. Eva's completed manuscript is anxious to weave its way onto the New York Times Best Sellers List. While waiting to announce its publishing date, she lives in her bubble of bliss and writes anonymous –but true – stories about her family and friends, love, healing, Bahrain and other exotic locales on her blog - *Tales of Dragons, Rabbits and Roosters.*

E: evalburns@yahoo.com
Blog: http://dragonsrabbitsandroosters.wordpress.com

FAHAD ALI

"I'm an young, aspiring writer from Australia. Writing is something I love. It is more than a hobby to me; it is something I have been doing for as long as I can remember. It is a part of my life, as natural as breathing or eating. It is my method of self-expression; my way of showing the world the content of my mind. It is my voice. I have a fascination with the interweaving of emotion and experience with written language. It is remarkable that something as simple as the alphabet, which is really just a series of arbitrary markings, can be strung together to make us experience

and imagine the richest scenes and deepest emotions. Enthralled by the almost-magical qualities of language, I began to write, at first as an outlet for my overflowing childhood imagination, and then as I grew older, as a medium with which I could articulate my thoughts and feelings. As Lady Murusaki wrote over a thousand years ago in the legendary *Tale of Genji*, 'Again and again something in one's own life, or in that around one, will seem so important that one cannot bear to let it pass into oblivion. There must never come a time, the writer feels, when people do not know about this.' Our emotions and experiences are transient—that much is apparent. My aim as a writer is to crystallise and preserve these evanescent sensations into a form that can be experienced by all. As Ezra Pound put it, 'Literature is news that stays news.' I write both prose and poetry spanning several genres. My literary inspiration ranges from the great classical writings of Catullus, Dante, and Homer, to the more contemporary works of J.R.R. Tolkien, Ray Bradbury, and Terry Pratchett. One day I hope to see my own works on a shelf beside the literary giants whom I admire, and hopefully inspire my readers, just as my own heroes have inspired me."
E: fahad.3li.9@gmail.com

FARIDAH SERAJUL HAQ

Faridah teaches educational psychology at the Bahrain Teachers College, University of Bahrain. She has a Ph.D. in Special Education and has been writing mostly academic articles for research in her area of specialization. She is originally from Malaysia but has lived in many countries such as USA, Mexico, Brunei, UAE and now Bahrain. She finds Bahrain a wonderful country to begin working on some creative ideas for her novel. She plans to write fiction with children living in adversity as the central theme of her future work. Like most writers, she aspires to produce a best-seller but for the time being she is satisfied if readers are interested in what she has to say about life and living in general.
E: faridah119@yahoo.com

FATIMA DINCSOY

Writing is something that has come very naturally to me ever since I was a kid. Any thought, feeling or event may prompt me to pick up a pen, and once something is playing in my mind I find it impossible to put the pen down until it has all been articulated. There are few things in life that I find as gratifying as having completed a decently written piece. I hope to share my observation of life, my perception of world events, and my fascination with the human mind by writing about it and communicating it to an audience, stimulating other people's minds while exposing part of mine. To me, this is what art is all

about. My interests span widely, so in addition to writing poetry, I am currently experimenting with writing for film, while re-kindling my old passion for song writing – with the purpose of singing on stage. Although I am German, I write in English and actually find it hard to write in my native language, probably due to the fact that I don't use it very much these days. So far, I have shared very little with very few people, as aside from my poem here, I have not had anything else published yet. However, I am looking forward to doing so in the near future.
E: fatima.dincsoy@gmail.com

HAMEED AL QAED

"A poet, writer and translator from Bahrain, my first poetry collection was *Lover in the Era* of Thirst. I published my second book of poetry, *Noise of Whisper*, in 2003. The second was printed in Arabic, but it included an English translation of the work by myself. This work won first prize in the 'Distinguished Book' competition for the year 2003. The competition is organised annually by the Ministry of Information in Bahrain. My third book *Alimentation of Violets* was published in March 2010 and it is also a bilingual collection of poetry (Arabic/English) translated by myself. In 2007, I published *Pearl, Dreams of Shell - Anthology of Bahrain Contemporary Poetry* in USA. It is a collection of poetry for twenty-nine modern poets from Bahrain compiled and translated by myself and is mainly distributed in USA and UK and can be found on Amazon.com. Many of my poems and other work have been published in Arabic newspapers, magazines and periodicals. I have also taken part in many poetry recitals in Bahrain and overseas. I translated many English and American poems, short stories and essays into Arabic, including the well-known *Van Gogh Letters* which I translated from English to Arabic. I also Translated *Nooran* novel, by Bahraini writer Farid Ramadan, as part of a joint graphic work with Jamal Abdul Rahim, a famous Bahraini artist. Some of my poems were translated into French and Russian as well."
E: hameed_alqaed@yahoo.com
W: www.hameedalqaed.99k.org

HASINA PATEL

Hasina Patel is a South African living in Bahrain with her husband Ridwaan and daughter Zaahiya both of whom she sees as her inspirations in life. An IT specialist by profession she has taken a break to be a stay at home mum and to pursue her dream of becoming a writer. *My Bahrain My Home* is her first of hopefully many published works, which pays homage to the country that has offered her and her family a very warm welcome and brought about many positive changes in their lives. She is passionate about travelling and would gladly drop everything to

travel the world with her family. She is currently writing her first novel which is a romance based in the Middle East.
E: thirtysumting@gmail.com
Blog: www.thirtysumting.wordpress.com

HEERA NAWAZ

Heera is a writer who specialises in writing feature articles, short stories and poems. She is also a teacher and trainer at BGS International Residential School, Bangalore, where she teaches English and French to high school students. She been educated in America, England, and India. Part of her schooling was done at Bishop Cotton Girls' School, Bangalore, and she attended college at Mount Carmel College, Jyoti Nivas College and Annamalai University. Heera Nawaz loves writing, and this intense and keen skill comes to her almost effortlessly. She has been writing short stories and poems on love, values and nature, and several of her pieces have been published in the *Deccan Herald*, Karnataka's main newspaper. Heera Nawaz has been influenced a lot by her parents, the late Mohammed Khader Nawaz and the late Mrs. Leela Nawaz. She stayed with her father in Bahrain for two years, and she feels that because of him, she has developed a keen interest to write about this beautiful island.
E: heeranawaz@yahoo.com

JIM SCALISE

Jim Scalise came from the US to Saudi Arabia to teach Computer Aided Design to Saudi Architects and Engineers, took up residence in Bahrain five years ago, and enjoys the island lifestyle here more than enough to warrant the long daily commutes to Saudi. US Architect and teacher, Jim has Bachelors and Masters Degrees in Architecture from the prestigious Tulane University of New Orleans. His first career was as architectural designer, builder and developer. His second career has involved teaching architectural topics to grade school, high school, college and vocational students, and to architectural/engineering professionals. "Exposing the fertile minds of grade schoolers to good design was my most unexpected architectural and teaching delight." Along the way Jim has received awards for both his own and his collaborative architectural projects, and for teaching. His favourite architectural project was as a member of the design team for the award winning New Orleans Rivergate Convention centre, a soaring concrete structure, ahead of its time and the world's largest thin-shell roof at the time. While a resident of the old historic and entertainment district of New Orleans, the 'Vieux Carre' - French Quarter, Jim also designed and renovated numerous antique buildings there. He notes similarities of the long established French Quarter preservationist

community with Bahrain's awakening to the importance of preservation here. For an international convention he created a three dimensional one-third scale model of a section of the French Quarter inside the Louisiana Superdome, including the huge famed St. Louis Cathedral, with Brennan's and other famed restaurants and jazz bands serving their fares from the model buildings. His extravaganza was awarded First Place in US Convention Theme Design. *IBM* and *Technology and Learning* Magazine awarded Jim Teacher of the Year Award for Louisiana and for the Southern US for an innovative project: teaching inner-city high school students Computer Aided Design by leading them in the design of a football stadium for their school. A televised documentary, *Teaching that Works*, was made of his classroom activities in that project and in another: helping a student design and develop a robotic hand that could pick up a Smurf ball and throw it through a model basketball hoop. The student won the State Science Fair and went on to be awarded a scholarship and then graduate as a Robotics Engineer. His third career is writing and lecturing about architecture, art, travel and other – and painting.
E: jim.scalise@gmail.com

JOANNE JONES

Joanne was born in Sydney, Australia in 1951, and moved to the political capital, Canberra, as a young teacher when she was twenty-four. Whilst always interested in writing, the combination of four children and a full-time teaching position meant that Joanne rarely found time to explore her interest in writing. Through her position as an English Literature teacher, however, Joanne nurtured her interest in creative writing but has also had a long term interest in journalism related to social issues. Until recently Joanne's contributions were restricted to occasional articles in local newspapers and letters to the editor. Creative writing was given expression by writing stories for her adult matriculation students in an effort to encourage them to write as well. The students often reacted positively to this approach rather than only studying the works of someone they did not know. In 2009 Joanne accepted a teaching contract at Bahrain Polytechnic to teach English and Academic Skills. The experience was very positive for her as she found the Bahraini people and culture very welcoming and embraced enthusiastically this first experience of living in an Arabic society. In this context Joanne became interested in teaching Middle Eastern Literature and suggested it as a possible future elective at Bahrain Polytechnic. Joanne appreciated and embraced the opportunities which were offered to learn more about Bahrain especially during the Bahrain Spring of Culture in March 2010. During this time she attended poetry readings at the Poetry House in Gudaibaya and other cultural events usually held at the Muharraq Heritage and Cultural area.

These were very special times for her. Travels to other fascinating places such as Oman, Syria and Jordan further increased her love of the region. Joining the Bahrain Writers' Circle was a very positive step in her development as a writer. At their meetings Joanne was able to meet other local writers and share stories and poetry with them as well as gain inspiration from their insights and encouragement. The Writers' Circle provided the discipline of monthly writing tasks which also became a fillip for her writing. Joanne is now living back in Australia, but one day plans to return to visit Bahrain.
E: joanne.mary.jones@gmail.com

KATHLEEN DODD

Kathleen Dodd was born in Liverpool. A mother of three, she has been teaching for forty years in England, Colombia and more recently in Bahrain. She has written numerous poems and short stories, some of which have been published, as well as a book *Sugar Butties and Mersey Memoirs* - a collection of poems and an autobiography about growing up in Liverpool.
E: kathdodd@aol.com

KEVIN HOWARTH

'Krazy' Kevin Howarth is a British radio disc jockey best known for his radio and television presenting in the Kingdom of Bahrain. He started his career as a DJ whilst living in Blackpool, and went on to win the UK DJ of the year in 1985 and was also voted Disco & Club Trade International Personality DJ in both 1985 and 1986. Since then he has been known as 'Krazy' Kevin. He has worked in Germany, Italy, Holland, Iceland, Hong Kong, Dubai and for ten years in the Kingdom of Bahrain, where he presented the Music Mania Television Show on Bahrain Channel 55 and host of the Radio Bahrain 96.5 fm Drive Time Show. Howarth has also been a regular writer for *Gulf Weekly* and *Bahrain Confidential*. Kevin is now living in Australia but misses the island very much.
E: krazykevindj@yahoo.com

LILLIAN MILLS

"I am currently writing my first book about my experiences in Bahrain".
E: lilofarabia@yahoo.com

LORRAINE CHARLESWORTH

Lorraine Charlesworth has written poetry from early childhood, it has been a comfort and a challenge throughout her life and it is something which today, she finds an obsession. Lorraine has had a varied career as a teacher, an exhibition florist, landscape gardener and the manager of children's play centres. She has lived and worked in the UK, Spain, Qatar, Egypt and Bahrain. In her travels she enjoyed watching people, and as an optimist has always been able to see the beauty of the world whilst recognising the terrible things man does to his fellow man. Her poetry is very much from her heart and inspired by her time in Bahrain. The stark beauty of the islands and the warmth of its people have been her stimulation for her book of poetry; *For love of Bahrain*, which reflects her deep love of the island.
E: loll48@hotmail.com

MADHAVI TIWARY

"My first rendezvous with writing was at college. My scribbling, which I fondly called 'poems', was proudly and regularly passed on to the like-minded class mates. We would exchange the little slips, dubbing them 'data' in the psychology class and savour each other's badly cooked write ups. After about four years of such expressions of passionate thoughts, there came a grand lull in my writing. Laundry lists, love and hate letters replaced all that writer's pride - 'data'. It took a decade for me to pick up writing again with zeal and zest. As a result, in the past few years I have written about fifty articles which were published in the editorial columns. I have written as many poems, most of which are still hatching in the warmth of my private closet. I hope one day I will feel ready to share them with the world. My articles were invariably written when I hungered to share my thoughts with the world. However, most of my poems were the direct consequence of some kind of personal flood happening in my heart. Hence, their fate generally was the bottom folder in my personal closet. My most cherished aspiration is publishing a joint book of my daughter's and my write-ups. A subsidiary dream, life permitting, is to write a book which could summarise my life's emotions in the form of a story that will leave the readers with a smile in their heart and with a storm in their minds. All those well wishing friends who want to comment, give ideas for my future endeavours, are welcomed to contact me."
E: madhavi.dwivedi@gmail.com

MAEVE KELYNACK SKINNER

"I arrived in Bahrain in 1976 to take up the position of PA/Secretary to the Chairman of one of the Gulf's oldest merchant families – and I'm still here! As all expats know; 'Bahrain is the world's best kept secret,' and despite little turmoil and traumas and the odd stressful occasion, living in Bahrain far surpasses many other places in the world in which to live, raise a family, work and play. I have lived overseas all my life, having been born in Penang, Malaysia, another tropical island with a similar easy going lifestyle as Bahrain. I've lived in Hong Kong, Sarawak, Kenya, Ireland, England, Spain, Italy and have travelled all around the world, enjoying wonderful experiences, meeting fascinating people and still never tire of discovering somewhere new to explore. My literary career began in Bahrain when I was invited to join Al Hilal Publishing Group by Ronnie Middleton, the CEO, who asked me to 'write a few articles on tourism and the hotel industry' and I've never looked back. I have since contributed to several pan-Gulf and international magazines, newspapers and trade journals including the *Gulf Daily News, Gulf Weekly, The Irish Times, Weekly Telegraph, Bahrain This Month, Arabian Knight, Bahrain Confidential, Arabian Woman,* Cathay Pacific in-flight magazine, among other publications. I am a former editor of *Gulf Falcon* (Gulf Air in-flight magazine), *Bahrain Gateway, Bahrain & Beyond* and was start up editor of *Oryx*, Qatar Air in-flight magazine. For the past couple of years I am fortunate to have been a member of a small and inspirational writing group whose members have helped me to complete a co-authored autobiography of my late father and encouraged me to write my own memoir and also to resurrect a novel I wrote about eight years ago, a romantic thriller based on the last island in the Arabian Gulf to discover oil".

E: maeveen6@gmail.com

MARY COONS

Mary Coons is the author of the award-winning books *Culturally Speaking: Promoting Cross-Cultural Awareness in a Post-9/11 World*, and *Safe From the Outside World: A Social History of Hanover, Minnesota*, as well as twelve privately commissioned family history books. Mary began visiting Bahrain in December 2005, and was immediately in awe of the Arab culture, religion, and people. As a professional writer, it was natural that she would seek out people to understand who they are and how they think. *Culturally Speaking* was the result of her drive to learn. Mary began her writing career with freelance articles more than thirty years ago, and has been published internationally, nationally, regionally and locally ever since. She is the founder and president of Pen & Ink Communications, a small business specialising in writing family stories / life histories, and business and travel article writing. Mary is the past

international editor of the *Bahrain Traveller* and the *Bahrain Telegraph* magazines. A former Bahrain resident, Mary has travelled extensively to the kingdom where she has delivered public and private presentations based upon her book's message. She and her husband, Bob Miller, are about to embark on a new journey in Doha, Qatar.
E: marycoons@usinternet.com
W: www.culturallyspeak.com,
W: www.marycoons.com

NADIA MUIJRERS

"As a teenager the worst homework a teacher could possibly assign was the writing of an essay. Math homework was always done first and essays were left to the very end – if I could have avoided them I would have. At university, I aimed at accountancy but somehow after a whirlwind of experiences the arrow ended up firmly rooted in the social sciences. It was during these years my natural abilities and affinities shifted without my realising. And they continue to shift. In what one of my dearest friends calls an act of self-hate, I spent my five years of work experience to-date in the finance industry. Somehow a few emails of rants and musings during the recession's troughs turned me into the 'oh you write well' kind of person. Wake up call: I can write. Today, a year or two after this epiphany, I have written my first little piece that will go beyond the boundary of the occasional email to friends. The rest I will leave up to whatever goodness change may bring. Armed with fancy degrees from Birmingham and Cambridge University in the UK, and with equally fancy experience at financial institutions in Bahrain, I have decided to rely on what I always should have: my curiosity. Aside from writing, areas of increasing interest to me include social entrepreneurship, international development, cognitive and social psychology, arts and crafts, yoga and meditation, and more. A quote I recently stumbled upon during a French film captures my intent more succinctly that I could ever explain:

'Me? I'm a failure
Prof. Albert Sorel taught me the little l know
He said You want to be what?
A diplomat
Are you rich?
No
Can you legitimately add a famous name to your own surname?
No
Then forget diplomacy
But what'll I become?

Curious
That's not a profession, not yet
Travel, write, translate
Learn to live everywhere.
Begin at once
The future belongs to the curious'
- Jules et Jim, 1962."

NATASHA KHAN

"Born in the literary heart of Pakistan (Lahore) and raised in a home rich with writings from all over the world, I was perhaps destined to develop a passion for reading. This soon grew into a love of writing. I started off writing for the school magazine, and eventually became a member of the editorial board. Later on, while I pursued a degree in political science, I wrote a bi-weekly opinions piece for the University of Southern California's weekly newspaper *The Daily Trojan*. Here, I was awarded the title of 'Most Passionate Journalist.' After University, I got married and moved to Bahrain, where I joined the Bahrain Writer's Circle and started my blog – Paki Girl in the Arab World. Today, I live in Saudi Arabia where I'm currently pursuing a distance learning degree in Law. In the meantime, I have completed a novel – a love story – which I intend to get published soon.
E: nmasroork@hotmail.com

NAWF AL BASSAM

Noof T. Al-Bassam is a freelance writer, innovative thinker and communicator. She obtained her Bachelors in Philosophy at the American University of Beirut (AUB) and Masters in Communications from the London School of Economics (LSE). Nawf is inspired by Horton's (in Dr. Suess' '*Horton Hears a Who*') philosophy, "a person is a person, no matter how small." She has passion for reading and writing in English, French and Arabic.
E: noufalbassam@gmail.com

OMAR AHMED

"I'm eighteen years of age, and hail from Yemen. My first writing experience was back in the summer of 2008 when I received an email from a friend, who compiled a short poem, mainly of lines stolen from different pop-songs. He asked me to try writing a poem and I thought 'Why not?' I am a huge fan of metal music and the poetry in its lyrics and abstract themes, so my first poem was

influenced by the music I loved. Encouraged by my friends and family I've never stopped writing since. I've written over ninety poems covering various subjects, frequently using dark themes and elements of Goth. I'm in a process of continuous hewing and growth, as I am obsessed and deeply interested in the working of the poetry machine. How words are carefully picked like the carpet, furniture and colours of a house, and how words get mixed and re-arranged in the machine to create the desired effect and impact on the reader's mind. It is abstract and a truly technical and skilful art of delivering ideas, of saying so much, yet writing so little. It's a melodious dance of words that inflame the mind! I enjoy every bit of this machine with immense pleasure. I'm not yet published, but hope that I will be one day. My dream is to reach out to masses and masses of minds and hearts, to send a message, inspire or make a difference through my words".
E: entersandman.ramo@gmail.com
Blog: http://omarahmed33.blogspot.com
Facebook: www.facebook.com/pages/Beneath-the-Oak-Tree/254953001224932

OSAMA ARSHAD

"I want to act in the movies. I want to sing. I want to dance. I want to start a charity fund to educate poor kids. I want to make people in Bahrain aware of global warming, and I want more. I want to make a difference and writing is a good platform to express my thoughts, feelings, aspirations and goals."
E: okai.91@gmail.com

PHARI POITIER

Phari Poitier's notable famous last name has granted her a few luxuries in life but it did not shield her from life's joys, pain, and tragedy; loves virtue, passion and heartaches; friendships loyalty, pleasure and disappointment. Through it all spawned a beautiful, brilliant being that is ready to share literary pieces of herself with the world.

POOJA RAJPAL KASALA

Pooja is a marketing and communications specialist, and has over a decade of work experience in the field of public relations, analyst and investor relations and executive communications. Pooja is from Bangalore, the IT capital of India, and is currently based in Bahrain with her husband Kamlesh Kasala. Apart from postgraduate certifications in public relations and human resources management, Pooja also has a masters degree in English Literature and an MBA. She enjoys

cinema and performing arts, and is passionate about travelling. In her spare time Pooja loves dabbling in new age healing and self–development programmes.
E: poojarajpal21@gmail.com

ROHINI SUNDERAM

"I grew up in several different parts of India as my father had been with the Indian Air Force, so I guess I was destined to be a nomad, or if nothing else tumble-weed. And, like human tumble-weed, I've collected experiences, ideas, words and different ways of looking at life. While at university I realised that I had started a life-long romance with words. I'd flirted with them as a child having once written a dramatic piece for my brother and sister, to whom I would tell all kinds of fanciful tales, which they would embellish with their additions, all this to pass away the long, hot, summer afternoons in India, when our parents were asleep. The affair with words and imagining led me to my line of work and I ended up becoming an advertising copywriter. A profession which, as Jerry Della Femina (a one-time advertising great) once said was 'the most fun you can have with your clothes on'. And that's what I have done all my working life. Now that I'm supposedly retired I continue to ply the trade as a freelance copywriter. However, alongside my commercial work I have always written other 'stuff'. These writings-on-the-side have included everything from dotty verse to flights of fancy sparked by a look, a person, a certain phrase or a change in the way the wind blew. Among these are: a short romantic novella, *Desert Flower*, set in Bahrain in the 1930's and published by Red Rose Publishing under the pen-name Zohra Saeed. I have also had articles published in the *Globe & Mail* (Canada) and T*he Chronicle-Herald* (Canada), and *The Statesman* (Calcutta/Kolkata, India) as well as children's stories. I administer a blog for my brother who had a stroke around four years ago, and my own blog: FictionPals both lately somewhat neglected. My blog has stories, verse, and other miscellany that I think might find an audience or at least other similarly inclined minds. My husband and I currently live in Bahrain and we have two children."
E: rohinisunderam@hotmail.com
Blog http://dlip.wordpress.com
Blog: http://www.fictionpals.com

S. KRISHNA KUMAR

"I was born and brought up in India. But I have lived in the Middle East. If childhood days are formative years, then my time in the Middle East are self-actualisation days. Thirteen years in Saudi Arabia, four years in Dubai, and now three years in Bahrain; these last twenty years have been a journey of realising most of the dreams that I set out with. Be it etching a career path, or providing

the family with all the comforts, or be it tangible assets that one always craved to collect. But the most soul-satisfying collectibles have been my lovely little family, the adorable friends, and the people - who walked into our life like angels. These angels have been what my life's journey has been about. There are no regrets. I have acquired and practised the art of public speaking and nurtured it into a professionally rewarding skill. As a public speaker I have written innumerable speeches and delivered them with gusto. The speeches have always been about people, about my experiences. Speaking and perhaps writing has always come naturally to me. Since I was seven years old, I have written poems. My collection is titled *Moods*, and I have relentlessly and unceasingly pursued writing. We Indians believe in astrology, at least most of us, and we take it seriously. When I was fifteen years old, a so-called astrologer predicted that I will never be able to write a short story of a few pages, let alone writing a book! I lived up to his prediction! Rather I made his prediction come true. Call it self-fulfilling prophecies. Now this is my only regret; that I believed him. But after several decades I now have a gnawing feeling that I could write... write a book. That I always wanted to. It is in my head. It is in the form of notes written in several pocket books, in my mobile phones, in my speeches. It is now time that it saw itself coming to life between a few hundred pages bound into a paperback! I have a story, or perhaps stories to tell. And that is why I thought, hmmmm… how about getting into the circles – the Bahrain Writers' Circle, and The Second Circle! Maybe the inner circles of my mind are ready to reach out to the outer circles. I am looking forward to meet new inspiring friends there."
E: Krsnarti@gmail.com

SHAUNA NEARING LOEJ

Shauna found a love of words as a youngster writing about walks in the forest in her native Cape Breton Island, Canada. Fast forward through a career in public relations and corporate communications which led to a keen interest in Internet communications. This interest was formalised by earning a Master of Arts in Communication with a concentration in Internet communications. Shauna's most recent writing endeavours include arts and leisure publications in the Kingdom of Bahrain. These experiences have brought profound insight into the rich history and culture of the island that has been her home for over five years. Shauna lives with her husband Morten and their three children, and hopes one day to also write stories for children.
E: nearings@hotmail.com

STEVE ROYSTON

"I live in the Middle East, was born in the UK, and have personal and business ties to the USA, Ireland, Malaysia, France and more than one of the GCC countries. In my blog I reflect on politics, education, business, books I read, music I hear, movies I see. I look at most things through the prism of history. I feel privileged to live in a region where spoken and written history began. The Middle East is a land of where civilisations, empires and great religions have mingled, mutated and succeeded each other, sometimes with violence, sometimes in peace. Sumerians, Hittites, Egyptians, Persians, Greeks, Romans, Phoenicians, Parthians, Byzantines, Umayads, Abbasids, Fatimids, Mongols, Franks, Ottomans, Saudis, French and British – all have contributed to the cultural and physical gene pool. The gods of Egypt, Babylon, Greece, Rome, Carthage and Mecca have fought for the hearts of the faithful, to be supplanted by the great religions of the Book – Judaism, Christianity and Islam. Today, the Middle East is still at the heart of things. The key to prosperity and deprivation, to peace and conflict way beyond its boundaries. It's a land of kindness, hospitality, resentment, envy, plenty, destitution, wisdom, foolishness and hope. You could say that of many parts of the world. But this is where western civilisation began. It's beyond compare in many ways."

E: sr59steps@gmail.com

Blog: http://59steps.wordpress.com

ZAHRA ZUHAIR

"I began writing at the age of fourteen. My first works were poems which I wrote at a stretch and never published. Shortly after that, I began to write short fictional stories which, unlike my poetry, I plan on publishing someday. I'm still a learner... Some of us know that we were meant to write. As writers, we are given the chance to speak up for those who cannot, or those who won't. Also, as writers, we have the ability to tell a story that no one else will tell or relate a fact no one else will relate. As writers, the chance we take or the stories we tell can make a difference. As a writer, I want to make that difference."

E: aezuhair@gmail.com

Blog: http://keeeptalking.wordpress.com

Blog: http://zuhairaekeeptalking.blogspot.com

ELLA PRAKASH – ARTIST

Ella was born and brought up in Bahrain. She had a passion of art from childhood and has dedicated herself in the artistic mission and challenge, the risk and realities of the royal profession. She has explored Bahrain heritage with fine art and abstract,

as she want to express her memories through colours of this beautiful island on canvas. Her abstract paintings present the world as if seen through a prism, with bold colours parcelled out into geometric forms that offer fleeting, exhilarating glimpses of bodies, streets and still life. The geometry of the Cubist aesthetic that structures the Bahrain-based artist's enigmatic compositions recalls works by Pablo Picasso and Georges Braque. In Ella's case, however, the choice of colours achieves a markedly different effect. Each interlocking, overlapping, super-imposed and contrasting hue provokes a different reaction in the viewer, as if we're not looking at a single canvas, but rather a whole range of artworks contained within one. The spectacular rhythm of colours, lines and brush-strokes infuses each subject with irrepressible inner dynamism. She believes that every work of art must carry a message. She shares the knowledge that she has gained along the years through teaching, hoping to help change lives along the way. She paints to influence people and show them the success that lies ahead of them. She continues to seek ways to lead to the development of her signature artistic theme expressed with her emotions. Her permanent collection is in Southern Nevada Museum of Fine Art in Las Vegas, also her work is exhibited and appreciated in the leading art galleries in Europe, USA and India. Ella lives in Bahrain, teaches and owns her own art gallery.
E: info@ellagallery.com
W: www.ellagallery.com

ACKNOWLEDGEMENTS AND SOURCES

THE EDITOR WOULD LIKE TO THANK THE FOLLOWING FOR THEIR KIND PERMISSION TO PUBLISH THE ARTICLES AND RE-EDITED EXTRACTS INDICATED:

The Birth Of A Pearl
© S Krishna Kumar, reproduced by permission of the author S. Krishna Kumar.

A Backward Glance
© 1997 Maeve Kelynack Skinner originally published in 'Irish Society Yearbook' and edited and reproduced by permission of the author
Maeve Kelynack Skinner.

Saar Surrenders Its Secrets
© 1999 Maeve Kelynack Skinner, originally published in 'Bahrain Gateway' and edited and reproduced by permission of the author Maeve Kelynack Skinner.

The Rare Bird Of Bahrain
© 1997 Maeve Kelynack Skinner, originally published in 'Bahrain Gateway' and edited and reproduced by permission of the author Maeve Kelynack Skinner.

Bokhara or Bust
© Maeve Kelynack Skinner, reproduced by permission of the author
Maeve Kelynack Skinner.

This Land is Mine, The Embrace and *Bahrain: Minarets and Palm Trees*
© David Hollywood, reproduced by permission of the author
David Hollywood.

The Journey Home
© Faridah Serajul Haq, reproduced by permission of the author
Faridah Serajul Haq.

From Another Country and *East West, North And South*
© Zahra Zuhair, reproduced by permission of the author Zahra Zuhair.

My Beautiful Bahrain, My Beautiful Anywhere
© Nadia Muijrers, reproduced by permission of the author Nadia Muijrers.

My Beautiful Bahrain and *Last Random Thoughts*
© DaVonda St.Clair, reproduced by permission of the author DaVonda St.Clair.

Sailors Come Sailors Go
© Phari Poitier reproduced by permission of the author Phari Poitier.
My Beautiful, Lovely, Exasperating, Expatriate Bahrain
© Rohini Sunderam, reproduced by permission of the author
Rohini Sunderam.
Land Of The Living
© Omar Ahmed, reproduced by permission of the author Omar Ahmed.
Snapshots From an Island
© Steve Royston, reproduced by permission of the author Steve Royston.
Images of my Beloved Bahrain and *My Pearl*
© Lillian Mills, reproduced by permission of the author Lillian Mills.
Bahrain - Architecture And Environs
© Jim Scalise, reproduced by permission of the author Jim Scalise.
New Beginnings, Pearl Epiphanies and *The Mystery of Bahrain*
© Bron Vanzino, reproduced by permission of the author Bron Vanzino.
Bahrain, A Culinary Oasis
© Anita Menon and Namit Bhatia, reproduced by permission of the authors
Anita Menon and Namit Bhatia.
Pearls
© Aaaron Maree, reproduced by permission of the author Aaaron Maree.
The Little Pearl Merchant
© Catherine Purchase, reproduced by permission of the author
Catherine Purchase.
Visiting Old Bahrain
© Shauna Nearing Loej, first published in *Bahrain This Month* and reproduced by
permission of the author Shauna Nearing Loej.

The Baker of Manama
© Ana Corradini Boreland, reproduced by permission of the author Ana Corradini Boreland.
The Two Seas
© Fatima Dincsoy, reproduced by permission of the author Fatima Dincsoy.
Ali And The Hummer
© Eva L. Burns, reproduced by permission of the author Eva L. Burns.
Beautiful Bahrain
© Fahad Ali, reproduced by permission of the author Fahad Ali.
Protection
© Joanne Jones, reproduced by permission of the author Joanne Jones.
Bahrain Is The Best
© Heera Nawaz, reproduced by permission of the author Heera Nawaz.
Hijab And Traditional Dress
© 2008 Mary Coons originally published in 'Culturally Speaking: Promoting Cross-Cultural Awareness in a Post-9/11 World' and edited and reproduced by permission of the author Mary Coons.
Manama Suq - A Cultural Feast For The Senses
© Mary Coons, reproduced by permission of the author Mary Coons.
Love's Gift
© Madhavi Tiwary, reproduced by permission of the author Madhavi Tiwary.
Hoora
© Hameed Al Qaed, reproduced by permission of the author Hameed Al Qaed.
The Arab Horse and The Village Clock, A'Ali
© 1999 Lorraine Charlesworth, originally published in 'For Love of Bahrain' and edited and reproduced by permission of the author Lorraine Charlesworth.
My Bahrain My Home
© Hasina Patel, reproduced by permission of the author Hasina Patel.

How The Pearl Got Its Lustre

© Nawf Al Basam, reproduced by permission of the author Nawf Al Basam.

Growing Up In Bahrain

© Dilraz Kunnummal, reproduced by permission of the author Dilraz Kunnummal.

Strange Place

© Osama Arshad, reproduced by permission of the author Osama Arshad.

Breathing Lessons

© Barbara Engel Khonji, reproduced by permission of the author Barbara Engel Khonji.

Bahrain

© Kathleen Dodd reproduced by permission of the author Kathleen Dodd.

A Newbie!

© Pooja Rajpal Kasala, reproduced by permission of the author Pooja Rajpal Kasala.

My Prince, My Princess

© Natasha Khan, reproduced by permission of the author Natasha Khan.

Memories Of My Life In Bahrain

© Kevin Howarth, reproduced by permission of the author Kevin Howarth.

ROBIN BARRATT

"I have developed a strong readership profile within the non-fiction, true crime genre specialising in books about security, nightclubs, bouncers, bodyguards, gangsters and other tough guys! I wrote my first book *Doing the Doors* in 2004, which is now a genre best-seller and can still be found in most high-street bookshops in the UK, and have since gone on to publish *Confessions of a Doorman, Bouncers and Bodyguards, Respect and Reputation* (co-authored with the UK's most notorious prisoner Charles Bronson) and *The Mammoth Book of Tough Guys*. I also write a biography titled *Maria's Story*, and for a while I also published and edited *Protection News magazine* for the close protection community, *The Circuit*, an on-line magazine for the British Bodyguard Association, and *On The Doors* - the only magazine in the world dedicated exclusively to Door Supervision. I am also a freelance writer and editor, and have written a large number of articles and editorials for a huge range of commercial, mainstream and business publications worldwide; from luxury lifestyle to rural life! For a while I was also Bahrain Country Editor for *Sur la Terre* magazine."

E: RobinBarratt@yahoo.com
W: www.RB-Media-Services.com